Taken in Hong Kong
December 8, 1941

Memoirs of Norman Briggs
World War II Prisoner of War

Compiled by
Carol Briggs Waite

*To Arthur,
a fellow NARFEr.
Carol*

PUBLISH AMERICA

PublishAmerica
Baltimore

First printing

ISBN: 1-4241-1301-6
PUBLISHED BY PUBLISHAMERICA, LLLP
www.publishamerica.com
Baltimore

Printed in the United States of America

To the memory of my father, Norman H. Briggs, a man with great strength of character, which carried him through many difficult times. He was an example of living right to all who knew him.

Acknowledgements

I am most grateful for the encouragement and support of my late husband, Charles. He stood by me in my grief losing first my mother, then my father. In clearing out the family home, I came across my father's memoirs of his experience of being caught in Hong Kong when the Japanese invaded the city, the same day that they attached Pearl Harbor, Singapore, and Manila. I also found some old letters which the Red Cross had returned, undelivered, some telegrams, and pictures from the prison camp. Although the family knew the story, I thought others should know of his first-hand experience and observations of the attack of Hong Kong. With the encouragement of my husband, this account of his experience will be shared with many, especially young people who may not have realized the far reaches of destruction during World War II.

I also thank my sisters, Kathie and Norma, who urged me to document to others what our father endured. This was a labor of love for us all.

Preface

This story about Hong Kong is connected with World War II but is not primarily about the war itself. I prefer to think of this story more in the light of human relationships, the action and reaction of individuals to the circumstances in which they found themselves, and how they considered or failed to consider themselves in relation to the community of which they were a part. The story is merely the telling of events possibly somewhat sordid, certainly not inspiring, but nevertheless human.

In the mess in which the world found itself during this war, all the right is not on one side nor all the wrong on the other. Humanity may be at stake, but it is still humanity, and the trials and tribulations of our daily existence must be met and solved. I prefer to look upon this chaos that we are in not so much as a war, but as a crusade, humanity's attempt to right itself. The story that I have to tell may not be full of courage and maybe some of the things told could well be left unsaid, but even so I have by no means lost faith in humanity.

The world as a whole from 1914 to 1918 and the ensuing interval of the peace lost much, gained little, and learned nothing. That will not be so at the end of this war. I firmly believe that we will emerge from this war a far better world than we had on September 1939. Not that it has been worth the price that we will have to pay, but then that is a part of living, that is humanity.

I have no ax to grind, no propaganda to put forth, and this story is in no way a criticism of ourselves or our allies, nor is it an attempt to condone or excuse our enemies. It is merely the unfolding of human events, possibly more stubborn than courageous, undoubtedly more selfish than inspiring. This I can only regret. I sincerely hope and confidently expect that at some future date I may witness and be a part of mankind building and working together in mutual trust and respect and that the foundation so laid will be firm and substantial. And, hopefully, simple and attractive, not requiring the veneer and niceties of the diplomatic boiled shirt society era that I hope was blown to pieces with the opening salvo of September 1939 and any fragments left behind effectively pulverized in the descending thud of December seventh. No matter of what race or color, we all make up humanity be we American, British, German, Japanese or the other nationalities the world around. So, in the words of James Russell Lowell, "The Present Crisis":

> For mankind is one in spirit and an instinct bears along
> Round the earth's electric circle the swift flash of right or wrong,
> Whether conscious or unconscious, yet Humanity's vast frame
> Through its ocean-sundered fibers feels the gush of joy or shame
> In the gain or loss of one race all the rest have equal claim.

Norman H. Briggs
August, 1942

Section 1:
Back to the Orient

Chapter I
Leaving Home

There is an old proverb among the Caucasian community in the Orient that to live in the Far East you don't have to be crazy, but it helps a lot. All I can say is, it certainly does. I counted myself one of the crazy community when I left my family in Pasadena, California, on August 14, 1941, to head back out to the Orient for my employer, Standard Vacuum Oil Company. My parents did not want me to go and, of course, neither did my wife, Ruth, as the situation in the Orient, with Japan's ongoing invasion of China, was ripe with peril. And war was raging in Europe with our allies trying to stop Hitler's advances. But oil was needed, and Standard Vacuum needed to keep the fuel moving. So, I headed back to my job. Instead of going back to Japan, the Company sent me to Hong Kong, as they were trying to get personnel out of Japan.

I was working in the marketing department of Standard Oil, assigned to Japan. When I signed up with the Company in 1928, the mode of operation was to have thirty years of service in one country. I was a green graduate from Pomona College at the time and had been pounding the pavement in New York City for several months looking for employment. I walked into #26 Broadway one day, the headquarters of Standard Oil, and inquired about any job openings. I got the usual line, "No, we don't have any openings."

As I was turning to leave, the receptionist added, "We don't have anything here, but if you're interested in going overseas, you might try the 13th floor for

Standard Vacuum Oil Company." Up I went to the 13th floor, filled out some forms, and, lo and behold, was offered a job in Japan!

Born near Boston, I lived there until my early teens. Then, with a short stop living in Fort Wayne, Indiana, my parents finally settled in Pasadena, California. I had never been overseas before. And never even thought of Japan before. But, what the heck, after working my way through college, I was ready for adventure. After six weeks of training, I arrived in Tokyo in early 1929.

Japan certainly was a culture change, but not an altogether unpleasant one. Although at more than six feet I towered over people and had to duck going into most doorways, the Japanese were always polite and very gracious. And, of course, they welcomed the oil companies that would bring them their much-needed fuel.

Actually, I considered myself very lucky to have a job, what with the crash later in 1929 and depression in the United States. And lucky to be in Japan, where foreigners could easily afford the luxuries of life, such as servants. I was first assigned to Kobe, then Osaka and Nagoya, later moving to the office in Yokohama, near Tokyo. I was also lucky to have met Ruth Buchanan, daughter of a Presbyterian missionary, who was then teaching college in Nagoya. We married in 1935.

But 1941 was a different matter. With the escalating war Japan was waging, first in Korea, and then China, the tension of the last couple of years was getting more intense. The Japanese were secretive yet always polite and gracious. However, you could never really tell what they were thinking. On the surface they would agree with you. What they meant or intended might be totally different.

September 1939 made us even more uneasy. Hitler was brutally invading Poland while Japan was doing likewise in the Far East. The United States was staying out of it so far, but things did not look good. In fact, the Company had urged all family members in the Far East to return to the United States for safety. My wife, pregnant with our second child, left in early 1940 with our two-and-a-half-year-old daughter, Katherine. Carol was born in July, and the family stayed in Pasadena.

In June 1941 I came home for my two and a half months of home leave. It sure was wonderful to see my family, and get to know my two little girls. And, yes, I was probably crazy to leave them again, but this was my job to support my family.

I left Pasadena Thursday evening, August 14, 1941, by train to San

Francisco, where I was booked to leave by ship to Hawaii via the Matson Line. When the train left, I took a walk through it to see if by chance there was anyone that I knew, but there wasn't. I smoked a couple of cigars and then went to bed. It was the best train I had ever been on. The berth did not have to be made up as you just let it down from the wall, already made. In the morning I just pushed it back up and there was plenty of room for dressing. We were about a half hour late getting to San Francisco, so I had breakfast on the train. When we got in, I went directly to the ship and got my baggage aboard. There was a wire from Lucy Gardiner, saying to meet her and Doris Davis at the St. Francis Hotel at noon, so I proceeded there.

I then called Morna Nock. She told me that Tom Nock, who was best man at our wedding in Nagoya, was still in Rangoon. Next I called Margaret McCaskey. Her husband, Mac, was in charge in the Kobe office, but Margaret said he had been transferred to Manila or Hong Kong, she wasn't sure which. But when Mac came to leave, the Japanese would not give him permission to do so. They were forcing all the Americans who were in charge to remain. It seems that the Japanese staff wanted some kind of a special bonus or discharge allowance, if the office were going to be closed, and they were holding Mac as insurance that such would be granted. Physically, he was perfectly safe and he could move around freely, but could not leave the country.

I met Lucy and Doris at noon, and we went out to lunch. We had to hunt around for a restaurant as there was some kind of a strike on and most of the places were closed. Both women seemed happy and well, although not pleased at the long separation from their husbands. Doris expected Jerry home by the end of the year, as he was due home leave from Singapore in October, but she hadn't heard anything definite.

We went back to the ship later that afternoon. San Francisco was cold and foggy, and when the ship pushed away from the pier at 6:00 PM, the city immediately disappeared. The first night was very rough, but I slept soundly till morning. My room was on E deck, right down on the water line, with a small port hole at the end. The ship was well loaded, so it was riding pretty well.

Ruth Briggs, Pasadena, California

Norman left last night on the train to San Francisco to board the ship. With all the trouble that Japan is doing invading China, the Company has assigned him to Hong Kong, rather than his usual post in Japan. I sure hated to see him leave again. He was only home for such a short period. And the girls certainly enjoyed seeing their Daddy. Kathie remembered him and had talked about him. But Carol, of course, was only a year old and seeing Norman for the first time this home leave.

He called from San Francisco and told me about his train trip. Also, he said he saw some Company wives who were living there, so he had quite a lot of news to tell. It was so good to hear his voice, but also I realized that it will be a long time before I would hear it again. These long separations are so trying. In the over five years that we have been married, we have been apart for two of our anniversaries, and together for just three. And now it looks like we won't be together for our next one in January. I just hope and pray that the world's hostilities will soon cease, and we can be together again as a family.

Chapter II
From San Francisco to Hong Kong

At the first meal aboard ship, I found there were three other men at my assigned table. Vic, who is also with Standard Oil, and Wessley Case and John Franz, who were on their way to India to set up an oil refinery for the British. They work for a New York engineering firm for petroleum equipment and have done work for Standard Vacuum, so they know some of the people at 26 Broadway. Their families are also at home. They too are taking the Pan Am Clipper from Hawaii, but were spending a week in Honolulu first before going on to Singapore, then to India.

Some others on board will be taking the same Pan Am Clipper as I am from Honolulu. There is a Procter and Gamble man who is returning to Manila. He came home last March with Vic, so they already know each other. Most of the other passengers are mainly Army, Navy and defense workers all going to the Islands. The men are going to work, the women to join their husbands, and several young women to get married. The atmosphere on the ship was about the same as on the President Coolidge when I came home; no one is free and easy as no one knows what is going to happen next. Most of the people going out don't know where they are going to live.

Since Sunday noon the sea has been like a mill pond, the sun shining over calm water. A pleasant breeze was always blowing. However, as we approached Hawaii, it turned hot and sticky. We docked on schedule in Honolulu on Wednesday, August 20, at 9:00 AM. I went immediately to Pan

American only to find out that the Clipper was delayed and wouldn't leave until Friday morning instead of Thursday. Before checking into the Moana Hotel, I had them weigh my suitcases. The big case was 58 pounds, and the small overnight one was 17 pounds, which came just under the limit of 77 pounds. They charge $2 a pound for any excess. I had already shifted my typewriter to the trunk with my other belongings to ship to Hong Kong. The typewriter weighed 17 pounds, which would have put me over if I had left it in the large suitcase. The trunk, however, with the typewriter in it, cost just $20.20 to ship.

After checking into the hotel, I went swimming and tried to use one of those surfboards. I had no success at all, but did get a lot of good exercise. I won't try that again, as the rental for the board is $1. This place is expensive, and the minimum price for everything seems to be a dollar. The room here is $7 a day which includes food, so that is not so bad but still not cheap. There is good bus service back and forth from town, so I use that instead of taxis. Everyone complains about living costs here and houses are practically impossible to get. I hear that three-room apartments that used to rent for $30 are now going for $60 to $75. Laborers, who have left the pineapple and sugar plantations and now are doing defense work, are sleeping in the parks.

I called Sven Dithmers and his wife. The Company sent them out here a couple of years ago. They have a nice place with a beautiful view and consider themselves very lucky as they just walked off the ship and right into a fully furnished house. They are members of the beach club which is right next to the Moana, so we had a swim there first before going out to dinner. They are enjoying life to the fullest here, but got word a few days ago that they are due to leave here September 5th on the Matsonia for Los Angeles. They do not plan to spend any time on the coast, but will go right to New York by train. They don't know what will happen there, but presumably Sven will have to go somewhere because he does not expect the Company will keep him in New York.

Mail was just delivered, and a wonderful letter from Ruth came with pictures of the girls on the beach at Balboa! It really choked me up to see my beautiful family. Now I would not see them again for a very long time. What a terrible way to live! Is it really worth it?? However, I tell myself that it will not always be this way. That is my one great hope. The maximum will be two years, and if conditions haven't improved by then, we will just take our chances and stay at home. We only live once, and to carry on this way for a few extra dollars—well, we'll just not do it, that's all. I will stand for this two-year period, but if we can't be together after that, I will find something else to do.

Friday, August 22, I got out of bed at 5:15 AM to get to the airport, about an hour from town. I got there some time after 7:00 AM, and then it took about an hour to get weighed and the baggage sorted. There were nine crew and seventeen passengers. With the mail and freight, that was a full load. The Pan Am Clipper left at 8:30 AM for the ten-hour flight to Midway Island. We got up to around 8,000 feet and could see quite a few islands and coral reefs. It is readily understandable why ships going directly from Honolulu to Manila have to be on the look-out as I think it should be very easy, especially at night, to run right into the reefs. I know they are all charted, but the bad weather is not.

The trip was very smooth, but crowded. Tomorrow I understand there will be seven fewer passengers, so it should be much better. We had some sandwiches and hot soup at about 11:00 AM and then at 3:00 PM a very nice cold buffet. There was entirely too much food, but we all enjoyed it. About twenty minutes before we landed at Midway, they pulled the shades and would not let us look out. It reminded me of dear old Louieland, my pet name for Japan, because it made no sense to me. After we landed there were no restrictions. I walked freely all around the place. They are putting up several oil storage tanks, as well as a pretty complete repair shop for airplanes, or at least that is what it looked like to me.

It was very hot and sticky there. The food was excellent, and the hotel nice, but not air conditioned. I was rolling in perspiration and thinking about having to get up at 4:30 AM for the next flight. Today, August 23, is Kathie's fourth birthday. I'm glad we celebrated her party before I left Pasadena.

The next morning after eating some breakfast and watching the baggage load, we finally left the water and headed skyward at 6:45 AM. It's 1,030 miles to Wake Island, and we cross the International Date Line, skipping a day. The airplane is not so crowded and we got a game of stud poker going. I won $9.15 and was the biggest winner. I hope they still want to play with me on the next leg of the trip. The Clipper got up to 9,000 feet, and the temperature there is just right, much better than the hot, sticky weather of the tropics. With fewer passengers, we were served a regular sit-down meal instead of a buffet.

We arrived on Wake at 4:30 PM Monday, not Sunday, which was the day we left. After checking into the hotel, I went for a swim. It felt good to have a little exercise, after sitting in the plane all day. The beach was beautiful there, and the water very clear, just like crystal. It was very refreshing.

The next day was a long flight: 1,530 miles to Guam. We passengers really had the trip organized with the game of stud poker going in good fashion. The boys paid me $10 yesterday, and in addition to that I won the landing pool of $10, by best guessing the time of arrival. That's the first one I have ever won in the twelve years of crossing the Pacific!

Guam is the largest of the islands where we have stopped and also the oldest as far as settlement goes. The total population is about 23,000. All the houses are one story, built about 10 or 12 feet off the ground. The place seems quite clean and at night the little town of Agona looked comfortable enough. Some of the houses have tin roofs, and some thatched. They have electric lights in the hotel and the town itself, but otherwise kerosene lamps are the order of the day. This place does not seem to be as busy as Midway or Wake. Both of those islands had a lot of construction work going on which has either been completed on Guam or not yet started. I imagine that both would apply as the Army has been here for many years. When we landed, the American passengers were given a permit, and we were free to go anywhere on the island except certain restricted areas. The others who were not US citizens could not leave the hotel compound.

The name of the Clipper I am on is the Philippine Clipper. About ten days ago the Honolulu Clipper ran into a coral reef taking off from here. There was no one hurt, but the plane was damaged. They now have it in shape and expect to fly it back to San Francisco tomorrow.

The next morning, August 27, we got up at 4:30 AM and the Clipper got off at 6:00 AM. After another long flight of 1,500 or so miles, we landed in Manila Bay at a place called Civite. It was about an hour by car to Manila. In both Honolulu and here I don't see why they couldn't land right on the water in front of the city, but I guess they know better. The ride to the city was typical tropical country and looked none too clean. Native houses were built off the ground, and the roofs were either corrugated iron or thatched. Sea water was generally standing under them with pigs and various other animals running around. The city of Manila, however, from what little I have seen, is thoroughly modern and fully American.

The stud poker was again pretty good on the plane, and I picked up about $12. So, from Honolulu to Manila, my net profit was about $40 which helped my meager assets some, plus a lot of fun in getting it. I'll probably lose some of the later games, but be that as it may. Most of the passengers are getting off here in Manila, but I understand others are getting on as they said the plane would be full.

We left Manila Thursday, August 28, at about 8:30 AM, a successful but uneventful trip. We stopped at Macao to discharge and take on mail which should have taken only about ten minutes. However, it seems that some of the papers were not made out correctly, so a whole new set had to be prepared which took the best part of 45 minutes. Although you can move around inside the plane, the space is very small and at this time of year extremely hot. They finally got things fixed okay, and about 45 minutes later we landed in Hong Kong.

Ruth Briggs, Pasadena, California

Norman is so wonderful. He has sent cables to me at every stop so I know things are going okay so far. The first was from Honolulu on August 20 when he arrived. He said the trip was ordinary. But he also said no stud poker! I know Norman loves to play poker, so obviously he was disappointed that on the ship there were no games going. Oh well, I'm sure he'll have plenty of times to play once he reaches Hong Kong.

The next cable was from Midway Island on August 23, Kathie's birthday. He said things were proceeding okay and thanked me for the mail he received in Hawaii. And, of course, said Happy Birthday to Kathie.

Cables also came from Wake, Guam, and Manila. On August 28 he sent a cable from Hong Kong, confirming that he was assigned there, as we thought. He also said the stud poker was good, so I imagine that he played on the Clipper flights and actually won!

It was so good to get the cables. I hope he gets my letters soon. I can't wait to get some letters from him to get some real news on how he is doing.

Chapter III
Arrival in Hong Kong

The sun was just setting when the Pan Am Clipper sea-plane arrived that Thursday afternoon, August 28. Hong Kong harbor was spectacular, with Victoria Peak, the top British residential area, ablaze in color while the busy dock area was in the shadows. But you could still see the bustling of the city streets, the jam-packed fishing boats in Aberdeen, and the ferry going across the harbor from Kowloon to Hong Kong Island.

Customs was no problem; the British were very accommodating. I opened my bags, but all they did was to glance at them and shut them up. Hong Kong seemed a fine port—no papers to make out. They did, however, have a list of the passengers, so that probably eased things red-tape wise. George Behrman met me, and after getting through the formalities with the customs, he took me to the Gloucester Hotel so I could check in. By the time I got ashore and registered at the hotel it was almost 5:00 PM, so the office was closed. George took me up to his apartment where I had dinner with the other two men who were living with him.

I must say my first impressions of Hong Kong were very favorable indeed, and the Limeys had certainly done a good job as far as the city itself goes. The downtown foreign business section was thoroughly British and most of the buildings of the old style architecture. The rooms were large with high ceilings and each floor had a balcony. The General Post Office was built in 1911, but I should say that most of the buildings were built well before the turn of the century. Some, of course, were more up-to-date which is really something to comment on being that they are British. Most of the hotels had lounges and air-conditioned public rooms, but the rooms themselves were not. The streets had traffic lights at main intersections which the vehicles follow, but not the pedestrians.

The residential section of the main city of Hong Kong, which is on Hong Kong Island, is in a section known as Victoria on the top of the mountain and known as "The Peak." It is probably around 1500 feet, if not more, above sea level. There are roads going up there for cars and buses, but the main public transportation is the Peak Tramways, a cable car similar to the one going up Rokko in Kobe, Japan. It is certainly a beautiful spot, and all the residences of course have a fine view of the harbor. There is about eight degrees difference in the temperature between the city and the Peak. We took about a seven mile walk before dinner, and made a complete circle. I must say that it is a beautiful place. The streets and sidewalks are all paved so that it makes it very convenient and easy to get around.

There are many single houses, but a substantial part of the living quarters seem to be apartments. They seem very nice and fully up-to-date. They are mostly from 4–8 stories high, and have automatic elevators, that is, no operators, or as the Limeys say: "No drivers, you just get in and push the button for the floor you want."

George Behrman has a very nice apartment with a large living room a good-sized dining room and two bedrooms, each with a bath. Three Company men were living there, but Watson left the day after I arrived as he was transferred to Rangoon. George is going on home leave soon, and wanted to know if I would take over his place. That seemed fine to me.

I will also be taking over George's job. The organization is somewhat different here than in Japan, but my work will apparently consist of running the gasoline and kerosene sales as an assistant to what is known as the Territory Manager. From what I can make out, the Territory Manager is about the same as the District Sales Manager in Japan. I will probably have to do a little traveling to Canton, Macao, and then up the coast to Swatow. I am glad that for the present at least I am going to be stationed here. The first plan was to send me to Rangoon, but at the last minute the plans were changed and they sent Watson down there. I don't know anything about Rangoon, but I would say off hand that I got the better deal.

The new General Manager here will be A. W. Bourne who is now in Singapore. Bourne, I believe, is about 48 years old and is one of the 'marked boys' as he was out here for several years and then transferred to London. I don't know the details and how long he stayed there, but anyway he has been pushed along. Parker was general manager here, and he went to New York as president. He has now stepped out and Schultz has gone in the number one job, so it looks as though Bourne might be the next president when Schultz moves on.

Of course, Hong Kong is fully British, but there is also a lot of military presence. The first is pretty hard to get along with, the second is difficult. When you put them both together, it is next to impossible. You see the British uniforms all over the place, and certainly a more conglomerate bunch would be hard to imagine. Different uniforms for each section of the Empire, and then the individual variations for the branch of service. They all dress for dinner, and it surely gives me a pain in the neck. The British Empire is about to crack, and to see all these fools sitting around in boiled shirts, some with monocles, drinking and eating, is a sight to behold. They are getting everything from America—boats, planes, and such—but they had better put a few of these silly fools out here to do some real work. Well, I will keep my mouth shut since it's their place here.

In the last few years, as Japan invaded China, thousands of Chinese refugees had come to Hong Kong. The streets were very crowded and commerce was flourishing. Hawkers were constantly calling out the wonderful claims of their products amidst the side-by-side shacks lining the road.

I was glad that my family was safe and sound in the United States. Hong Kong was not a place I would want them to be at this time, and certainly not Japan, as the Company was trying to get all our people out. Hong Kong has been a British Colony since 1840 and a free port. Commerce made it a city that rarely slept. Business deals were made during the day and other deals went on all night. The British kept things in order. Sort of. I learned early of the normal routine for business. Begin work a little after 9:00 AM. Repair to the bar across the street for a quick gin at 11:00 AM. Then back to the office, returning to the bar for lunch and more serious drinking at noon!

So I wasn't all that apprehensive about being shipped to the office in Hong Kong. The British had earlier introduced me to one of their favorite drinks, Pink Gin. Just pour the gin over ice, with a few splashes of bitters. A fine drink to help one live in the Orient. Yes, you don't have to be crazy to live in the Far East, but it helps. All kidding aside, the British did have things running smoothly at the time. England was at war with Germany, not Japan. And no one thought Japan foolish enough to launch an attack on British soil.

I well knew at the time that I was going right into the midst of trouble, but even with all the preparations going on, and forerunners of armed conflict on every side—supplies, troops, and most of all conversation, rumors without end—I would still have bet my last dollar that everything would be all right. The British went on about how they could hold Hong Kong, that the Japanese would never get it and if they did get into a serious situation, immediate help would come from Singapore. However, the stock British expression was: "When is the balloon going to go up?"

Ruth Briggs, Pasadena, California

I finally received my first letter from Norman after he arrived in Hong Kong. It seems he knew some of the Company men there, and I was glad to hear that he got a nice apartment on the Peak to share with some others. And his job seems agreeable to him.

I'm glad he didn't have to go to Rangoon, even though Tom Nock apparently is there. He would have enjoyed working with him again. But Hong Kong seems much more civilized. Although I know he's not too fond of formal dinners that the British are prone to, I'm sure he'll find other things to his liking, like getting a regular group to play poker with him. Hopefully, that will make it a little less lonely for him.

The girls here keep me busy, which really helps. During the day, time passes by fairly fast. It's the evenings, after the ritual bath and bedtime stories are done, and the girls asleep, that I feel sorry for myself. I keep telling myself, however, that I'm not the only one. There are many women here whose husbands are in the military and in danger daily. So, I'll count my blessings that Norman is a civilian and, hopefully, in a safe place.

The car was delivered on August 31, a green Chevrolet! Norman ordered it for me before he left. He is so thoughtful. He knew I would need help getting around doing the normal errands and shopping. With two babies, a car will make it so much easier for me. I've driven a little bit before, as Ma and Pa have a car. But I'll have to practice and get used to it.

Chapter IV
Getting Settled

I moved into the apartment on the Peak on September 1. It's quite ample, with one bedroom off the entrance hall which Lee Cramer has. Down the hall, the next room is the dining room, with the living room opening off to the right. There are sliding doors between, which usually stay open so that the two rooms are practically one. The kitchen is to the left with the other bedroom to the right. The front bedroom has its own bathroom, and the rear bedroom has two bathrooms, so no one has to share which is very convenient. George and I have the rear bedroom. A small balcony, separated by steel frame glass doors, is off the living room, which gives a perfectly marvelous view looking out over the harbor. It also gives us a nice cool breeze. I am generally soaked through with sweat from walking up from the tram station, but it does not take long to get cooled off up here. Everybody says that the hot weather is about over, although whites are worn until the middle of October.

George has a dog named Tiger, named that as his markings are just like one. Tiger's one great aim in life is to go walking. So, my usual procedure when I get home is to take Tiger out for about an hour walk. This suits me fine as I get some exercise and there are really some very fine walks around the Peak.

My next order of business is to see if I can rent a practice room to play the piano. I might see if I could rent a piano to have at the apartment, but I would not want to annoy the boys or the neighbors by my banging. If I can rent a practice room, then I can go whenever I want and no one will be bothered.

Maybe I will be able to find a teacher too.

Everything would be fine if Ruth, Kathie, and Carol were here. Although we've been separated before, I guess I'm getting old, as every time I think of home I begin to crack up and tears come very easily. The next Clipper will be out here September 12. I hope it brings another letter. I plan to have one ready to send to Ruth by then. Ships are going out too, but very few, and no schedules are given, so I'll spend the extra money for air mail.

The office is closed Wednesday afternoons as well as Saturdays, which is something new to me. However, I have no objections to that! George has a sail boat which he charters. Last Wednesday afternoon two other men in the office and I went out for a sail. When we started out the weather was fine, but we ran into a couple of squalls and got completely soaked though. Regardless, we had a good time.

Later that evening one of the Chinese agents gave a party. Although different from the Japanese parties, the principles were about the same with bowing and scraping going on. However, there was no sitting on the floor as they had regular chairs. There were twelve of us and we sat around a table. There was a circular revolving tray with various dishes on it to which we helped ourselves. All in all, there were about seven or eight courses. I do not have any idea what they all were, but the main ingredients seemed to be chicken and pork. Like a Japanese party, it ended fairly early. We were all home by 9:30 PM.

Thursday, September 4, McCaskey walked into the office. He was on the American President Lines' President Garfield on his way to Manila. He had a lot to say about Japan, but the main fact was that he was out and hopes never to see the place again. About 50 Americans got out of Kobe on the Tatsuka Maru for Shanghai. When the freezing order came, their bank accounts were no good. It seems that you could draw up to 500 yen a month, but you had to have it in a Japanese bank. Some of his personal property he got rid of, but most of it he just packed up and stored in the office. It seems that there was no great difficulty in doing this, although after the freezing order, nothing could be sold without a permit for both the seller and the buyer. To leave the country you had to have something like five different permits from various government departments and evidently this was done on purpose to cause delays and to prevent or at least make it very disagreeable for people to get out. They were particularly hard on the British and Mac says unreasonably so.

The only one left in Shukugawa, Japan, now is John Allison. He moved back into his old house in the missionary compound. It surely must be a lonely place. Harry moved to Shioya, taking Oscar, our dog, with him. He was hoping to be transferred to New York, and even had a visa, but Mac said a cable had just come from Switzerland saying nothing doing, so Harry is stuck in Japan.

Mac said that those leaving are due for furlough and there seems to be no move to completely close up the Company in Japan, although there is very little business to do, and what there is, the Japanese staff could surely do. Mac says there is no physical danger and except for being annoying and troublesome, things are just about the same as they were when I left. However, you cannot move about freely unless you have a special permit.

Just before getting on the ship to Manila, Mac received a wire to remain in Hong Kong. I suggested he move into the apartment when Behrman leaves.

I spent the better part of Saturday going all over town hunting for a place where I could practice the piano. I went to all the piano stores, but there was no interest in renting pianos, and no practice rooms. They just wanted to sell me one. I then checked at some of the schools. The nearest is a Catholic institution, St. Joseph's School. I finally found someone in charge to talk to. They only have one piano which is in the general auditorium, and it would be free from 4-7 PM daily. They had never received such a request before, but agreed that I could use their facility. So, I'm glad that I found a place to give me something to do outside of the office and the American Club, which I have just joined.

The American Club is in an air conditioned building and is mainly a luncheon club. However, the boys do go there after the office. It is also the main center for poker, but the stakes are too high for me there. The quarters are somewhat small, but they have a dining room for men, a lounge, and then a place portioned off for a mixed (men and women's) dining room. The library is in the lounge, and then they have the bar and the poker room.

Wednesday, September 10, I had lunch with Mac. He told me he resigned from the Company and is going home. He had received a cable from Margaret who was having a very difficult time going it alone at home. Apparently, she could not abide the separation anymore, and said if he stayed out here it would tell her he did not care about her or their son anymore. Mac said his family came first. He was afraid of what she might do, so home he goes. I don't blame him. I think things are looking to clear up in the Orient, but we all have to make our own decisions. I think there is a fairly good chance that families will be permitted to come back next spring. I don't think the China business will be completely settled by next spring, but I do think it will be a lot nearer to a solution.

Last Thursday, Paget took the Company launch and some customers for a party down the bay. There were about twelve of us in all, half of whom were Chinese. The others were British with the exception of Paget and me. Swimming was the order of the day, but my swimming trunks were in Manila. I had gone swimming at Wake and hung my trunks up in the plane to dry. Naturally, I thought they would stay there until Hong Kong, as I gave them to the steward. But, they were taken off at Manila. Hopefully, they will be in on the next Clipper flight. Even though I didn't swim with everyone else, I got cooled off being away from the city. We got back about 8:00 PM.

Friday night Paget and I took the Company launch again for the week-end calling on agents who live on two nearby islands. The main purpose was business, but also pleasure as Paget asked along several of his friends. We expected to get back Sunday night, but were delayed until Monday morning. Typhoon signs were up all week-end, but did not hit Hong Kong full force until Tuesday. When I went home later, the glass doors on the front of the apartment had been blown in! We had to move the furniture out of the living room into the dining room. The typhoon was at its height about 12:30 on Tuesday. The office was closed because transportation was tied up. Most of the Chinese staff live on the mainland in Kowloon, and the ferries were not operating.

With what little I saw of the Chinese way of living over the week-end in calling on the Chinese agents, I can readily understand why Japan has gone as far as she has in China. With the dirt and the filth that the Chinese live in and the entire indifference to their surroundings, it is no wonder that some outsider could walk in and with a little organization take over to a limited extent. However, this very indifference of the Chinese is absolutely a stone wall to going any further mainly on account of their numbers. I think Japan has gone about as far as she will get because she cannot mass her numbers against the Chinese and still maintain control.

The islands that we sailed by were perfectly beautiful, but the mess that the Chinese make in living on them is something to behold. Animals live far better than the main bulk of the Chinese that I saw on this trip.

Ruth Briggs, Pasadena, California

I just wrote Norman that his Aunt Irene passed away. She was his father's only sibling. Carol was named after her, as she was born on Pa's birthday. Norman was extremely close to her son, Malcolm, as they played together as children in Boston. Pa was making plans to go East to see her as we knew she was ill, but that trip didn't happen in time. Fortunately, her illness was neither painful nor unduly long, and the end came quietly and peacefully.

I've now put our savings account in my name, as Norman suggested. I removed his name and foreign address on the bank records and also on all utilities, so there would be no question of any of our accounts being frozen. I am getting $90 living allowance from Standard Oil for separation compensation, and Norman has allocated part of his salary that the company sends directly to me.

Kathie has made friends with a little girl who lives on the next block, but our back yards back up. There is a little gate they can go through, so it's very convenient. Before that, I was taking her back to Ma and Pa's neighborhood several blocks away to play with friends. So this is much better for me, and they have a lot of fun together.

I plan to drive the car up to Santa Barbara to visit my brother, Walter. Edith, his wife, is great, and the two girls, Lynette and Marcia, are close to Kathie and Carol's age, so it should be a lot of fun. This will be the first time I will drive the car a really long distance, which is a little scary, but I am looking forward to the outing.

Chapter V
Down to Business

My trunk finally arrived on September 23 with my other belongings, including the typewriter. So now I feel like I'm really settled in. J. B. Emmert, the man in charge here in the office, is retiring and leaving for home the end of the month. The staff gave him a very nice piece of carved ivory, presented to him at a dinner at the Hong Kong Hotel. It was not a particularly late affair, as it started at 8:30. I was home at 12:30. It was the usual dinner with speeches and all. Every Saturday night they have a dance at the hotel, and some of the boys went from the party into that, but I beat it for home. The place was all full of Limeys with their boiled shirts. With the British Empire at war I thought it best to stay out of there. Another reason was that it would probably be fairly expensive. I am going to see how things go here in money matters before I start going around. I wish there were some cheap yen here, but so far that market has not developed.

Since I joined the American Club, I always go there for lunch. I have not started going there yet after the office, which I should probably do to meet a few of the boys. My usual routine after the office is to stop and bang on the piano at St. Joseph's for about an hour and then go home and take Tiger out for a walk. By the time I get back, it is time for dinner. Next month perhaps I'll stop by the Club and see what the boys are doing. The most popular place around here seems to be the Hong Kong Hotel. Why, no one seems to know, as it is about twice as expensive as the Club.

The Hong Kong government at the present time is in a swell mess. They have been building air raid shelters all over the place. It seems that there have been quite a few of the boys who have been making money on the side. One Limey has already shot himself and another one tried to take poison, but he did not take enough. There are inquiries every day, with a Chinese girl, Mimi Lau, mixed up in it somehow. Most of the Limey wives are in Australia, and I bet the mail will be hot when they hear about it. Yep, the old Limey Empire at war wants help from America. Probably 90% of the stuff we ship across the Atlantic is mixed up in some sort of racket.

I spent a week in Macao, leaving Hong Kong September 26, returning on Friday, October 3. The four-hour boat ride there is pleasant, certainly much better than the place itself. Macao is a Portuguese Colony. I must admit that the Limeys have done a much better job with Hong Kong than the Portuguese have with Macao. Hong Kong is at least clean, which is more than I can say for Macao. I stayed at the Grand Hotel, although it certainly isn't a grand place. It's a concrete building, about eight stories high and maybe 5 or 6 years old, or at least old enough to have the new worn off. It made me think of Louieland all over as it was built just like they would do the job. And, nothing worked, except the elevators which were Otis. Dirt was everywhere, but I did not spend a great deal of time in my room, so I guess I can't complain too much.

The main interest in Macao is gambling, and all that goes with it. The boat schedules from Hong Kong are arranged so you can leave Hong Kong after office hours and get back in the morning before opening time. Some people, of course, stayed for several days, but the boats were always full.

We have two agents stationed here. In addition, several of our other agents from various parts of China were there, having been driven out by the Japanese. They all gave me a party, with the main purpose of indulging in a game of chance. We played five-card stud poker. The biggest raise was HK$15, (equivalent to US $3.50), so the game was not too unreasonable. After the first night, they wanted a game every night. As I had nothing else to do, it passed the time and was fun besides. The boys took me for HK$70. The usual procedure was to start about 6:00 PM, quit at midnight, have dinner, and then go home. They would never think of eating earlier, but fruit was passed around, so we always had something. They said that this conformed to life in Macao, as the rich Chinese stayed up all night and slept all day. The hotel was right in the noisiest part of town. It was practically impossible to sleep, so after I did get back I spent a good part of the night looking out the window watching the people go by.

Saturday afternoon the agent took me in his car for a drive around the place. There was a small residential section that was not too bad. That is where the richer Portuguese, or rather Eurasians, lived. I very much doubt if there are any true Portuguese there. There were also quite a few Germans living in Macao. When the Limeys kicked them out of Hong Kong that was about the only place they could go. The total population is about 300,000. When I visited the Water Department, they said the per capita consumption was about 3 gallons per day. I think the ratio at home is about 25 gallons per day, which explains the filth in Macao.

Macao is on what they call the West River Delta, on the Pearl River going up to Canton. The Louies now control Canton and all of the country immediately surrounding Macao. One of the main activities was smuggling supplies through the Louie lines. But the Japanese caught on, so now the only way they can do business is directly with the Japanese. The Chinese agents are perfectly willing to do business with them if there is enough of a kickback.

A month later I went to Canton for a week. The Japanese were trying to have things done their way. But, it is entirely different from my experience in Japan. People feel free to talk back to them here, which we did not dare do in Japan. Canton, now known as Quangzhow, certainly was bombed; block after block was just nothing but ruins. From the condition of the buildings left standing, I think the Japanese did the Chinese a favor. The brick buildings that were left were very dark, with not the slightest chance of any light or air getting through to the inside.

I got back to Hong Kong on Monday, November 3. The summer clothes have now been put away, although the weather is none too cool yet. In the middle of the day it gets pretty hot, but the morning and evenings are fine. Up on the Peak it is cool enough, but also very windy. I understand during January, February and March the Peak is usually fogged in all day. But down at the harbor the winter sun gets through.

I did not get a chance to do any banging on the piano in Canton, but am back to my usual routine of going to St. Joseph's after work. They have now given me a key to the auditorium and also a small cabinet where I keep my music. Before I always had to go find the number one boy, which always took around ten or fifteen minutes. Every once in a while one of the brothers comes down to talk, and we pass the time of day. They seem to be a very friendly crowd and don't inquire into any personal matters. The ones I have met are Americans. I am not making much progress on the piano, but it gives me something to do and makes the time go by quicker. It also keeps me out of the lobby of the Hong Kong Hotel, the booze place of choice after office hours.

Everyone here expects war between Japan and America, and there are quite a few bets on the matter. In spite of all the talk going on, we are still selling oil to Japan, even if it is in greatly reduced quantities. I don't think there will be war, but I admit it looks pretty dark. There is a large amount of bluff with the Japanese, and no reason why they shouldn't play that game as they have always been successful with it. The uncertainty is very unsettling. At one point it looked as if they were going to come around, but I guess they were just out for position. The more I see of it, the more I think McCaskey was right to resign and go home. It sure is tempting to think about not staying the two years that the Company wants me to, but instead to be home with my family.

On Friday I went to a piano recital at the Peninsula Hotel. Chun-Wa Lau, a piano teacher here, played some Bach, Schumann, Handel, Tchaikovsky, and Beethoven, as well as a couple of Mozart and Chopin pieces I sometimes bang out. She was very nervous which caused her to make some mistakes, but it was a pleasant diversion for me. Her students flooded the stage with flowers for her afterwards.

Word just came through that Pennybacker and Grant Whitman are being transferred here, with Pennybacker slated to go to Rangoon. I don't know about Grant. The Company seems to change assignments at the last minute, as I was originally supposed to go to Rangoon. I imagine Lillian is pleased to have Grant out of Japan and in British territory. Even though she is British, she'll just have to stay in Pasadena as families are not allowed to join us. Maybe by next spring things will have cleared, and our families will be able to join us. If the Company is transferring more men here from Japan that would indicate to me that the situation in Japan is not too good, but that the State Department must think that actual warfare in Hong Kong is not on the boards.

On Wednesday morning I was out in the Company car on business accompanied by a Chinese salesman. There was a low flying airplane right overhead. Coming in the other direction from us was a Chinese on a bicycle. He decided to look at the airplane rather than where he was going. The next thing anyone knew, there was a crash, and he was in a heap by the side of the road. As he hit the car straight on and the car went over something, I surely thought he was injured badly. But, luckily, it was the bicycle we ran over; he had been thrown clear. He knocked the front headlight completely off, messed up the radiator a bit, and put a dent in the hood. We had been going very slowly, but as he was coming down a hill, he had a little speed on. I jumped out of the car to see how he was. He had been knocked out, and had a bad cut on his head, and some cuts on his feet and hands. In addition, he had a stone jar of soy sauce on the back of the bicycle which had broken all over him. He certainly was a mess. We put him in the car and went a short distance to a police station. I insisted that he go to a doctor, so we took him in the car. They cleaned him up, and you would never know that it was the same guy. He had probably never been so clean before! He was not seriously hurt, and his mother came to get him as we left the doctor's office. His bicycle, of course, was a complete wreck, and it will probably take him some time to earn a new one. I am glad that we had the chauffeur and not me driving.

It's now the middle of November. I just got a nice long letter from Ruth with a note from Kathie enclosed. The formal picture of all of us that we had taken before I left was packed separately and arrived the same day. I sure wish my family were here, but it's wonderful to have this picture. It's really good of little Carol. Kathie's shyness shows, and I don't think it's great of either Ruth or me, but all in all it's a great family picture. Ruth asked what I wanted for Christmas, as she's getting organized for family gifts. I wrote back for her not to send me anything as there is nothing in the way of food that I need. We have Sunkist oranges every morning, and plenty of coffee, sugar, candy and other provisions. As for other material things, I don't want them to cart around or look after here. Under present conditions, the less that we have out here, the better off we will be until the war is over and we are back to normal living. I told her to get something small for my parents, and also get something for herself and the girls as I cannot send anything from here without an export permit which involves reams of papers. There is not much Christmas spirit in this, but I guess it just can't be helped.

I have a new roomer who moved in when Lee Cramer left. Max L. Ulrich is with the Company's Operating Department. His wife and son are in Westwood, Connecticut. He is very nice and also a good stud player. He has spent most of his time in Thailand and French-Indo China.

We now have a regular stud session going at the Club every Monday night from 5:30 to midnight, with time out to eat. It's a very congenial crowd and we set the limit at HK$10, or $2.50 US. It's a little high for me, but I'll try to hold my own. It is business stud pure and simple, and although we have a lot of fun, I personally would like it more if the limit were smaller. The HK dollar and the yen are equal as far as official rates go. In Japan only the big shots played for

2 yen, but down here that seems to be nothing. On the black market it was nothing in Japan. That is one thing I surely miss here, for it made expenses much cheaper. Well, it is a good game of stud, and although it is a little stiff, I think I can get by without losing my shirt.

Last Monday when we played the Hong Kong government decided to have a blackout. I had been through enough of those in Japan, and hoped it could be avoided here, but that's not to be. We started as usual, and played until 1:30 AM. The boys paid me for staying up, but I missed the last tram home. With the black-out, the taxis would not run. I ended up going home with Bradford, and slept on the couch in his flat which was walking distance from the Club. Bradford is with General Motors and knows the entire Japan bunch.

Later in the week Max and I decided to go to the movie show and see Buck Privates which had just arrived in town. The shows start at 5:30, 7:30, and 9:30. All seats are reserved, and you have to go at the stated times which is actually a good idea as you are not bothered during the show by people getting up and leaving or coming in. The British do have some good ideas once in a while. We went to the early show, so we were out to have dinner as usual at the apartment.

In November the weather turned cooler. However, only last week it was warm and I was wearing the tropical worsted suit that I bought in Boston. The papers here are all full of the Japanese business and negotiations of Saburo Kurusu, Japan's special envoy in Washington. I am more convinced than ever that they will never settle anything and the talks and posturing will go on until the European mess is over. I don't think Japan is going to back out of China, and America won't put on any more pressure, so the threats will go on both sides.

A boatload of Canadian troops arrived in mid-November. I don't know just how many, but I think I heard there were over 1,000. Everyone is in a uniform here—the Canadians and all the other branches of the British services. In early December we heard that British battleship *Prince of Wales* and cruiser *Repluse* arrived in Singapore. The newspapers were full of warnings to Japan that the British meant business and were fully prepared for any eventualities that might take place. Yes, you don't have to be crazy to live in the Far East, but it helps a lot.

Ruth Briggs, Pasadena California

I miss Norman so much. We were apart before when I came home early during my pregnancies with Kathie and Carol, but those were normal times. Now with the war in Europe and the Japanese invading China, things are very scary. I try to carry on in a normal fashion so the girls won't know how worried I am. And it's a great support having Ma and Pa Briggs so close here in Pasadena. They're a great help. I'm also lucky to have my parents, who retired from their mission work in Japan, on their little chicken farm in Pomona Plus I have three brothers close by—Don in Pomona, Walter in Santa Barbara, and Ed in Riverside.

It was wonderful having Norman here on home leave, especially for him to share Kathie's fourth birthday (celebrated early) and Carol's first! And the car he bought me before he left is a wonderful convenience. But the news between our government and Japan is not good. I heard on the radio that Washington rejected the Japanese proposals of November 20 because some features conflict with part of the general settlement under consideration, or some such bunk. Not good. German troops are advancing to Moscow, and the British North African offensive was blocked by tanks commanded by General Rommel. The world seems to be falling apart.

I'm glad the girls keep me hopping as it takes my mind off of worrying about Norman. I keep telling myself the company will keep him safe. I worry about him daily, but especially so when I pull the blackout shades down each night.

Section 2:
The Attack

Chapter I
Before the Attack

Saturday noon, December 6th, I left the office and headed for the American Club to have lunch. On my way over I stopped at Watson's store to pay a bill and presented a HK hundred dollar note. The girl said she was very sorry but with the weekend coming on they had deposited their surplus in the bank just a few minutes before and, as she wanted to keep what small change she had, would I please pay the bill on Monday? I replied in a joking way that possibly Monday might be too late. She did not think so, and I continued on my way to the American Club fully expecting to pay the bill on Monday. The bill remains unpaid.

Arriving at the Club, I sat down at a table with several men, including the American Consul General and two men who had just arrived from Shanghai. The first item of interest in the conversation was that the American gunboat, the "Mindanao," had sailed at midnight, Friday, for Manila. This seemed somewhat strange as the boat's regular patrol was between Hong Kong and Canton, China. We discussed the various implications of what this might mean, all of course bearing on the outbreak of hostilities.

The rumor was also circulating that the crews of merchant vessels had been ordered to their ships and that they might be sent to Singapore at any moment. The conversation continued along this line all through lunch, and although opinions were expressed to the contrary, it was the general consensus that nothing would happen at least until spring. That shows how much we knew about it.

Lunch finished, I sat around and read for a couple of hours and then went and practiced the piano at St. Joseph's College. Finishing with this, I did not want to go home and sit around the apartment alone, so went back downtown to a movie. After this, I went and had a bite to eat at the Dairy Farm and then took the Peak tram, the cable car up to the top of Victoria's Peak, arriving home shortly after 10 o'clock and went directly to bed.

Sunday morning I got up about 8 o'clock and had breakfast at 8:30. The help served it as usual, having no special comments to make. The Sunday paper was there, and after reading that through I was none the wiser as it had the usual items about how well prepared the British were in the Far East, and Japan had better move very cautiously. Having read enough of this, I tossed the paper to one side and decided that I would go down and bang out a little Mozart on the piano. Accordingly, I left the apartment, telling the servants that I would be back at 1:00 for lunch. Going down and back in the Tram, I did not pay any particular attention to the conversation going on around me, but there was certainly nothing to cause any special comment as far as I could see. The tram had the usual number of people on it, some with golf bags, others with tennis rackets, some going downtown, others going to church. There was no excitement, and as far as I was concerned, it was just an ordinary Sunday. There was no particular comment about war or peace, and everyone was going along as usual. People had no expectation whatsoever that their usual procedure would be rudely interrupted by the bursting of bombs.

After lunch and a short rest, I took Tiger for a walk around Luguard Road which encircled the Peak at the top and gave an excellent view of the harbor. This was the first time that I noticed something strange. I thought there were fewer ships in the harbor than usual, and even then I noticed one or two leaving. I recalled the conversation at the luncheon table of the previous day, about ships going to Manila and Singapore, but even then it made no profound impression upon me. After all, Hong Kong was a busy harbor, and I could not see where the departure of a few ships would have any direct bearing on a declaration of war, but I was to find out differently.

I stayed out with Tiger for most of the afternoon and returned to the apartment just as the sun was setting. I had dinner at 7:30 and was reading when Mac returned about 9:00 o'clock. Mac (M. L. Ulrich) and I shared the apartment together, and he had been away for the weekend sailing. Coming back in the Peak tram, Mac said he overheard conversation to the effect that the volunteers had been called out. I told him that I had heard nothing nor had I noticed any particular activity going on in the city during the weekend. I believe I mentioned the incident at Watson's, not having change for a hundred dollar note. We passed the time with conversation for the next hour or so, and then went to bed expecting to wake up the next morning to the usual daily go-along.

The expectation came true. I woke up at 7 o'clock, and as far as I could tell, it was the usual Monday morning—Sunday, December 7, in the USA. I went into breakfast at 7:30. The table was set and the morning paper there. Mac came in and sat down, and the boy served breakfast as he had always done. Then the phone rang. Bob Booten was on the other end and said that Pearl Harbor had been attacked. He said the Japanese planes had come into the harbor and hit all the ships, sinking them! Bob and I had done a lot of kidding in the office about the war question, and I really did not believe him, thinking it was some more funny business. We discussed it back and forth for a minute or two and then hung up.

I went back to the breakfast table and was telling Mac what Bob had said when in came the boy. He did not have his usual white serving jacket on, but was wearing his military uniform, which was a coverall, his gas mask, tin hat, and first aid kit. He informed us that he had just received orders to report at the ARP headquarters, the Air Raid Precaution. Mac and I both looked at each other and thought there might be something to the Pearl Harbor story after all, but as yet were not fully convinced. We finished our breakfast and left the apartment in time to catch the 8:00 Peak tram to go to the office.

Although I miss them terribly, I sure am glad that Ruth, Kathie, and Carol are safe in Pasadena.

Ruth Briggs, Pasadena, California, December 7

Ma and Pa Briggs came over for dinner after bringing Kathie home from church. After we ate, Carol, the ever-perpetual motion child of seventeen months, went down for her nap. It wasn't until after she woke up that we learned the war had started! She was playing around in the living room, and in one of her blitz-maneuvers she climbed up on the couch and turned on the radio. I usually listen to the news once a day, and then some music stations, and she loves the music. But this time a special news report was on—Pearl Harbor had been bombed by the Japanese!

TAKEN IN HONG KONG
DECEMBER 8, 1941

What we had feared had happened. War with Japan! What a tragedy in Hawaii. Many ships and lives were lost! With the Japanese attacking the US at Pearl Harbor, I worried again about Norman in Hong Kong, with the Japanese armies so close in parts of China! The radio has been serving me steadily ever since. The next morning I heard that Japan had also attacked Hong Kong, Manila, and Singapore! I hope Norman made it to one of those air raid shelters in time. I'm so worried I don't know what to do, except try to think straight and keep as busy as possible and think of all the people that are worse off than we are.

I called up Lillian Whitman and learned that Grant is on a ship en route to Singapore! Then I talked to Mrs. Enikeieff, whose husband is still in Japan. She said maybe the Japanese wouldn't put him in a concentration camp since he is white Russian. Then she said that the Chief was put in jail for ten days! He took a picture of his dog in his own backyard, and they caught him, took away his Kodak, and put him in jail. They never bothered to look ad the picture until ten days later. When they found out it was only a dog, they let him out!

I am trying to be calm, and trying to show the optimistic side as much as possible to keep up Ma and Pa's spirits. Ma told me she had a dream last night that Norman telephoned her and had gotten on the last clipper out, and we should meet him at the airport. Oh, if it were only true!

Chapter II
The Attack

Halfway to the station we saw planes over Kai-Tak, the airport on the Kowloon side. The anti-aircraft guns, or ack-acks, were firing, and we saw white circles of smoke in the air where the shells had burst. They had conducted all sorts of maneuvers during the past month, and we still weren't sure that this might not be some more practice rather than the real thing. When we got to the Peak tram station, however, we were finally convinced that it was the real thing. The balloon had gone up this time for good.

Going down in the tram, everyone was talking about Pearl Harbor, the damage done, and that Japan had declared war on Britain, America and Holland. When I walked from the lower tram station to the office, people were running back and forth. It was evident that all knew the war was on!

Turning the corner at Queen's Road into Pedder Street, the first thing that greeted our eyes was the newsboy hawking a special edition with big headlines "Roosevelt Sends Special Message to Emperor." I didn't know whether the Emperor had sent a message, and this was the reply, or whether it was about the attack? In any event Hong Kong was being attacked. Mac and I continued on to the office only a block away.

Arriving there, we had no doubt that the war was on all right. We were the first two members of the foreign staff to arrive, and only a very few of the Chinese and Portuguese staff were in the office. The first remark that greeted me was from a member of the Chinese staff: "You Americans have got your chance now; you will have to clean them up. We have been fighting them for four years."

The office was in confusion as there were very few people there, and those that were there were running around trying to obtain information. I had a couple of phone calls with members of the staff saying that they could not get to the office and wanted to know what the situation was downtown. I had been in the office about 15 minutes during which more of the staff arrived. The sirens started again, which meant the Japanese were coming back for another visit.

The office was one of the oldest buildings in Hong Kong, and therefore about one of the worst places you could be in during a raid. There was, however, an air raid shelter in the basement, and we told the Chinese staff to either go there or over to the Hong Kong Hotel, which was a modern reinforced building. There were three Americans in the office by this time, and we decided to make a run for the American Club which was a little farther away than the Hong Kong Hotel, but would be less crowded. The Japanese planes were over the city, but we made it. The planes circled over Kai-Tak, but neither machine-gunned nor dropped bombs as they were evidently over for a check up and observing the damage done on their first visit. The machine guns were going ack-ack, but the Japanese were high and well out of range.

When the Japanese planes came over the first time, there were six or seven planes of the Chinese Navigation and Aviation Corporation (CN & AC) on the ground. These planes flew between Hong Kong and Chunking. Also, swinging from her moorings was one of the Pan American Clippers which was on the shuttle service between Hong Kong and Manila. The Clipper was waiting orders for departure, but there were no passengers aboard nor were there any on the CN & AC planes. The Japanese came over and machine-gunned the Clipper and all the planes. All immediately burst into flames. The Clipper burned to the water line and sunk, and the planes were just a mass of ruins. None of the planes was loaded, and the people that were on the ground at the time ran for the hanger. As far as I know, no one was killed or even hurt. The Japanese did not bomb the airfield; they only machine-gunned the planes.

When the second raid was over, Mac and I decided that we had better go back home and pack up the things in the apartment. All the furniture in the apartment belonged to a man home on leave, and we had the apartment during his absence. However, he had been active in Air Raid Precaution (ARP) work. As a precaution against some such thing as this happening, he had an empty grease drum in the apartment for packing things like silver, linen, blankets, and other ornaments that he had left behind. With the assistance of the cook, everything possible was put in this grease drum. This, together with one or two small packing boxes which were also filled, we put in the store room. I then packed one small overnight bag with as many essentials of clothing as I could and also one wardrobe suitcase. These were packed with the newest clothes that I had, leaving in the steamer trunk my older ones. The idea was that if we did have a chance to get out, I could in all probability take the overnight bag and possibly the suitcase. I was leaving the older clothes behind, not the new ones for the Japanese army and the Chinese looters. Mac was doing the same thing, and we finished both the packing of the apartment, as well as our own personal belongings, shortly before noon. The cook wanted to know if we would have lunch there, but we said no, that we would go downtown to the Club and see what the latest information was.

The rest of Monday was spent going back and forth between the office and the Club whenever the air raid alarm sounded. The Club was on the fifth floor of the Hong Kong and Shanghai Bank Building, which was one of the newest buildings in Hong Kong. It was a modern reinforced structure, as were also the Gloucester and Hong Kong Hotel buildings. These, plus the air raid tunnels, were the safest places to be in if you could make any of them from where you were when the alarm sounded.

The Club was the main gathering place for the Americans and consequently left more space elsewhere for others. The Japanese planes kept coming over all afternoon, but did not drop any bombs on the city. Their main purpose was observation and to cover their troops coming into the New Territories adjacent to Kowloon. The ack-ack guns were going which kept the Japanese planes high. They went for some of the ack-ack gun emplacements on the outskirts of the city, but they really did not open up on the city itself until Wednesday.

As darkness fell, we expected some night activity. Consequently we stayed at the Club as the apartment was right at the top of the Peak and thus an excellent target. However, everything was peaceful and quiet as the Japanese were apparently going to operate only in the daytime. We had one alarm shortly after 10 o'clock, but this was a plane from the CN & AC coming in, which the British thought at first was a Japanese plane. At about 11:30 we decided to go home. The city, of course, was in complete blackout. We took the Peak Tram home. Walking from the upper station to the apartment, we could see the scene below us. It was a complete blackout, except for one or two lights in the city, as well as an occasional light on the boats in the harbor.

Tuesday morning came, and the Japanese planes were right on schedule flying over the city about 8:00 o'clock. The ack-acks went into action, and the Japanese went for these by bombing the emplacements in the outlying districts, but not as yet in the city itself. They were very high, and their main purpose was still observation and covering their troops moving towards Kowloon.

Although a good part of Tuesday was spent keeping under cover, we did try to keep some semblance of an organization in the office. The main thing was to keep the oil supplies going, and the Hong Kong Motor Bus, operating on diesel, was one of the most important. The main supplies were in Kowloon, and we knew that supplies would have to be stored on the Hong Kong side, so our main attention was given to getting them over.

We had some bulk storage on the Hong Kong side, but our main installation, Laichikok, was across the harbor in Kowloon. As the Japanese were stepping up the tempo of their raids, the Chinese at Laichikok quit work. Everyone naturally thought that an oil installation would be one of their first targets. At about 3:30 in the afternoon I got a call from the installation that they wanted me to come right over. I took the Company launch and went.

When I arrived, Mills, Larson, Suter, Sanger, and Williams were already there. Mills, Larson, and Suter lived on the installation, and they had their families there. Mills had his wife only, and she was on duty at the Kowloon Hospital. But Mrs. Larson had three sons ranging from seven to fourteen years old, and Mrs. Suter had her eight-year-old daughter there. It was decided that it would be better to send the women and children to Hong Kong. They had no particular place to stay so I suggested that they go to my apartment as I was going to spend the night at the installation. There were two bedrooms which could be turned over to them, and Mac could sleep on the couch in the front room. I could not reach Mac by phone, so I wrote him a chit which they could take with them.

This was the first home to be broken up in Hong Kong, and the first American refugees of the war there. The expectation was that they would return to Laichikok later, but I think we all sensed in our bones, the women especially, that they were leaving for good and would never see their home again. They hastily packed a few suitcases with their own and the children's clothing. These were put aboard the launch. Several trips were made back to the house to get some more odds and ends that they thought of separately at the last minute. They were finally aboard the launch with their bags and bundles, farewells said. Although they were only going across the harbor, it was a grim departure with the reality of war.

I don't know why the women and children were still in Hong Kong, but perhaps they had planned to return home with their husbands on their next home leave. I know the company advised us, and the State Department has also requested, that all family members leave months ago. Again, I certainly was glad that my family was safe. War is no place for women and children, and I certainly had no desire to be in the middle of it myself.

Dick Sanger went back to Kowloon and Mills, Larson, and Williams stayed at the installation. Felix Suter and I went to the Kai-Tak airport. We drove two tank trucks full of aviation fuel. With the heavy plane traffic of people leaving, we were asked to drive the tank trucks directly to the planes for refueling. This was certainly the first time I had pumped fuel into an airplane. I finished before Suter, and drove my empty truck back to the installation.

Just as night was falling, a small British tank with four Chinese soldiers on it came into the installation. They said they had been sent in by the British military to guard it. Four men to guard a big installation! It looked ridiculous, but no one said anything. They took up their position on one of the piers along the waterfront. The sergeant in charge of the detail took up his post at the main tank truck entrance.

In the middle of the Hong Kong harbor and right opposite the installation was an island known as Stonecutter's. This island was military headquarters and supposed to be fortified. They had troops, barracks, and heavy guns on the island. Just how many of the latter I don't know, but they did have several 9.2 inch guns. Soon after dark, probably about 7 o'clock, Stonecutter's opened fire on the Japanese who were coming into the New Territories and marching towards the city of Kowloon. I would say the Japanese at this time were about ten or twelve miles away. Stonecutters only fired one round at a time, but it kept up all night long at regular intervals. About every seven or eight minutes they would let one go.

It was exactly one mile from Stonecutter's Island to the Standard Oil installation and when they fired, the flash of the gun lit up the whole compound. It also shook the entire house, which was a frame building, and then we would hear the screech of the shell as it went over. The Japanese were not replying, as evidently they had not gotten their field pieces near enough yet. I was afraid that there might be a dud or a shot fall short. If one fell in the installation and hit a full or empty fuel tank, there would only be one result—a disastrous fire.

At 1:00 AM Suter returned from Kai-Tak. He was dead tired having been on the go since early the previous morning. He attempted to get some sleep, but I don't believe he got very much with Stonecutter's firing away.

The main road to Castle Peak and the New Territories ran right back of the installation. Traffic was going on all night with supplies and troops going out. There was also some traffic returning which were probably the empties coming back for more, but they also must have been bringing some wounded in. At about 3:30 in the morning, Wednesday, the sergeant on duty at the gate received a phone message to evacuate the installation as the Japanese were very close. He informed the soldiers on the tank; they cranked up the engine and putt-putted out of the installation. Our main defense and protection, one small tank, was gone!

We had a launch standing by with steam up, the crew sleeping aboard, for just such an occasion as this. We were all awake in the house, and I ran down to the waterfront and informed the crew to be ready as we were leaving. Stonecutter's was still firing away. Larson's kitchen was full of tinned goods, and he wanted to get as much on the launch as possible. I think we put several gunny sacks full aboard. Mills had a couple of cedar chests packed with his family belongings, such as silver, linen, and so forth, and he wanted to load these.

I could not see any sense in this myself. Here we were told to evacuate the installation by the British military because the Japanese were right behind the Kowloon hills and were expected to show up most anytime. Stonecutter's was still hammering away, but in face of all this we must use up time loading household chests! I was considerably annoyed, and it seemed extremely foolish to me, but if that is what they wanted to do, I would give a hand and stand by.

We got the cases loaded all right, and all assembled on the launch with the exception of the five Indian watchmen who were the only ones left. We told them to come too, but they said no, they would stay and guard the installation. We told them it didn't need guarding anymore, and it would be much safer in Hong Kong than to be taken prisoner there. They still refused to come. I did not think of it at the time, but they knew the Japanese would not touch them. They would stay behind and turn the place over to the Japanese and secure their liberty. Anyway, it was a perfectly safe bet and probably all agreed to a long time before. If the Japanese were stopped and did not get to Kowloon, they were safe. If the Japanese did come, they would turn everything over to them and still be safe.

We pushed off around 4:15 or 4:30 AM. It was the first time in the history of Laichikok that it had been left without a Westerner on the premises. Just as we were casting off, a plane roared out over the harbor from Kai-Tak, with all engines wide open, and climbed just as fast as she could up into the sky and into free China. At that time we expected it back that night, but it proved to be too late. This was the last plane that ever left Kai-Tak. We drifted out into the middle of the harbor and waited until daybreak. We would not dare approach the Hong Kong side in the dark, as we certainly would be fired on by the British troops and sentries.

When daylight came about 7:15 AM, we tied up at Blake's Pier. Suter and I went to the Hong Kong Hotel to get some breakfast, and the rest went up to William's apartment at St. Loan's Court. Service was going on in the hotel as usual, but all the windows were boarded up to prevent the glass from shattering. We read the morning newspapers which stated that a few Japanese had gotten in over the border, but that the British lines were holding and the "situation was well in hand." Now, all together boys!

Well, be that as it may, with breakfast finished Suter and I went over to the office. By that time, Wills has also arrived back. We called military headquarters on Stonecutter's and asked them about the evacuation of Laichikok. They said, "What evacuation?" We told them what had happened, and they said that they had given no such orders and knew nothing about it. If any such orders had been given, they must have come from Hong Kong headquarters and suggested that we call there.

We called the headquarters on Hong Kong, and they said they knew absolutely nothing about it as no such orders had been given. They said they were still holding Kowloon, and the military had received no such orders nor were they thinking of evacuating. No one could account for the order.

I did not realize it then, but the answer was the Japanese Army's Fifth Column. The sergeant took the message over the phone and thought that he was talking to British Military Headquarters, but he wasn't. He was talking to some English-speaking Chinese or Japanese. I say, this was not realized at the time, but soon became clear.

That being the situation, the thing to do now was to go back to Laichikok, take some money with us to pay some coolies, Chinese workers, in advance, and see if we could not get the bulk containers filled, as well as remove the tin goods to Hong Kong. Upon arrival at Laichikok, our plan was to inform the head Indian watchman that we would pay the coolies in advance and for him to pass the word around. It would probably take two hours for the word to get around for any workers to show up. We knew they would show up if they were paid in advance.

In the meantime, we were going to deliver two tank truck loads of aviation gasoline to Kai-Tak. The plan was to leave the tank trucks at the airport as it would be easier to bring the trucks to Hong Kong from there rather than from Laichikok, if it proved necessary to do so. Also, in the event that any other planes happened to come in, the tank trucks could be run right out to the planes for refueling. Mills was coming over later, and he would pick us up at the airport in the Company car to take us back to Laichikok.

Ruth Briggs, Pasadena, California

The Japanese have now attacked Hong Kong, Singapore, and Manila! I haven't heard much, as the news did not give much detail, just that the Japanese were there. On December 9 I received a cable from Standard Oil in New York advising me that all staff in Hong Kong were safe. Thank the Lord! I imagine the British are well-fortified, but I know the Japanese to be real methodical and organized. Ma and Pa Briggs came over right away to be with me, and many of my neighbors have also come to give me much-needed hugs. Kathie knows something has happened, and I've tried to explain to her as simply as I can without alarming her. Carol, of course, doesn't realize what has happened, even though she knows there is some sort of gloom over me. She goes about her normal activities, and Kathie is a great help in entertaining her.

After several days of sketchy news from Hong Kong, I only know that the fighting there is continuing, as it is in Singapore. Although Norman is a civilian, I now know how my friends and neighbors feel who have husbands and sons in the war in Europe. And now we are in full military combat with Japan too! Our loved ones are far away and in constant danger. And there's nothing we can do, except pray and take care of each other.

My emotions are in a turmoil. I was born and raised in Japan, my parents are Presbyterian missionaries, and I love many Japanese people. Why do we have to fight? I have always prayed for love and peace and find it hard to understand imperialistic tendencies of countries. Hitler is awful, taking over Europe. So many people killed! But the Japanese! I know it's a small, crowded country, but why oh why can't we settle things differently. I just wish Norman were home with me. Or I was with him. This not knowing what he is going through is hard.

I plan to drive to Pomona to visit my parents soon. I need their strong faith to bolster my faith in humanity and to have them tell me that Norman will be all right.

Chapter III
The Oil Facility Attack

The plans set, Suter and I pushed off around 8:15 or 8:30 Wednesday morning. About halfway over in the Company launch, the air raid alarm went off. We could be expecting the Japanese any minute! We stopped the launch as all movement ceases during a raid. The planes never came directly over, but they were at the far west entrance of the harbor. We saw bombs fall in the water and heard machine guns. We had no idea what the planes were after, but as they were flying very low, they must have seen troops. Fortunately, they did not come anywhere near us. Soon they disappeared over the hills, and we proceeded on our way.

Arriving at Laichikok, we informed the head watchman to pass the word around that we would pay in advance for workers. We then went to the garage to get the tank trucks, but there were none there. The watchman informed us that the Chinese chauffeurs were afraid to bring them back to the installation and had left them on the road on the way back from the airport. I don't know the exact circumstances as to why these trucks were left in the street, but it looks to me like some more 5th column work. To abandon trucks is in itself a sign of despair, and it certainly would have a demoralizing effect on the civilian population to see equipment openly abandoned and left in the street.

Suter and I set out to find the trucks. Fortunately, they were not far from the installation. They were empty and headed away from the installation. It is very seldom that an empty tank truck leaves an installation. They come in empty, but go out full. Were these tank trucks going to be turned over to somebody? They either thought better of it, or got scared out of it. It seemed very peculiar to me. Fortunately, they had left the keys in them. Suter took one truck and I the other. We turned around and went back to the installation.

None of the Chinese workers had yet returned, but Suter was fully familiar with all the valves and pipe lines. As the filling tanks were full, it was a simple matter to fill the tank trucks at the loading rack. We only filled one truck at a time, however, which Suter did while I was keeping watch on the main road back of the installation. If I saw any Japanese coming down the road or over the hills, Suter and I were going to run for the launch with the hope of getting to Hong Kong. I did not want to get caught and taken prisoner in an oil installation, as we certainly would be classed as military prisoners whether we actually belonged to the military or not. That is, assuming we lived to be taken prisoners.

While I filled the tank trucks, a very peculiar thing happened. Near to and behind the installation was a sharp ridge of hills. A low flying plane came over and started machine-gunning the far side of the ridge. You could see every part of the plane very distinctly, but there were no distinguishing marks on it whatsoever, neither Japanese nor British. Because there was no ack-ack firing, I assumed the plane must be British. It paid absolutely no attention to us filling the tank truck. Had he wanted to, he could have very easily gotten us. The plane was not British, however, for the simple reason that they had none. So it must have been a Japanese plane machine-gunning retreating British troops.

This plane gave us some cause for concern, but we finished loading the tank trucks and headed for the airport. Suter took the lead truck, and I followed. We agreed that if an air raid came while we were on the way, we would draw up to the side of the road, leave the trucks, and hunt for shelter. With bombing and machine-gunning going on, we thought it best to be as far away as possible from 1,000 gallons of high octane gasoline. Fortunately, that problem never arose, and we got our load safely to its destination.

I will explain here about the Chinese Navigation and Aviation Corporation—CN & AC. Monday and Tuesday nights they were running loaded planes all night long to the nearest place in free China behind the Japanese lines that they dare land. They would then come back for another load. Thus, the shuttle service kept up for those two nights. We saw the last one go out about 4:30 Wednesday morning. The first night they took out the crew of the American Clipper. They also took considerable tools and machinery out from the repair shop. This was all good work. We were eager to keep the gasoline supplies going so that there would be no delay or interruption in the service.

However, if we knew then what we know now, we probably would not have been so eager. A considerable part of the passenger business on these two nights was in taking out rich Chinese and their concubines. The price was whatever you had and whoever could pay the most got the space. We heard that the prices ranged from $2,000 to $4,000 per passenger for the shuttle to free China. The last load that went out on Wednesday morning took the ground crew with them, so that was good work done anyway. Maybe the concubine story is exaggerated, and there weren't as many as reported. Anyway, it was well worthwhile to get the Clipper crew and the ground crew out. If a few others slipped in, well more power to them.

My only regret, in hindsight, is that after helping to fuel the plane, I stupidly did not insist on going aboard. If so, my story here would have ended. Unfortunately, my mind was not working at its best for my own welfare, and I remained to return to the oil facility to help protect the Company's assets for Hong Kong.

Mills picked us up in the Company car as agreed, and all three of us went back to Laichikok. I went to the superintendent's office. The floor was covered with demolition material—wires, dynamite, and so forth. I asked what this was. It seems that during our absence at the airport, the British military had come around and said that they were going to blow the place up or at least get it ready to push the button. They had everything with them but the fuses. They said they would leave what equipment they had, go and get some fuses, and then return to do the work. They never came back!

We had heard that the British military also went into the Texas plant with demolition equipment. They had not forgotten the fuses there and went right to work, wiring the whole plant. All that was necessary then to put the entire plant in flames, preventing the Japanese from getting valuable supplies, was to push the plunger.

They got the work completed about 4:00 PM when the sergeant in charge received a phone message to the effect that they were going to delay destruction of the plant because they were going to hold Kowloon. They needed the supplies and could use them immediately, and thus he should remove the caps and report back. Thus, the Japanese got another good installation with a lot of oil in it!

In my opinion, this was pure 5th column work. I don't believe the phone call was from headquarters, but was some English-speaking Chinese or Japanese. It just shows that war orders should never be given over the phone. I can see no plausible reason whatsoever for the British changing their first decision. It must have been the Japanese 5th column.

Well, to return to Laichikok, we locked the small superintendent's office with the demolition stuff in it because the Chinese coolies had begun to arrive. We did not want them walking around this demolition material, or we would all be going up over the Kowloon hills much sooner than we expected, as one good kick and off it would go.

There must have been around one hundred or so Chinese coolies. We lined them up and paid them off. They got about two or three times their usual pay, but this was one time when we were not disputing the price. One of the Portuguese employees arrived. He made out the receipts, and I paid out the money. As soon as a worker received his money, he reported to Mills and Larson who were getting the loading organized. As the workers were paid, we told them that there was a steam launch at each end of the waterfront. If anything happened while they were at work, they were told to go immediately to the nearest launch, and we would all get away from the installation. Filling and loading had actually started, and I should say there were only about twenty-five or thirty more workers in the line to pay off. Anyway, the major part of the money was gone as I had only a little over $600 out of the original $3,500 that I brought with me.

Then I heard the air raid siren go off. This had no sooner stopped when I heard the word "fire." I turned around and looked out the window. There was a huge column of black smoke rising from behind the godowns, or warehouses. I did not know exactly what had been hit, but there was a fire in the installation and that was sufficient for pandemonium to let loose!

There was only one exit from the office, and all the workers rushed for it at once. Fortunately, no one tripped, and all got through it in some fashion or other. While waiting for them to get through, I jammed the odd cash in my pocket, shoved the receipts in the desk drawer, and banged it shut. The two steam launches were at each end of the waterfront as planned, but as luck would have it, all the workers rushed for one launch, the Standard-Vacuum.

There were a hundred or so coolies on board, and they were hanging on just like flies. The captain was waving his arms trying to get them off as he said the boat would capsize; then he asked Suter and me to order the workers off. With an oil installation afire, do you think anyone could get any of the workers off the Standard-Vacuum? Not on your sweet life.

Only a machine gun would have removed those workers off the launch. Mills and Larson had not shown up yet, so I told Suter he had better take the Standard-Vacuum and go and I would get the other two and follow in the Eagle, the second launch at the other end of the installation. The Standard-Vacuum pulled away, weaving from side to side with its over-loaded human cargo. Why it did not capsize will never be explained.

I rushed up towards the Company house and met Mills just coming out. I told him, "The Eagle is down at the pier. Let's find Larson and get out." He said he was going down to the pump house to start the engine and try and put the fire out. I looked at him as much as to say, "Are you crazy?" The British military had been in that morning and said that they are going to destroy the place, and now that it was afire, what point was there in trying to save it? We would only be saving it for the Japanese. I told him I was taking the launch as it was the last transportation left, and he had better come now if he were coming at all. He said he would not go, that he was going to start the pump engines.

I left him and raced down to the waterfront. Turning the corner of one of the buildings, I ran into Larson in the Company car. I told him I had seen Mills and that Mills was going to stay and start the engines. I said the Eagle is here and let's take it and go. Larson said that he was going to drive the Company car into Kowloon and suggested that I go with him. He opened the door. I still don't know why I did it, but I jumped in. There was the Eagle standing right by us in the water and of all the dumb things to do, I jumped into the car. We raced along the waterfront and had to go around three sides of the installation before we could get out on the main road. We came face to face with the fire. The flames were twenty-five or thirty feet high, and there were huge columns of black smoke.

We were on the windward side, and I could see that by driving through this we would miss the flames, but we would have to go right through the smoke. I asked Larson if he were going to drive through that. When I heard him reply "Yes" I said that is enough for me and to please let me out. He stopped the car, and I jumped out.

I was now back at exactly the same point at which I had left Mills. I raced towards the waterfront which was 700 or 800 feet away. When I got there, the Eagle had given up all hope and was about 200 feet away from the pier, headed for Hong Kong. I gave a yell which I guess you could have heard all over Hong Kong harbor. Anyway, the Eagle came back and got me. We headed for Hong

Kong. The only ones on this launch were me and the crew of five Chinese.

By this time the air raid was in full progress. Their main objective was Stonecutter's Island. Japanese naval boats were in Deep Bay throwing shells over the Kowloon hills. They had not yet got the range, so were falling short. The water between the installation and Stonecutter's was just one huge mountain of spray with bombs and shells striking the water.

We set out in the midst of this for Hong Kong. I immediately went up to the wheel house. One of the crew and I lowered the glass windows so that they would not be broken from the concussion and cut us to pieces. We were getting soaked from the spray of the shells falling into the water, but we never got a direct hit. (If we did, I would not be here to tell this story.)

The captain was weaving in and out and whenever we would get a good soaking from a shell spray, he would joke, "Well, I missed that one." We were in this direct line of fire for about five or six minutes, but it seemed like an eternity. Once out of the direct line of fire we were pretty safe. The Japanese had only one objective: Stonecutter's Island. They were not wasting any shots on anything else.

About three quarters of the way across the harbor we stopped. All traffic had ceased. We were well out of the range, and we had a grandstand view of the attack on Stonecutter's Island. The planes were overhead dive bombing the gun emplacements, and the navy was still sending the shells over from Deep Bay. The shells and bombs were hitting the island, as well as falling short as the huge geysers of spray indicated. A small British gun boat which had been outside and evidently attacked by larger Japanese boats was coming in full speed, at the west entrance of the harbor. The planes noticed it and tried to dive bomb it, but the gun boat weaved back and forth. It was successful in missing every one of them, but there were no two ways about it. That little gun boat was sure in a hot spot.

In the middle of this the other launch, the Standard-Vacuum came alongside with Suter on board. As soon as they were clear of the installation and at the first convenient place, the captain had put all the Chinese workers ashore. He did it before she capsized, which I consider mighty good luck as well as good work. Suter came and joined me on the Eagle. There was nothing else we could do but just stay there until the raid was over. Unless they made a general attack on all shipping in the harbor, we were fairly safe, as the chances of a stray shell coming over our way was somewhat remote. Or so we thought.

We looked back at Laichikok. It was evident that the fire was greatly diminished. Someone had either gotten it under control, or it was burning itself out. Things quieted down, the air raid sounded all clear, and so we headed once again for Blake's Pier on the Hong Kong side.

Upon landing, we went straight to the office. In about twenty-five or thirty minutes, Mills and Larson came in. They had gotten together and taken the Company car to Kowloon and then come across on the Star ferry. Mills said he never hoped to have such a ride as that again. Larson was driving and gave the car everything it had. They went through the streets of Kowloon at 80 miles per hour, across intersections and all. Later, Mills maintained that after going through the entire attack of Hong Kong, the bombing, the shelling and everything else connected with it, his worst experience was still that ride from Laichikok to Kowloon. I could well understand Mill's feeling all right. I don't believe there was much difference between that ride and the launch missing the Japanese shells, or rather the shells missing us. One hundred percent pure luck.

We were now able to piece together what had happened at Laichikok. An incendiary bomb had landed in the compound. Although I could see that no tanks or godowns were hit, I knew that something else was burning besides the bomb itself. There is no question but that the bomb was intended for Stonecutter's and not for the installation. The bomb had struck in an open space, but it had hit and severed a gasoline pipe line. It so happened that the gate valve to the tank to which this line was connected was closed. So the fire did not go any further and merely burned out the gasoline in the pipe line. This seems somewhat incredible, but that is what actually happened. An incendiary bomb drops in the midst of an oil installation, and the only thing that burns is a few hundred gallons of gasoline in the pipe line! Alright, now you tell one!

From the way the Japanese were working on Stonecutter's and avoiding Laichikok it was very evident that this was being done on purpose. The Japanese had it planned all right; they knew they would get Hong Kong. They weren't going to destroy any oil on their own accord as they would need it themselves when they got there. The Japanese would not bomb Laichikok and the British would not destroy it. So who was to get it? You guess.

Ruth Briggs, Pasadena, California

I had a good visit with my parents. In my bones I know that Norman is still all right. Having the prayers and abiding faith of my parents have helped my frame of mind somewhat. Thank goodness they are retired from their missionary work in Japan, and my brothers and sister all are living in the United States now.

The girls enjoyed themselves, as always, with Mother and Father. Kathie enjoys putting on Father's big rubber boots and helping him feed the chickens. She goes inside the coop with Father and thinks she is being a big help. Carol stays outside, but grabs a fistful of corn and sticks her pudgy hand through the chicken wire to feed the chickens, then turns around with a big grin, like saying "what a big girl I am!"

Mother gave Carol a piggy-back ride, and then took Kathie for a ride around the little farm on the back of her bicycle. I wish I could come here more often, but I have to be careful with the gas rations.

The news reported that Japanese forces occupied Bangkok, Thailand, without opposition, and German troops started pulling back from the Moscow area. Dutch aircraft from the East Indies went to Singapore to bolster British defenses, but the British ships Prince of Wales and Repulse were sunk off Malaya. There is no more news from Hong Kong. And Father has not heard from anyone in Japan. I guess I have to believe the old saying that no news is good news. At least that's what I tell myself.

Chapter IV
Air Raids, Food and Shelter

The air raid alarm went off again around 5:00 PM. We rushed out of the office and heard the planes were already overhead. As there was not sufficient time to make the American Club, we headed for the Women's Club Room in the Gloucester Hotel. It was very crowded, but we managed to squeeze through the throngs of people. Mac was there, and he told me what he had been doing since I left him on the previous morning.

Late Tuesday afternoon he had received orders from the Hong Kong Billeting Committee that we must get out of our apartment. This we fully expected, as the Hong Kong Government had been working for months on a billeting plan. They had plans of every house and building in Hong Kong and had worked out how many people could be taken care of on a room-by-room basis. A large number of Chinese and Portuguese Government employees lived in Kowloon. If hostilities broke out, the plan was to bring them all over to Hong Kong Island where the main city and government were.

All of Kowloon was being evacuated, and many more came over than they had ever made plans for, throwing the whole billeting system into confusion. When the Larson and Suter families arrived, we tried to have the billeting committee assign them to our apartment, exchanging their assigned place to whomever else they had planned to put there. The committee would not listen to this. We had to get out of our apartment, as well as the Larsons and the Suters. There was absolutely no sense to this move, and we went to the

American Consulate about it. They could do nothing, as the billeting was entirely in the hands of the Hong Kong Government. As there was a war on, we decided to follow instructions, rather than to argue for common sense.

Mac, the Suters, and I were billeted in the Company house, 459 the Peak, which was called Altadena. The Larsons were billeted elsewhere. We all got out of the apartment as told. However, not one single person moved in; far as we knew, the apartment remained vacant! This was duplicated over and over again. People got out of their quarters and moved elsewhere, and their own apartments remained vacant. It was just one complete mess from start to finish. When people saw the way it was going, many moved right back into their own quarters.

However, Mac had moved mattresses, blankets, and bedding from our apartment to Altadena. There were finally 23 of us at Altadena, and these extra mattresses came in very useful. As there were not sufficient beds for all of us, we put the mattresses on the floor and slept on them. When the air raid was over, Mac and I took the Tram up the Peak, went to the apartment, got our personal belongings, and took them to Altadena. I was certainly thankful that I had packed on the first morning of the war, as all I had to do now was to carry two suitcases. We helped the Suters and the Larsons to get moved, arriving back at Altadena just a little after dark.

The company house, Altadena, was a very large and pretentious one. It was the residence of the general manager. Even with 23 people, there was ample space for us all. We were certainly far better off than many others. The house had four bathrooms upstairs and a wash room downstairs, which showed that it was thoroughly American, as a British house of the same size would have only one bathroom. This was commented on by some of the later arrivals who were British. They counted themselves lucky to be quartered here rather than elsewhere.

The first night at Altadena there were only nine of us. I well remember dinner that night. There were two rooms downstairs that were thoroughly blacked-out, so that we could have the lights going. These were the library and the dining room. We sat down to dinner to a table fully set—napkins, linen, silver, and china. In fact, the whole table was set for a formal dinner party. The boy had just been told there would be nine for dinner; that many people meant to him a dinner party. The fact that a war was on made no difference to him. This was not the first war he had seen, and if the master was entertaining, why that was okay. The servants were carrying on just as usual. The fact that a little scrap iron was being thrown around was not going to interrupt their routine, at least not at present.

We all sat down, many of us all dirty as we had not been to bed at all the previous night. I myself had not shaved since Monday morning, and it was now Wednesday night. But what difference did that make? The serving boys were in their white coats, flowers were on the table, and the dinner party was on, so let's go!

We had roast lamb that night, and I think we all felt that it would be the last nice dinner we would see for some time. Second helpings were passed, and I don't think anyone refused. At least, I didn't. It was quite a contrast to what we had been through the last three days and especially to what lay before us. It was rather unreal to be sitting here in comfort and being served by the boys in their white uniforms. It was the last such meal that we would have, and I think we all sensed it although no one said anything about it. Cigars were even passed, we had coffee, and the meal was over. No one had had much sleep since the war started, and several of us had not been to bed since Monday night. Within a half hour after the meal, which must have been about 9:00 PM, we were all in bed.

We were not to stay in them long, however. At 10:00 PM I was awakened by a whistling noise going over the house. I was in the same room with Henry Durreschmindt. He got up, began to dress, and said, "You know what that is, don't you?" I replied no, and he said it was shells. The whole house was up in no time. Several of us went out on the front porch, which overlooked the harbor and Kowloon, to see what was going on. On the Hong Kong side the British had 9.2 inch guns on Mt. Austin and Mt. Davis. These were firing into the Japanese troops behind Kowloon. The Japanese were replying as they had now brought up their field pieces. We could see the flash in the sky of the Japanese guns and then hear the report. We could also see the flash of the British guns right behind us, and we decided that this was no place for us to be viewing the scenery.

The basement of the house had two rooms and also an "L" shaped passageway. One room had the furnace in it, and the other room was entirely free except for a few odds and ends of furniture that were stored there. We decided that we had better take the spare mattresses and put them on the floor in the basement. Some of us lay down and tried to sleep, and several others sat in chairs on the long side of the "L" passageway. Shells were going out and coming in. Although they were not exploding anywhere near us, we still thought the basement was the best place to be. The shelling continued for a couple of hours. We would take occasional glimpses out of the corner of the window or go outside to the back garden, looking over toward Kowloon.

The city was in complete blackness. All that could be seen was the flashing of the Japanese guns behind the hills of Kowloon, and the flash of the British reply from Hong Kong. This lasted until about midnight, and the night sounds changed to complete silence. Some of us remained in the basement and slept, but most of us went upstairs to bed.

The next morning, Thursday, December 11th, we got up and had breakfast about 7:30 AM. After breakfast, three of us—Mac, Suter and I—set out for the office by walking along Barker Road to the Tram station. We had just about reached the Tram station when the air raid alarm went off. We could hear the planes coming over. It was too far to go back to the house, so we ran for the shelter of the Tram station. The Japanese planes were after Stonecutter's again. When they got through working it over this time, it was silenced forever. The British did not evacuate it until a day or so later, withdrawing the men at night, but they never fired another shot.

The Japanese planes came over in groups of three in a "V" formation, dive bombing it from one end to the other. We could see the bombs hit the buildings. Several dropped into the water. Fires were started, but these did not last long. While watching the raid, an Englishman joined us to take shelter. We mentioned we had heard over the radio that the "Repulse" and the "Prince of Wales" were sunk in Singapore. The Englishman said he did not believe it, that it must be just pure 100% Japanese propaganda. Well, he could see some more Japanese propaganda right before his very eyes. Hong Kong was being blasted to pieces, and not a British plane anywhere around. The British still thought they were invincible.

With the raid finally over, we took the Tram down to the office. It, and every place else, was a mad house. The Chinese agents were there, wanting to get hold of as many supplies as possible. Most of the supplies were taken over by the military; furthermore, we were in no position to make deliveries. From the previous night's activities, we knew that the Japanese were almost into Kowloon, and we needed one more tank truck on the Hong Kong side. Suter went over and got one of the trucks that we had left at Kai-Tak the day before. This was certainly a good piece of work; he got it over to Hong Kong just about noon.

In the middle of the morning, Al Bourne, the general manager, called a meeting of all the American members of the staff in his office. He had just received a phone call from Sir Athol MacGregor, the Chief Justice, who wanted the Company to take over complete policing duties of one of the downtown air raid tunnels on a 24-hour basis. If the Americans did this, it would release the British for more important work. MacGregor said that this would be one of the most effective ways that we could help. As long as this involved no oath of allegiance to the British Crown, it was okay. I remember distinctly this question coming up; all of us felt exactly the same about it. We would do any work that they wanted us to do, but no oath of allegiance. We were one hundred percent American and would remain so. A schedule was fixed up, and we immediately took over the operation of the tunnel.

Just before leaving the house that morning, Mac had received a phone call. The British wanted us to work on the Food Control on the Peak; we agreed to do so. For this reason, I was counted out of the tunnel work. Mac and I reported the next morning, Friday, to help with Food Control. Our first order was to get three bags of rice and some coal to our house. Mac got hold of a truck, and we got the task accomplished. This turned out to be crucial, as I do not know what we would have done without those supplies later on. The number in our household increased to 23 British and Americans. Some brought Chinese servants with them, so the total number of people was 38. Food became a problem. The servants were in just as bad a way as we were. When the Europeans were ordered out of the houses, the servants generally had to go too. Some had families to which they could go, but many didn't. Furthermore, if they stayed by their employer, they realized their chances of getting fed were much better.

Food to the Chinese is everything; we were to learn this lesson ourselves. They had starved before, but we hadn't. I think they realized much more than we did what was really ahead of us. We did not need 15 servants at Altadena, but we surely could not turn them away. Where there is rice, the Chinese will stay. Although we did not have all we wanted, we had enough to keep us together for awhile.

We had air raids all day long. A considerable part of our time was used up in going back and forth between the office and the Club or other shelters. The South China Morning Post was still being issued, giving the summary of the military situation. It was a summary alright. I think the civilians knew more about it than the so-called High Command did. The military advised us that we could expect shelling on the north side of the Island, which was the city, but not to become alarmed because it would only be light stuff—mostly nuisance shelling more than anything else! Nuts! There is no such thing as nuisance shelling. Shelling is shelling. If anyone doesn't think so, let him be a civilian caught on an island like rats in a trap with no means of escape, the enemy overwhelming in numbers, and your own forces commanded with utter confusion.

In the middle of the afternoon Larson came in and wanted to contact his family. He had not seen them since they left Laichikok on Tuesday afternoon. I told him where they were, but he did not know how to get there. Plus, he had clothes in addition to other items he wanted to get to them. These were at William's apartment where he had been staying. Larson had the Company car and wanted me to go with him to show him the way. There was absolutely nothing that I could do in the office now, so I slammed the desk shut and went with him.

We had just arrived at the apartment when another air raid came. This was one of the newer apartment buildings on Kennedy Road, the first road level on the Peak. There was a good basement in the building and most everyone went there. Larson and I, however, stayed on one of the inside corridors. It was a modern reinforced building, as safe a place as any. The planes came right over the building. They were after the Naval Dockyard which was not more than half a mile away, as the crow flies, if that. The ack-acks were going, and bombs were dropping very close to us. Finally, the raid was over, and the building and we in it were fortunately not touched.

We decided it was then too late to take the car up the Peak and get back before dark, so we divided up what things he wanted to take to his family, and we went up by Tram. The Tram was full of refugees from Kowloon. They had been half the way across the water then the raid came. People said that several bombs had dropped near the ferry, and they had been soaked by the spray. They also said that the planes had machine-gunned the ferry. Although no one was killed, one man had been hit in the leg with a bullet.

These ferries were always crowded. If the Japanese had purposely gone after them and machine-gunned them, there would have been many killed. The man who got his leg injured was probably hit from a shell fragment. I don't know. I did not actually see this ferry coming over, as Larson and I were keeping under cover.

These people also reported that the British were officially evacuating Kowloon. The police force had left, and looting was going on all over the place. The last act of the British military before they left Kowloon was to mount a machine gun on a truck and drive up and down the streets shooting into the crowds in order to stop the looting. Rumors were rampant, so this may not have been true. It certainly sounded bizarre to me.

When we reached the top of the Peak, I showed Larson where his family was and then went back to Altadena. We all gathered in the library, heard each other's stories and experiences, had dinner, and went to bed. We were again awakened about 10:00 PM by the exchange of shells and all went below to the basement. Shortly after 11:00 PM there was a terrific explosion which shook and rattled all the windows in the house. It came directly from downtown. We took a peep out of the window and also from the front porch, but could see nothing.

The next day, we learned what had happened. At the west entrance to Hong Kong harbor there is a small island known as Green Island. On it was a lighthouse. This belonged to the Hong Kong Harbor Office, and they had 8.5 tons of dynamite in an ordinance storage. The military decided that this should be brought to Hong Kong. They could not get sufficient coolies to do the loading and unloading, so got six Europeans as volunteers.

The exercise was all mapped out on a time schedule, leaving Green Island at a definite time, passing other points on the way at specific intervals, arriving at Blake's Pier, Hong Kong, at 11:00 PM. Nothing showed up at that time. About five minutes later the sentry on duty heard or saw something in the harbor moving toward the pier. Without any further questioning, he took up his rifle and fired. Up went 8.5 tons of dynamite with all on board!

Just what exactly went wrong, no one seems to know. Maybe they had just changed the guard shortly before. The information I got was the sentry on duty knew nothing about any such shipment arriving. Evidently, with all the red tape, all posts had been informed but this one!

In my observation, this was typical of the way the entire Hong Kong campaign was conducted. Totally disorganized, untrained troops, and poorly officered. But then, I guess war does cause mass confusion and panic. No one was killed in this explosion except those on the lighter, but every pane of glass was broken for blocks around on the waterfront. All the glass in the buildings on Pedder Street was shattered. The only reason many other people were not killed or severely cut is that it was night. With the curfew on, no one was out. My office was on the third floor of the Union building, facing Pedder Street. Several days later I went in; it was just one perfect mass of shattered and broken glass.

The next morning, Friday, December 12, was the last breakfast we were to have with fresh fruit and eggs. If I remember correctly, we had one apple each and one egg. Once in January we had another apple, but that was to be our last fresh fruit until we boarded the ship for home on June 29th, 1942.

Ruth Briggs, Pasadena, California

It's now December 12, four days since the Japanese invaded Hong Kong, and I haven't heard any more word from Standard Oil. The only news is what I've heard on the radio. I finally couldn't stand it anymore and put in a call to Standard Oil's headquarters in New York.

When I got through, they couldn't tell me much, as they hadn't heard much either. They did get another cable that said all office personnel were accounted for and assisting the British in manning the air raid shelters and helping with food distribution. They also said they tried to maintain some oil services, but that was now out of their hands.

That's not much news, but at least it's good news, I think. Since the cable said all personnel were accounted for, I have to believe that Norman is all right. What he must be going through is certainly not all right.

I took the children over to Ma and Pa Briggs for a visit and told them the news from the New York office. Then, while they were entertaining the children, I went to church for a little quiet time by myself to pray for Norman's safe return.

Chapter V
Ship Scuttling and Shelling

After breakfast, Mac and I were ready to leave the house to report to the Food Control for our assignment to pass out food rations to the Peak residents. Several of us were on the front porch looking out to the harbor and Kowloon. We noticed that the few ships that were in the harbor were very low in the water, and some were listing. It struck us all simultaneously. The British were scuttling their ships!

During the war and afterwards, I saw quite a bit of the captain and the chief officer of the Swedish ship, Ningpo. In June, 1941, the Ningpo was in Singapore, and the stern of the vessel was struck by a floating mine. The propeller was blown off and considerable damage done to the aft part of the ship. Repairs could not be made in Singapore for some reason or other, so the Ningpo was towed to Hong Kong via Manila, arriving sometime during November. The Ningpo was to go into dry-dock about the middle of December. In anticipation of this, the boat had been fully bunkered and provisioned for 6 months. The purpose of this was to save time so that upon release from dry-dock, she could immediately put to sea.

The Hong Kong Government came to the Captain and told him to scuttle his ship, or, rather, that they were going to do it for him. The Captain refused to let them scuttle his ship, pointing out that it was a neutral vessel sailing under the Swedish flag. Even if the Japanese took Hong Kong, they would not touch his ship. Furthermore, the boat was damaged and could not go anywhere under her own power until repairs were made.

The Hong Kong Government said that this made no difference. They wanted the ship scuttled, for which they would be responsible, making settlement after the war. The Captain, of course, could do nothing so said okay. But he wanted a few hours to get some of the provisions ashore. The Hong Kong Government said nothing doing, it must be scuttled immediately. The Captain pointed out that it had just been refueled and stocked with provisions for six months. It surely would be worthwhile to take time to save this. The Captain and his crew of thirty men could live six months ashore on the food, thus saving that much of the Colony's food supply. The reply was that no time could be lost; down she went.

The Hong Kong Government took a launch and went from ship to ship in the harbor, scuttling them all with no advance notice. The members of the crew that were aboard saved their personal belongings, but those that were ashore had no chance to do so.

The method of scuttling was merely to open the sea valves and then to abandon ship. One or two turned over on their sides, but most of the ships settled on the bottom. You could see the super structure or the masts, depending on the depth of the water. To raise a vessel that has been sunk by merely opening the sea valves is not a difficult task. I did not see the Hong Kong harbor myself after January 24th, at which time none of the ships had been raised.

By June, however, the report was that every one of these ships had been raised and was in the service of the Japanese. The Japanese came in with the full equipment, sent the divers down, closed the sea valves, put the pumps to work, and up came the ships. If a proper job of scuttling had been done, the machinery would have been dismantled, demolition bombs would have been put in the engine rooms and elsewhere, and the ships blown to pieces. There were around ten ships in the harbor at the time, and now all were in the service of the Japanese. Just think what a little thought and planning could have saved!

After watching the ships being scuttled, Mac and I started to leave for the Food Control Headquarters at the Peak Mansions. Just as we were going down the steps, the air raid alarm went off, so we headed for the basement. About an hour later the all clear sounded.

The Peak Mansions was an apartment building. The Food Control had taken over an apartment on the ground floor as an office. All the entrances to the building were protected by sand bags and sentries were on duty. Mac and

I went and reported to the man in charge and his assistant. I don't know what these men did in civil life, but if they were anything more than Tram conductors, they were about two classes ahead of themselves. If you gave them a switch poker, a red and a green flag, and put them at a track intersection to control traffic, I am certain they would throw the switch the wrong way, flag the trams through, and then wonder what it was all about.

Be that as it may, these were the two guys to whom we reported and from whom we received instructions. The head one took us into another room where there were several comfortable chairs. You would think it was a business conference we were attending and that everything was okay with the world...except for the fact that there were a few bombs dropping outside, and a little scrap iron being thrown around. Minor details.

The Food Control had taken over two private houses on each side of Magazine Gap, where two roads meet making one which leads up the Peak. We were to go to these houses and be in charge of receiving and distributing food. We received what few instructions there were. Mac went to his location and I to mine. My spot was #513 the Peak, a private residence owned by a Swede by the name of Homer Hallgrin. He was an ARP warden and his house was also post #58. He was assisted by a Dutchman; they relieved each other on four hour shifts.

They were supposed to be advised from headquarters by phone when raids were approaching, but often the raids were overhead before the advice came. Their main purpose was to give all the assistance possible to civilians and report casualties or damage after the raid was over. They had the thing set up on a semi-military basis. Messages would come over the phone such as yellow, red, and so on, indicating the proximity of the enemy. Conversation over the phone would start or close with "Message starts" and "Message ends." A log book was kept of all calls. It looked impressive, but that is about all there was to it. Hallgrin said it was all bunk, but the Dutchman thought he had a big job!

When I arrived at the house, I took an inventory of all the food that there was and phoned this to the headquarters so that they would know what supplies should be added. The stock was not great. I had in the neighborhood of 3 cases of corned beef, 2 cases of tinned corn, 3 cases tinned peas, 50 loaves of bread, 1 bag of rice (220 lbs.), and several other odds and ends. I did not know the exact number of people I was to feed, but I think it was around 25 or 30. At noon, four Chinese ARP wardens came around for food. They told me the number for whom they were getting food, and I would hand it out to them and make a record of it. We had a ration schedule of so many ounces of each article per person.

As this was the first day that the post was established, I did not expect that it would get into full operation, but I certainly expected that more work would be involved than this. I stayed at the house all day, during which we had several raids, both bombing and shelling. Fortunately, we did not get any direct hits. After the last raid was over, around 5:00 PM, I phoned Mac, and we arranged to meet at Magazine Gap to walk home to the Company house, Altadena.

We arrived there just before dark and all gathered in the library to hear about each other's activities of the day. Some had been driving trucks, others on duty in the tunnel, still others on food control work at various places on the Island. Everyone was busy doing something.

After dinner we turned on the radio and listened to BBC, London, which we referred to as the British Bullcasting Corporation. We heard that citizens of Hong Kong had repaired to their impregnable fortress, the businessmen were joining the armed forces, and thus Hong Kong defenses had been increased by 2,500 men.

The BBC announcer also said the Peak was honey-combed with air raid shelters. Our nickname for BBC was more correct than anyone will ever know. There was not one single air raid shelter on the Peak. There were tunnels downtown and shelters in various sections of the city. We listened to some more of the usual line of propaganda. As it was all quiet outside, we decided that we had better get a little sleep while the getting was good. We all turned in for the night.

I think it was after midnight when we were awakened, not by heavy gun fire as we had been the previous nights, but by machine gun fire. We got up and took a look outside. The British had search lights going, and they were playing back and forth across the waterfront on the Hong Kong side. We could see tracer bullets being fired. The search lights would only be on a few seconds at a time. I am not certain, but I think they were mounted on trucks, because the location would change. I don't think they had lights in each place that they showed up. There was heavy and continuous machine gun fire. When the search lights would play along the waterfront, we could not see any men in boats, but it was very evident what was going on. The Japanese were trying to land.

From the position of the search light, the Japanese were going to try to land right in the city itself and not in the more isolated sections of the Island and then work in. Apparently, in this first attempt they were not successful, because it was two weeks more before the Colony was to fall. They did take it by landing in remote sections and then working into the city. However, that night they were trying to land in the city. If they had gotten that close, things were really getting serious. This attack lasted around two hours, after which all became quiet. When the firing stopped, we knew the Japanese had not landed this time, at least in force. Although we had considerable apprehension, we nevertheless went back to bed, hoping that we would not be routed out later at the point of a bayonet.

The next morning Mac and I went back to our respective locations. The work was exactly the same. At noon four Chinese wardens showed up for food. Each day was practically the same. I could see no point at all in keeping one man at a place to do one hour's work a day. The Chinese cook could have done what I was doing just as well, although the food would probably have disappeared a little faster.

One day over the radio I heard that they needed truck drivers. I thought I could be of much more use doing that than dishing out food to four Chinese every day so I called up headquarters on the phone and offered my services as a truck driver. I said that in my opinion I was of no use where I was and as long as the truck did not transport troops or military supplies, I was willing to serve civilian needs anywhere. He thanked me for the offer, but said that just at present the food control did not have any trucks at their disposal. He said he would keep me in mind as a truck might show up any minute that would need a driver.

Hallgrin's house was about 1,000 feet up on the Peak. Directly below us on the waterfront was the Naval Dockyard. We had an excellent view here of the Hong Kong waterfront and the city of Kowloon. We could see any activity that was going on, and we saw plenty! One amusing incident happened which I think is worth recording. Every social upheaval brings new works, new phrases, and forms of expression. Hong Kong was no exception.

Do you know what the word SHEMOZZLE means? Well, I didn't until I heard Hallgrin use it. The Japanese shelled the Naval Dockyard every day. Hallgrin and I would go out on the front porch occasionally and watch the proceedings with a spy glass. This was a very foolish thing to do, and we soon cut it out. The Japanese were in full possession of Kowloon. They were over there with glasses watching every move on Hong Kong. If they should happen to see us looking at them with glasses, they would think that we were a military observation post and thus would let us have a few little reminders that would go boom, boom! As I say, we cut this out. But one day before we did, Hallgrin and I were out on the front porch watching the shells explode in the Naval Dockyard. Hallgrin was rocking back and forth in his chair. Every time a shell exploded he would turn to me and say, "Briggs, Briggs, this is one hell of a shemozzle!"

I arrived at Hallgrin's generally before the Japanese opened up for the day. When they did, the opening salvo was directed at a couple of houses right above us which were known as the custom houses. They were not real custom houses, but the people who lived in them worked for the customs. Maybe the British had put a couple of machine guns in those houses or troops or supplies in them, I don't know. But the Japanese shelled these houses steadily for about two hours. It was really surprising the small amount of damage done. The shots fell short, long, to one side, and then the other. But they also got direct hits. You would think that the houses would be demolished, but they weren't.

I had just finished giving the food to the four Chinese wardens when, BANG!, a shell exploded right in the front yard. There were five of us in the house at the time. The minute the shot landed, we knew that we were the target. We all raced to the front door, opened it, and stood in line. The shots came over at fairly regular intervals. If you waited until one exploded and were still able to move, the chances were that you could get 300 or 400 feet away before the next one came over. That is what we decided to do, wait until the next shell came over. If it didn't get us, we were going to run like hell down the Peak. The next shot came and hit right square in back of the house. We were now bracketed and the next one could be right on the button.

We raced out of the door. I was the last one out, but we did not go very far before I was the leader. I passed those other four like nobody's business. The road leading down the Peak was dug out of the side so that going down on the left hand side was an embankment and on the right a steep drop. The road was paved, bordered by a small stone wall about three feet high on the right. When I would hear a shot coming over, I would lay flat on my stomach on the side next to the stone wall with my arms folded over my head. As soon as the shell exploded. I would jump up, run another 300 or 400 feet, and so on until I got pretty well down the Peak and hopefully out of the range at which the Japanese were aiming.

Of course, these shots sounded much nearer than they probably were and just how close in feet they came I don't know. They were hitting the embankment right above me and the fragments were whizzing over my head. If I had been standing, I am certain that some of the fragments would have hit me. Anyway, I never want to spend another two hours like I did that afternoon. After every shell came over I thought of Ruth, Kathie, and Carol…would I ever see them again?

The other four had found what they considered to be a safe place up a little ravine, so they stayed there and did not follow me down the Peak. However, I didn't see any ravine; I was moving too fast. When the shelling stopped, I walked back up and found them. We returned to the house to see what damage was done. The servants' quarters had received a direct hit, putting a hole right through the roof. There were no other direct hits on the house, but several shells had fallen in the front garden and on both sides of the house. Windows were broken, but there appeared to be no structural damage. Shell fragments had come through the windows, hitting furniture and knocking plaster down. The front room and dining room were messed up. We picked up quite a bit of scrap iron.

The main point of the attack that afternoon was Magazine Gap. Traffic from Hong Kong proper and from Wanchi, another section of the city, meet here at Magazine Gap, an important center for transportation. What the Japanese were trying to do was to make the Gap impassable. The shell holes, I would say, were three to four feet in diameter and probably two feet deep. There were plenty of them, but trucks and cars could still go around or through them very easily. It is surprising to me what reinforced concrete will take in the way of punishment. I thought that after two hours of shelling there would be nothing left.

Evidently, right in the midst of the shelling a car had tried to make a run for it. A small car was right in the middle of the road at the Gap and had received a direct hit with a shell or at least a large fragment of one. A hole was torn right in the top. In the back seat was a British soldier with his head blown to pieces. What had become of the driver I don't know as the front seat was vacant. By the position of the body and the blood all over the back seat, it was evident that the victim was a passenger. A British squad came along, pushed the car to one side, removed the body, and continued on. I proceeded on home.

Mac and I talked it over that night and decided that we were not going back to Hallgrin's house to man our food posts. They had moved troops into this section and it was no place for a civilian. Furthermore, we were not going back there to spend all day to do one hour's work of a very minor nature. Al Bourne, the general manager, agreed with us one hundred percent to by all means to keep out of there.

The next morning Mac and I went to the Peak Mansions to report that we were not going back to the posts assigned us. Just as we arrived, an air raid siren blasted. No one was there, but we left a note that if they wanted us to do anything else not in a military area, we would be glad to help. If we heard nothing, we were going on tunnel work downtown, which is what we did. Later that day the military took over the area, ordering the Food Control, ARP, and all civilians out. Mac and I were just one jump ahead of them.

Our apartment, the Hillcrest, was only a short way from the Peak Mansions, so we headed there. As soon as we got there, another raid came and the planes were right over us. The apartment building was right on top of the Peak and an excellent target as far as visibility goes. It was a modern reinforced concrete building, or, rather, a brick building, so we beat it for one of the inside corridors. Everyone else went to the basement.

The planes were not after us, but there was an anti-aircraft battery about 500 feet away that they were targeting. We never got a direct hit, but bombs were dropping all around us. Planes came over dive bombing all the time. We would hear the hum of the motors, the roar of the dive, then the bursting of the bombs. One formation after another came, but we lived through it all and that is all that counts.

All the days from now on were practically the same—bombing and shelling, and shelling and bombing. There were two raids on the Peak in which the Japanese just shelled from top to bottom, then again from bottom to top. The Peak is made up of several road levels, such as Kennedy Road, Macdonnel Road, Mar Road, Barker Road, and so on. The Japanese took the Peak level by level, shelled everything from side to side, and then from top to bottom. They didn't miss a thing.

The first of these attacks came around 8:30 or so one morning. Al Bourne and I were sitting talking in the front hall, waiting for the rest of the household to assemble for breakfast when, BANG, the whole house shook. A shell had exploded in a small embankment in the garden right square in front of the house. We looked at each other and knew that the target was us.

The rest of the house needed no warning call, and we all headed for the basement. About half of us were down there when the second shell came over and exploded to the side of the house, shattering windows and shaking the whole structure. I think there were twenty-four of us in the house at the time, including twelve servants. The shelling was so terrific that we did not dare stay in the room in the basement, but rather in the short end of the "L" shaped corridor which was around fifteen feet long.

The two hours that we spent in the basement that day I think were the worst of the entire attack. We had endured well over two weeks of this stuff, no one had much sleep, and we were all pretty well on edge. The children were crying and wanted to know when it was all going to end; the women were nervous. In fact, we all were.

The servants were looking at each other as much to say, "The next one is going to be a direct hit, trapping us all in the basement." Planes would come over one wave after another. We would hear them coming in the distance, the hum of the motors, the roar of the dive, and then BOOM, BOOM, BOOM!

When the planes would come out of their dive and gain altitude, the shells would come over. The shells had a very sharp cracking explosion, the bombs making a heavier dull sound, but both had plenty of stuff in them. It sounded like the New York Sixth Avenue Elevated train coming over. In fact, I think every piece of scrap iron that we ever sold to the Japanese came over that morning. The Japanese won't be short of scrap because all they have to do now is pick it up in Hong Kong. A nice sensation—American planes in the air, powered by American gasoline, and dropping American scrap iron on American citizens!

The house shook continually for two hours, with windows, dishes, and everything else falling down. Fortunately, the house never got a direct hit, but shells fell on all sides, in the front, to the right, to the left, and to the rear. But when they hit they were well above the house, as the ground the house was built on was leveled out of the hillside. Right in back of the house was an embankment.

Finally, the bombing and shelling ceased, so we went up to see what was still left standing of the house. The dining room was just one complete mess. Had any of us been in there when the shells exploded, I doubt any would be alive to tell the tale. Above the fireplace was a very large mirror—completely shattered. Plaster had dropped from the ceiling as well as from the walls. The windows were all broken, and the furniture nicked, dented, and gouged where shell fragments had hit.

At the entrance to the dining room leading into the hall were massive solid oak doors about four inches thick. These were closed during the shelling, but shell fragments tore right through them. We picked up shell splinters four to five inches long that had come right through the doors. We guessed these shells had exploded outside only about 60 feet away. One of the front rooms and the sun porch, right off the dining room, were also in a mess, but not as bad as the dining room.

Upstairs there was one bedroom and bathroom that were approximately over the dining room. These were in very bad shape. Every fixture in the bathroom was damaged. The wash basin was completely demolished. Shell fragments had gone right through the wardrobe in the bedroom. Plaster was all over the place. Practically every house on the north side of the Peak was in the same condition.

We picked up all the scrap iron in the house. Believe me, we had quite a pile! Outside all the drain pipes were broken. The house was stucco and several breaks on the walls and corners were blasted away, but still not a shell had pierced the house so there appeared to be no structural damage.

There was a small ravine right in back of the house. I don't know what the Japanese thought was there, but they poured shell after shell and several bombs in there. I'm sure glad they did that, because if all the shells and bombs that exploded there had hit the house or even the garden, I don't believe there would have been much left of us.

Measuring in pounds, I don't know what the shell fragments would be that we picked up in the house. Most were in the vicinity of three inches. We picked up one shell butt and by putting the pieces together, we figured it was nine inches in diameter. That told us that the Japanese had naval boats outside lobbing a little message over the hills. Nuisance shelling, my eye!

After this raid, there was no water on the Peak from the city mains. It never freezes in Hong Kong, so all the water pipes are above the ground, in plain view along the road levels. The Japanese had gone for the main pipes on every road level, so that settled the water question. Before this modern system had been installed, each house had a well. Most of these wells had been abandoned, but not filled in. They were put to immediate use. At Altadena we were very fortunate as we also had a swimming pool. The morning the war started, Henry Durrschmidt had it filled up. We had 38,000 gallons of water! We had to carry it into the house, but at least we had plenty of water.

The Japanese blitzed the Peak a second time, but for that session I happened to be downtown on tunnel duty. Thank goodness I missed it. More nuisance shelling you say?

After quitting the food job, I joined the Company men and took my turn on duty at the air raid tunnel. This tunnel work was to keep the morale up of the Chinese more than anything else. Our tunnel had three entrances and was one of the largest in Hong Kong, built to hold 18,000 people. In the middle of the tunnel was a diesel engine which ran the forced ventilation system. We had electric lights, but the power went off on December 18. After that we had to use kerosene lanterns. It certainly was a good thing the forced ventilation system was built to operate independently of the electric current.

There were two of us on duty at a time. We had two shifts, one day and one night. Our main purpose was to show the Chinese that we were not fleeing town and to help them (and us) remain as calm as possible through it all. I think it was very worthwhile. As a colony run entirely by foreigners, if the Chinese saw that we stuck to our post during these raids, I think it gave them more confidence.

We went through the tunnel a couple of times an evening to see how things were going. Sometimes we would have to make some minor corrections in adjusting people and getting them to move over to make for more room. We had night sticks, but never had occasion to use them in any serious manner. There were Chinese wardens who did any man-handling necessary, but we were always in the background if further assistance seemed necessary.

What a mass of humanity! I thought I had seen collections of people before, as Hong Kong was always a crowded city. But I had never seen anything like this that assembled in these tunnels at night. Imagine the dirt, filth, and the worst of all the smell, with 18,000 people. There was a toilet in the middle of the tunnel. Although this was used, I don't think it was used by any more than around half the people. The rest just took care of themselves where they were. There was a drain in the middle of the tunnel passage ways, covered with cement blocks. Between every block there was a space of several inches. The Chinese were pretty good at hitting this opening. They were certainly expert spitters, and their aim in other matters was not too bad either!

Walking through that tunnel looked just like a big steam shovel had picked up a load of human beings and dumped them down, then dropped another pile on top of them. Just one mass of bodies, leaning and tangled up in each other. Arms, legs, bodies intertwined, babies crying, old men coughing and spitting, women nursing children, and so on far into the night. There were no assaults, but life was very much on the sexual side.

The main fear of concern of the Chinese was that someone would get in the tunnel with a knife or revolver. Everyone was searched by the Chinese warden as he or she came in. One morning about two o'clock a Chinese warden told us that a group of Indians had come in at the other end of the tunnel who were armed. We went to investigate. As luck would have it, they would be at the other end. We had to go through all that dirt, filth, and odor again. But Herbie Rea and I set out. There were around eight Indian policemen who had come off duty. They had come into the tunnel to sleep, leaving their guns in the police station across the street. We told the Chinese warden, who passed the word around so all the Chinese in the tunnel felt easier.

Ruth Briggs, Pasadena, California

On December 22 I got an early Christmas present from Standard Oil's headquarters. They had just received a cable from Hong Kong, dated December 15 that everyone was safe! Now I can breathe a little easier, and maybe the knots in my stomach will ease.

I spent the day getting ready for the upcoming holidays and trying to keep my mind off how lonely it will be without Norman here. The news on the radio said that Japanese troops have crossed over to Hong Kong proper from Kowloon. That is not good. And Wake Island has fallen to the Japanese. Sometimes I think that I just won't listen to the news anymore, but I really can't do that.

The girls "helped" me make three different kinds of cookies. They both took turns stirring the dough until it got too stiff for them. They really enjoyed using the cookie cutters. Carol picked out the bell and the Christmas tree for her cookies, and Kathie had the star and the candy cane, so they were both happy. They could hardly wait for them to cook and cool so they could put the colored icing on. Talk about a mess, but it was fun!

We also made shortbread cookies and regular chocolate chip cookies. Some of the chocolate chip dough got eaten before cooking, but I guess that won't hurt.

Tomorrow, while Kathie's at nursery school and Carol's napping, I'll tackle making a few pies.

Chapter VI
Christmas Day Surrender

Toward the closing days of the attack, we knew the Colony would fall. We were greatly concerned about the tunnels. What would the Japanese do? Would they repeat the Nanking business—come to the tunnel entrance and throw in hand grenades? If they did, where would be the best place to be? If near the entrance, we would probably be killed by the grenade. If we went farther back, we would surely get stomped on and suffocated by the Chinese. Certainly pandemonium and riot would follow the minute a hand grenade was thrown in. Well, this was crossing a bridge before we got to it, but it shows some of the things that were going through our minds.

Throughout the entire attack of the city the Japanese operated on a time schedule. If you wanted to get anywhere, it was generally safe to do so before 8:00 AM, as they seldom opened up before that. Similarly in the evening, it was generally safe between 5:00 PM and dark. The attacks usually lasted about two hours, then stopped for an hour or so. Just what the reason was I don't know, but I presumed to let the guns cool off. Apparently they did not have sufficient guns to keep going all day long.

When on tunnel duty, we would leave the tunnel as soon as it was broad daylight, around 7:15 AM. I would head straight for Altadena, about 1,200 feet up the Peak. I think my record time from the Hong Kong & Shanghai Bank Building to the house was 23 minutes. I was soaked through with sweat when I got there, but I was not about to slow down. On several occasions I had just made it when the shells started to come over. Once I was within five minutes of the house when the Japanese opened up, but I made it okay. I lost 20 pounds, most of it from running up and down the Peak in nothing flat.

In the early days of the European War and the bombing of London, I remember that the Germans never hit anything in London but hospitals and churches. In fact, from the newspaper accounts, I thought there were no other buildings in London but what were covered by these two classifications, as according to reports, nothing else was hit. I could not understand the reason for it, as it seemed peculiar to me that the Germans would bomb only hospitals and churches and nothing else. After seeing the British operate in Hong Kong, I now understood perfectly. In front of every hospital in Hong Kong, or within its immediate vicinity, they would set up anti-aircraft guns. The Japanese would dive bomb the guns and, of course, the hospitals would be hit. There were large open spaces there which were good for gun emplacements, but even so, I can't understand why they put guns in these locations.

The Carnossa Hospital got hit, the French Hospital, and the Naval Dockyard Hospital. On Christmas Eve the British moved troops into the War Memorial Hospital on the top of the Peak only to receive a two hour shelling on Christmas morning. There were also a couple of guns about 700 feet from the hospital. The only hospital in Hong Kong that wasn't hit was the Queen Mary which did not have a gun emplacement anywhere near it.

During the last few days of the attack, the British placed men in strategic locations of the city for sabotage work. Men were to go to places such as the electric plant and await further orders before doing any damage. I was astonished to learn that they chose men in their late 60s for this mission! Tom Pierce, Devoux, and Rodgers were assigned to the electric plant, but never heard a single word from headquarters. The next thing they knew, in came a Japanese officer, drew his revolver, shot all three of them, and then threw them over the sea wall! The British had such poor communication that they probably had no idea that the Japanese were that close to the city. The British communications were ancient and out-of-date. Going around the city later, I saw field telephone wires and sets all over the place. The Japanese did not waste any time stringing up wires; they had portable field radio phone sets.

In withdrawing from the New Territories and Kowloon, the British never destroyed a thing. They had a fine military road out through Castle Peak and up to the border. The bridges, road and everything were left intact. The Japanese could roll their guns, field equipment, and tanks right over the road. Later a Japanese was asked whether he came over the hills or not. He replied,

"Why bother to come over the hills? The roads were in perfect shape and we had no trouble whatsoever in using them. Good road builders, the British!" The Canton and Kowloon Railway was not touched at all, but left in working condition for the Japanese. Bridges, locomotives, rolling stock, machine shop, round house. Not a thing done to them. Incomprehensible, but so.

I have already told about the supposed plan to destroy the Texas and Standard oil installations. The British did put one shot into a Texas godown which burned up a few thousand units of kerosene. But the tanks and everything else in the installations remained for the Japanese. Every day during the attack we expected to see Laichikok fired by the British and go up in flames. I think maybe one shot was fired which put a hole in a tank and let out a few gallons of kerosene. But it did not catch fire and no further attempt was made to destroy the installation. So the Japanese had all the supplies.

British Navy did have four tanks of mostly kerosene and fuel oil in Kowloon, which the British destroyed by gun fire. The tanks burned fiercely for several days, flames leaping 50–60 feet in the air with huge and dense columns of smoke. Fires flared off and on for a week or so. The APC also had eight tanks on the Hong Kong side which the Japanese fired on, destroying most of them. Several farthest away from the waterfront remained intact, so the Japanese had the contents of these when they arrived.

The official reason that the British gave for not destroying all the oil installations was that there was a hospital for lepers right in back of them. Dr. Sylwin-Clarke, head of the public health service of the Colony, said that on account of the nearness of this hospital, the installation could not be fired as it would endanger the hospital full of patients. What? And they had put gun emplacements near all the other hospitals? I think the military just goofed, and used Dr. Sylwin-Clarke as a front, relieving the military from responsibility.

The Japanese 5th column was one of the most vicious things I ever saw. It is almost impossible to give an adequate description; you had to see it to believe it. There was absolutely no way to combat it. The British could not move a gun from one point to another but that in five minutes the Japanese would either be over dive bombing it or shelling from Kowloon. The speed of this information was amazing. Everywhere the British turned they were sold down the river. There seemed to be no solution to this problem.

During the siege of Hong Kong there were two peace missions which came over under the white flag. I remember both of them very well, although I do not recall the exact dates. The first came when I was still on the Food Control work at Hallgrin's. We were on the porch looking over the harbor. They had been shelling the Naval Dockyard right below us. They ceased firing, and one of the Star ferries pushed away from the Kowloon side. Across the front of the ferry was a white banner which had "Peace Mission" on it. They also had a white flag flying. We watched them dock at Queen's Pier through our spy glass.

The Japanese officers came ashore, as well as soldiers and guards with rifles. I presume their bayonets were fixed, although we could not distinguish that clearly. But the Japanese never went anywhere without fixed bayonets. The British came down from Government House and met them. I don't know what terms the Japanese offered, but the talk lasted around 30 minutes. Then the ferry, which was one the British had not scuttled, pushed away and returned to Kowloon.

As soon as they got there the shells started coming over again, so we knew that the terms had not been acceptable. They aimed for the Naval Dockyard again. Along the side of the yard was a traveling crane. The piers along the waterfront were of concrete and the buildings brick. They pounded this yard steadily for around two hours. Amazingly, only minimal damage was done. The traveling crane was a twisted mass of steel, and one shell went through the roof of a godown which started a fire. The fire department arrived right away and had the fire out in a few minutes, a very efficient piece of work. If the fire had spread to the munitions stored there, it would have been a different story.

When the second peace mission came over, the Governor, Sir Mark Young, is reported to have given the Japanese this reply: "The Chinese are in back of you, the British in front of you, so come on." Actually, there was nothing in back or in front of them except the hollow dimness of Harrow, Eton, Oxford, Cambridge, and the Old School Tie. The Japanese came on all right.

Talking to some British a few days later, they told me, "Why, Sir Mark could not surrender the Colony; it would ruin his whole career." Enough said.

The statements about the Chinese being in back of the Japanese was one of the most conceited lies and vilest piece of propaganda that I have every seen handed out. The Hong Kong Government issued official communiqués in which they stated that there was a large Chinese Army coming down in back of the Japanese to the relief of Hong Kong. Sir Mark knew that this was not true. He was trying to keep up the hopes of a doomed army and the morale of a civilian population caught like rats in a trap. The Japanese had their main base at Canton which was only 90 miles away. The Japanese would not start a major military operation on Hong Kong with a large Chinese force in the immediate vicinity. If there had been any large force, the Japanese would have dealt with that first.

To confirm that no Chinese Army was nearby, when the Japanese did get Hong Kong, they gave the army the run of the city for several days, then moved most of them out, leaving only a sufficient force to police the city.

If the British would have come out and said we are outnumbered and outmaneuvered, but let's fight, the morale of the entire colony would have been much better. However, British pride would not do that. I think it was worse than Pearl Harbor. The Hong Kong Government deliberately went out of its way to mislead the people; Pearl Harbor just went to sleep.

From December 22nd to the surrender, the Japanese were going back and forth across the harbor from Kowloon to Hong Kong, landing just below North Point. They had a steam launch with a barge roped to the side, bringing supplies over in the daytime and men at night. As far as I know, not a single shot was fired at them. The only explanation I can think of is that the British could not lower their guns sufficiently to bring them to bear on the Japanese and the smaller British field pieces must have been put out of commission by the Japanese air power.

This traffic went on for two or three days. The Japanese were piling up supplies on the waterfront. One afternoon the British did put a shot into the midst of a good quantity of supplies stacked up and set the whole thing afire. It was small rounds of ammunition, and we could see the fire and hear the shots going off round by round for several hours.

The last two days of fighting in Hong Kong were just one terrible nightmare. The British were taking over hotels and private houses, making forts of them. They had machine gun nests in the Repulse Bay Hotel and in private houses on the Peak. It seemed to me the British were fighting the war with tactics and equipment of 100 years ago when they first took Hong Kong. When the Canadian troops moved in on the Peak, they had no British officers who knew the terrain nor did they have any maps. When the Japanese came in, they had loads of maps.

It was also reported that when the Canadians and Japanese came into contact, the Japanese always shot first. That is just a mere matter of training. Take any kid 18 or 20 years old, which most of the Canadian troops were, and put him up against a professional soldier, and of course the latter will shoot first. And a kid who has never been in battle is hesitant to kill. This is no criticism of the Canadian troops, but it is a severe criticism of a government that would send them out with no training. There were about 2,500 Canadian troops, and some of them had been down in Bermuda, then transferred to Hong Kong. They were seeing the world and thought they were on a pleasure cruise. They had only been there several weeks before the war broke and in the boiled shirt tradition, they were widely entertained, but not soundly trained.

During the last week of the attack, leaflets were dropped by the Japanese appealing to the Chinese, and particularly to the British Indians, to cease resistance against the Japanese, desert the British, and come over to the Japanese side. The leaflets were worded to the effect that if the bearer presented it to a Japanese soldier, he would be immediately taken to an officer and would be assured of receiving kind treatment. These leaflets had pictures on them, showing the British crushing the Chinese and the Indians, the latter having practically nothing, whereas the British had the best of everything.

I have no idea of how many people made use of the leaflets. But I do know that a considerable number, particularly Indians, either went over to the Japanese before the British surrendered, or did so immediately afterwards. I heard reports that several people saw groups of Indian soldiers, 25 or 30 in number, throw down their rifles and hold up their hands when they were confronted by the Japanese. Their surrender was accepted, and they were put to work by the Japanese as policemen and guards.

The last few days were all alike, shelling and bombing, bombing and shelling. On Christmas morning the Japanese opened up as usual about 8:00 AM and kept pounding away for most of the morning until a little after 11:00 AM. We expected them to start up again after noon, but nothing happened. We were certain another BOOM would come any minute. But at 2:30 we got a call from the American Club downtown, saying it was all over, the Hong Kong Government had surrendered.

We all gave a sigh of relief. As the silence was explained, we went out onto the porch and the garden to see what was going on. We could hear small arm ammunition going off and see columns of black smoke arising in several places. The British were evidently destroying what they could by shooting their small arm shells and burning kerosene and gasoline supplies, which they had in small quantities at various places on the Island. Around 3:30 PM the Japanese Navy came in through the west entrance of the harbor. There were a couple of heavy cruisers, four or five destroyers, some auxiliary supply ships and some merchant cargo boats. This was a real blow to the British...the

Japanese Navy coming in and taking possession of Hong Kong!

Around 5:30 a lone plane came over at a good rate of speed. He dove and released a stack of bombs on the Naval Dockyard. Evidently he had not been informed that Hong Kong had capitulated. He straightened out from his dive and flew over Kowloon towards Canton. These were the last missiles thrown on Hong Kong.

I looked towards the west. There on Mt. Austin in the setting sun was the Rising Sun flag. The attack on Hong Kong was over.

Ruth Briggs, Pasadena, California

Today is Christmas. Ma and Pa came over several days ago to help me put up a Christmas tree. The girls are all excited and loved decorating the tree. Of course, most of the decorations are on the lower branches, but it looks lovely anyway. Ma and Pa came over Christmas Eve to stay with the children after they were in bed so I could go to church. I feel Norman's all right; my heart tells me he's still alive. I hope my special prayers are reaching him.

Kathie woke me up early Christmas morning. She insisted on checking out her stocking right away, so we got Carol, who was awake by this time, and went downstairs to see what Santa brought. I let them get the goodies from their stocking, then open one present from Santa. I said the rule was to wait to open the other presents when their Gram and Granddaddy got here. They checked things out, but managed not to open any others until Norman's parents came.

I took some pictures so Norman could see them when he gets home. I'm not saying if he gets home, but when he gets home.

The next day I got a late Christmas present from New York. They had received a cable from the American Consulate at Hong Kong, dated December 25, saying all Americans were safe! Yes, there is a Santa Claus!

Section 3:
The Occupation

Chapter I
Japanese Takeover

I still think the best thing I ever heard about the Orient is that you don't have to be crazy to live there, but it helps a lot. On Christmas day, December 1941, the Japanese officially occupied His Britannic Majesty's Possession, the Crown Colony of Hong Kong. The Hong Kong Government capitulated that afternoon, or, according to the Governor, Sir Mark Young, it officially "ceased resistance." Regardless of the technicality between "surrender" and "ceased resistance," the Japanese took Hong Kong, and the niceties of the British boiled shirt diplomacy were at an end as far as the Colony was concerned.

The number of armed forces on each side was a big factor. The general consensus of opinion was that the British armed forces consisted of the Middlesex, the Royal Scots, the Royal Rifles of Canada, the Indian troops, and the Hong Kong volunteers, totaling in the vicinity of 10,000 to 12,000 men. The Japanese had about 25,000 to 30,000 men, with another 25,000 in reserve. If absolutely necessary, the Japanese had further reserves of up to 100,000 men at the main Japanese base at Canton, only 90 miles away.

The losses on both sides were very heavy. The Middlesex and the Royal Scots were all but completely wiped out, and the Canadians lost a great number of men. No Indians were taken prisoners, and those that were alive when the Hong Kong Government ceased resistance were set free. I heard that there were about 4,000 British in the military internment camp, which means the British lost about 8,000 men.

Thus, being so out-numbered, and with antiquated equipment, the British put up a fight, even if they were fighting in confusion and disorganization. Japanese were the attackers. Their losses must have been much more, probably in the vicinity of 15,000 men, which is the figure I later heard.

The Japanese took Hong Kong in 17 days, and I think they were as much surprised as anyone else. The Japanese had planned on at least a two or three month campaign. When they took it in 17 days, they did not know what to do with it as they had no organization set up to handle it. Several sources told me that the Japanese went to the Hong Kong Government and asked them to keep the police force, the fire department, the sanitary department, and, in fact, all the civilian activities in the Colony and to operate these under the supervision of the Japanese. The reply was a flat NO. The Hong Kong Government was not going to be accused of cooperating or working with the enemy in any way.

The result was a complete mess. The British would not run it; the Japanese could not run it. The Japanese had no organization set up for running a civilian community. All they had at hand was a military machine, and now that they had captured Hong Kong, this was needed elsewhere. They gave the freedom of the city to the troops for several days, and then moved them all out to the Philippines, Malaya, or wherever they were needed to capture more territory. They only left sufficient troops—around 2,500 men—in Hong Kong to police the downtown section of the city and guard their own supplies.

The first visit at the house we had from the Japanese was on December 26th. They came in sometime during the afternoon. All 23 of us were in the house when they arrived, plus 15 Chinese servants. Around eight Japanese came in. The officer in charge spoke very little English. The soldiers were the regular shock troops; they had fixed bayonets, and it was easy to see that they were veterans, men who really did the work of capturing the Colony.

Their uniforms were torn, patched, ragged and dirty. They had on the Japanese rubber-soled shoes, split in the middle. It was not hard to see they were tired and worn out, that they had been fully employed for the past 17 days.

The officer asked if we were British or American. We replied both, then gave them a list showing our names, ages, sex, and nationality as requested. They also questioned the servants as to whether any of us were military and if any soldiers were hidden in the house. They also asked if any military equipment, such as arms and ammunition, were in the house.

The Japanese went through the house, inspecting every room. They satisfied themselves in a general way that we were civilians, then asked for something to eat, particularly wanting milk. When we gave it to them, they made the servants taste it first to be certain that it was okay. Then they posted a notice in Japanese in the front hall saying the house had been inspected. Later they put a wooden sign up at the main front entrance to the driveway, which showed that the property had been inspected and entered on their records.

This was the first of an interminable number of visits, sometimes subject to around three or four visits daily. They would vary in size from a couple of Japanese officers to up to seven or eight soldiers. They generally walked through the house, looked into every room, and always asked the same damn fool questions as to how many we were and so on. They gave us all sorts of Japanese papers and certificates written in Japanese to be shown to the Japanese group, but they were always ignored by the next officer inspecting the house, who would wave his hand, perhaps give a grunt, inspect the house, and then issue his own papers or none at all.

They didn't seem to know exactly what they wanted; they were just out on an inspection tour. These visits were very annoying, and we were always apprehensive because we never knew what they might do. We had several very unpleasant visits, one in which we were physically threatened with revolvers. However, we never came to any harm, nor did they ever make any attempts on the women and children in the form of rape or anything approaching it. As far as we were concerned, they were nuisance visits. Sometimes they would stay only a few minutes, but other times a couple of hours.

When they came, we always assembled in the downstairs hallway. When they went from room to room, one of us generally followed them around to which they did not object as they wanted us to point out things, answer questions and so on. This following around probably saved some trifling with personal belongings such as razors, fountain pens, and other small things that they could easily pick up and put in their pockets. If they had, we would never have said anything. It was all theirs for the taking, but when people are being watched, they are more or less prone to leave things alone; hence, the purpose of our going around with them.

During the first two weeks of the Japanese occupation, they brought in about forty or fifty cargo boats which were empty. These went alongside the docks in both Kowloon and Hong Kong and left fully loaded, taking absolutely everything they could lay their hands on. Hong Kong was full of a vast store of supplies such as food, machinery, and military equipment, but particularly food. The Hong Kong Government counted upon and was prepared for a blockade. They had enough food to feed a million and a half people for six months.

The Hong Kong government had what they called the dispersal system. The plan was to move the population out of the city itself and establish smaller groups of people in various parts of the Island in what they called dispersal areas. They had warehouses built all over the place which were crammed full of food. Not just one, but several to a dozen in each area. These were only one story buildings, but were about fifty feet long, so they held a huge quantity of food—Australian corned beef and mutton, jams, dried fruits, margarine, syrup, canned potatoes and, in fact, all manner and description of food of a stable quality.

The American Red Cross had 500 tons of cracked wheat. The dock yards and machine shops were full of supplies, and the military equipment consisted of machine guns and ammunition in an appreciable quantity. The Japanese got all this and much more. The first two weeks were the most active. They would load up a dozen ships, make up a convoy, and off they would go. Whether the stuff went back to Japan or some place else, I don't know. But even by the end of June, they had not removed everything.

Ships were put right alongside the Standard Oil installation and all the package goods were taken away, such as gasoline and kerosene in tins, lubrication oil in drums. They did not touch the bulk stocks, as evidently they were going to use those supplies for local purposes. The most valuable supplies, such as the high grade marine oils and industrial oils, were moved out without any delay. What a haul this was for the Japanese! It should have been all destroyed by the British, but that did not happen.

As far as I know, they took only goods that belonged to the British Government, and the British and American firms and nationals of those countries. They did not touch goods belonging to Chinese and third-country nationals. The supplies of the big department stores such as Sincere's and Wing On were left intact. These stores were in business by the latter part of June.

They collected all the motor cars in Hong Kong and parked them on the cricket field and in front of the Hong Kong & Shanghai Bank. When they had a sufficient number, they just pulled a ship alongside and on they went. I have no idea how many cars and trucks they got, but it was a big number, at least around 800 or so. This was looting on a large scale, but under strict supervision.

There were rumors without end about internment. Some had it we were going to Formosa, now known as Taiwan, others that we would be sent to Canton. By the middle of January, it seemed fairly evident that it would be either Kowloon or Hong Kong Island. The British Central School in Kowloon was considered a very likely place. Around January 20th it was pretty certain that we would be interned on the Island, with Stanley being mentioned. Stanley is the Hong Kong prison, still operating as such today. We had visions of looking out of a small cell until the war was over. I think this was the first time in history that the entire foreign population of a city was to be interned. As there were no precedents, it only gave a broader base for more rumors.

Ruth Briggs, Pasadena, California

Happy New Year. The day after Christmas the news said that Hong Kong had fallen to the Japanese. Which means that Norman is a prisoner, if he's alive. I know he's alive, I just know it. He's got to be. I hope the Japanese distinguish between the military prisoners and the civilian prisoners. I know them as wonderful people, but that was in good times. They can be brutally cruel, and they will follow orders right down the line with no questions asked. But Norman knows the Japanese. He knows that you should never offend them. He will survive.

Although it was very meager, Pasadena did have a Rose Parade. I walked the three blocks to Colorado Avenue with the girls to show them the beautiful flower floats. The smell of the flowers is wonderful, like a fairyland! A little make-believe to help us survive during this awful war.

What will this year bring? Will the war be over this year? Will I see Norman this year? I can only hope and pray.

Chapter II
Entertainment and Coping

We had some amusing visits at the house from the Japanese and some that weren't so amusing. One of the former happened a couple of days after Hong Kong fell. A small party headed by an officer who spoke very little English came in. The Company had bought a brand new Buick car the latter part of November; the purpose of the visit was to get the car. The Japanese officer came in, sat down, and said, "Ah, you have motor car?" We replied we did. "My captain, he—, he—, thinking, he thinking, he need, need, motor car." We said the motor car was in the garage. The Japanese would fumble with his sword, drum on the table, suck his teeth, and then every few seconds would come out with "My captain, he—, he—, think—ing, thinking." To make a long story short, they decided to take the car to their thinking captain. Believe it or not, they gave us a receipt for it!

The car was quite a haul for them. There were six or seven Japanese in the party, and they were just as pleased as children with a new Christmas toy. You could see it all over their faces that they were going to take this car back to the company commander, present it to him saying: "See what we found, the best car in Hong Kong." Brand new cars were at a premium, and they would certainly get special recognition by bringing back such a prize.

They could not start the car, so pushed it out on the road. It had the gear shift lever on the steering post, and these Japanese had never seen one like that before. They fumbled and fooled around with it for ten or fifteen minutes, climbing in and out, sucking their teeth, commenting on how good it looked. They got tangled up in their swords, doors and fenders were scratched with their hobbed nailed shoes. They stood on the bumpers, and in fact were all over the car except actually on top. They finally gave up as they could not get it started.

They then asked us to please drive them downtown, and they would bring us back. We then told a little fib and explained that as it was a brand new car, we did not know how to drive it either! They were greatly surprised at this and asked why we had a car. "Oh," we said, "we have a chauffeur." "Chauffeur, where is he?" We replied that he was an Indian, and we had not seen him since the war started. This statement was not strictly true as he had been up to the house several times. But he had not been near the place for the past week, and we did not know what had become of him. There was one thing certain: we were not going downtown if we could possibly help it. They fooled around some more, and finally got the car going by pushing it. When the engine fired, they all jumped in and off they went.

We never expected to see the car again, but miracles do happen. That next afternoon, they brought the car back, put it in the garage, and thanked us for its use! That night at 10:00 PM, there was a knock on the door. The first words from the Japanese was, "Ah, my captain he thinking, he—, he—need, motor, motor car." They took the car for keeps this time. We never saw it again.

Another house visit that wasn't so pleasant occurred one afternoon during the first days of the occupation, when all the Japanese soldiers were given the freedom of the city. A car drove up to the front of the house and four Japanese privates got out. Three came into the house while one stood guard outside. They were on a private looting job, looking for small things of value like rings and watches. One of the soldiers drew his revolver and stuck it into our stomachs saying, "Bullets! Bullets!" meaning that if we offered resistance they would shoot. They took watches and fountain pens and such. One person had a very nice gold watch which he prized very highly that had been in his family for years. They went through all the men's pockets; one man had his watch hidden in his back pocket, which they missed. They did not go over any of the women, but just gave them a looking over. One of the Japanese slipped upstairs and went through the rooms up there. My watch and fountain pen were in one of the dressing table drawers in my bedroom; they opened the drawer, but amazingly took nothing out! In my suitcase I had my wallet in the midst of some clothes. He rummaged through this, saw the wallet, and took it, getting a good haul as I had $300 in it. This was the only instance that I heard of them taking money, as generally they were not interested in it.

Everything was theirs for the taking anyway. They knew that they would be there for only a few days, and Hong Kong money would be of no use to them elsewhere, but watches would. They had only been in the house about twenty minutes when the guard outside gave a yell. All three dropped what they were doing and immediately beat it. They all got in the car and drove off. They had no sooner gone than a regular patrol of Japanese officers came by. The guard had seen the officers and, of course, they did not want to be caught on a private looting expedition. This was true all over Hong Kong. The men were given the freedom of the city; it was understood that they could do and take anything they wanted, but it must not be done in the presence of officers.

One of the favorite tricks of the Japanese was to stop you on the street to ask what time it was, and then take your watch away. I saw several soldiers with two wrist watches on each arm. They were sure nuts about wrist watches and also cameras. It took us a very short time to figure out that whenever we left the house, we first hid all our valuables. After this, whenever a visitation came, money, watches and other small valuables would be put in back of chair cushions, thrown under book cases, or anywhere that it was most convenient. Thus, we never lost anything more, nor were we threatened.

Downtown, around twenty-five or thirty Europeans were living at the Hong Kong University when the Japanese came in. Some Japanese soldiers also moved in, just how many I don't know, but there were quite a number of them, around forty or fifty, I believe.

One night, time was hanging pretty heavy on the Japanese hands, and they decided that they wanted some entertainment. They sent a note to the Europeans and told them to report in the assembly hall. Of course, all reported, but it was somewhat in fear and trepidation because they had no idea what was going to happen.

When both the Europeans and Japanese had all assembled, a Japanese officer got up and explained in broken English that they wanted a little entertainment. To start everything off, the Japanese would entertain first. A Japanese solider got up and played a couple of pieces on the piano. Then a group of soldiers sang some Japanese songs. (Knowing the Japanese, I can well imagine what the songs were, so it was probably just as well none of the Europeans understood them.)

Then the Japanese officer got up and tried to explain, in his broken English, that their part was now finished: "Japaneseu, we—we—now, finish, we—, we make end." All the foreigners were seated in the front row. Right in the middle was a fairly large woman. The Japanese continued, "Now you people, you—, you make merriment for Japaneseu, you—, you—. He then opened his mouth wide, yelled at the top of his voice, and very abruptly pointed at the large woman, saying, "SING!"

Having no choice, she got up and sang. I don't know what, but sing she did. When the Japanese told you to sing, you damn well sang. Later, this was one of our favorite pass words in camp. We would pass someone, point abruptly, and then holler, "SING!"

Of the 23 of us in the house, there were fifteen men, five women, and three children. After the Japanese took over Hong Kong, we never left the house except for absolute necessities such as food. We did not want to risk being picked up on the street by the Japanese nor did we want to leave the house empty or unprotected. We always left sufficient men in the house so that the women and children would not be alone. If trouble did occur with Chinese looters, we wanted enough men in the house to put up some resistance or go for help.

Felix Suter was one of our number. As he was Swiss, he had a pass and could go freely about the city. As soon as the Japanese took over, he went to the Swiss consul and then to the Japanese military to get an arm band, showing that he was a third-nation national, or neutral. He helped us out considerably, going back and forth downtown getting food and other supplies. Also very helpful were the three Swedish officers from the Swedish ship that was scuttled. Never a day went by but what one of them came around to see if he could do anything for us.

Between December 26th and January 5th I think about everyone in the house made at least one trip downtown with Suter or one of the Swedish officers. It was impossible for them to carry everything that was purchased, so we had to go along, hoping to get by without being stopped or questioned. Every time we left the house we were never certain that we would get back. When we went, we distributed money all over ourselves—some in our shoes, linings of hats, coats, inside pockets, and most anywhere else that one could think of. The idea, of course, was that if we were held up by either some Japanese or Chinese, they might miss a few spots and not get all we had.

Watches and other small valuables were left at the house. Each of us had a small bag packed, because we did not know when we would be ordered out. Furthermore, if any of us did not get back from these shopping trips, the rest of the household would probably be ordered out shortly, and it was hoped that they might be able to bring our bag with theirs. We were all expecting internment, and, if so, it would be most likely in one place.

One little incident was quite funny to me. One of our number, an Englishman, decided that he wanted to go downtown, but was not quite sure of himself. He thought he would be much better protected and would not be picked up by the Japanese if he had a letter from some person whom he thought was of importance in Hong Kong. He went to the house of the Chief Justice of Hong Kong and got a letter stating his purpose for going downtown. The body of the letter was legible, but the signature could have been made by any two-year-old. We Americans just smiled, as we could not see of what importance such a letter would be.

To be on the safe side, he decided to take this letter to the Japanese Consulate, that is, what was formerly the consulate. He thought if he had their official "chop" or signature on it, he could show this to any Japanese soldier if he were stopped. He waited around the consulate for a couple of hours, finally getting in to see the consul. The Consulate officer took the letter, looked at it, and asked who the signer was. The Japanese knew perfectly well who the signer was, but he was going to rub it in a bit. When the reply came, "the Chief Justice of the Crown Colony of His Britannic Majesty's Possession, Hong Kong," the consul looked at the bearer, handed the letter back, and said, "Sa, Chief Justice before maybe big man, but now all finished, no more important, sa, thank you, good-bye."

On December 28th the Japanese held their Victory Parade on Queen's Road. The boats in the harbor were dressed, and they had an air display of forty or fifty planes, including stunt flying. We did not go downtown, but saw it from the house. The air display was the main thing, and they came over in much bigger waves than they did during the attack. One of the purposes probably was to show us exactly what they did have and how much more damage they could have done to downtown Hong Kong. However, we did not need to be convinced, as we were well aware of that fact already. The British did not have one single plane!

The Japanese had loud speakers going and bands playing. We could not see the reaction of the Chinese downtown, but the servants did not seem greatly excited or impressed. We heard shouting from downtown, but it was all in Japanese, not Chinese.

Ruth Briggs, Pasadena, California

The news doesn't have too much on Hong Kong anymore, since it's now held by the Japanese. I sure wish I knew what is going on. Is Norman in prison? Is he with the other Standard Oil people? Is he getting enough food? I know he's smart and he knows the Japanese people, so he can probably help the other company people, as most of the others were not in Japan before. And his sense of humor hopefully will carry him over some of the rough times I know he must be having. I don't know why, but I think of the Rudyard Kipling poem, "If you can keep your head while all about you are losing theirs and blaming it on you…" Norman is steady, and will be a calming influence on others, I think.

The New York office finally called me. They still don't know much, but are assuring me that Norman's okay. I don't know how they know, but as long as they say it, that's fine with me. I wish I knew more, but it makes me feel better when they say that the Standard Oil personnel are all accounted for in Hong Kong. They will be sending a portion of his paycheck directly to me from now on, until Norman is back home. At least that takes the financial worry off my shoulders.

I just wish I knew more about what Norman is going through and wish that I could help him in some way. I don't even know if I can write him or send him anything. I try to keep the household going in as much of a normal fashion as I can. That's all I can do.

Chapter III
Hawkers and Looters

For two weeks after the Japanese came in downtown, Hong Kong was some place! Queen's Road was just crowded and packed with people all day long. Where all the Chinese came from and what they were doing, no one seemed to know. There were two streams of people going up and down both sides of the road all day long. It just seemed as if the east part of the town was moving west and the west to the east section. The Chinese seemed to have no purpose, just going up and down Queen's Road.

The hawkers certainly had a Roman holiday. They set up stalls on both sides of Queen's Road and "went to town." The main items were food, but they had other things for sale too, such as tobacco, razors, shirts, socks, and other small items of clothing. Prices, of course, were double and three times what they were before the war. We thought at first that all of these goods for sale were looted and stolen, and no doubt many of them were. All the shops and stores were closed, as the Japanese had not had a chance to take them over and take an inventory.

The stores and shops owners, therefore, would give some of the employees an arm-full of goods, send them out the back door, and tell them to go and set up a stall on Queen's Road. When the supplies of the stall had been sold out, they would return to get more. I have no idea what the number of the so-called legitimate stalls were and those operated by the looters. There were a large number of both.

Apples were 50 cents each. Bars of candy that were 15 and 20 cents before were now selling at 50 and 60 cents. Half pound bars of chocolate were highly prized at $2.00. The main items were tinned corned beef, corned mutton, and condensed, powdered and evaporated milk. You could bargain and, especially for large quantities, you could get them down a little, but not much. They knew that there would be no more of these items, and prices would be going up rather than down.

The looters, however, did not have a large stock on hand, so they liked to sell their stuff for what they could get, and then go out and loot some more to set up business again. Turnover was something to them, so they would shave the prices. Lugging suitcases of tinned goods up that Peak, believe me, was some job. I lost quite a bit of weight during the shelling running for cover, but I know I lost more lugging stuff up the Peak.

Other looting was done on the British and American residences on the Peak. The houses that were not destroyed by shell fire or incendiary bombs were well destroyed by the Chinese looters. In fact, many of the houses looted were in far worse shape than those destroyed by bombs. The Chinese would go into a house in gangs of eight or ten, saw up all the furniture such as grand pianos, chairs, tables, rip out the window cases, and tear up the floors. After they had demolished everything else, they would rip down the staircases and saw them up. There would be absolutely nothing left of a house when they had finished with it. In some cases, they would drive trucks right up to the front door and then go to work. When they weren't as well organized as this, they would tie up the sawed furniture into bundles, put it on their backs, and walk off. These gangs were mainly composed of women, or at least women participated to a large extent. There would usually be sufficient men to guard the party so that they would not be attacked by other looters.

From Altadena we would watch them go to work on the houses all around us. Some of this looting was done in broad daylight, but the major part of it was carried on at night. Whenever we would see a gang of looters coming, we would assemble in the front yard, all 23 strong, so that they could see how many we were and that the house was occupied. We did not attempt to interfere with looting of other property, because we had no means of interfering. Furthermore, we were afraid that if we started a policing job and stopped looters, it would only be a question of time before they would gang up on us and clean us all out. We held to the policy of protecting ourselves, minding our own business, and let others do what they could.

One thing the Chinese didn't want was the boiled shirts and penguin suits, or women's dinner dresses and high-heeled shoes! The Peak was just strewn with tuxedos and formal wear. The Chinese had no use for British boiled shirt dinner parties and all the refinements of so-called polite society. Thick Chinese rugs were a dime a dozen. All other clothes such as regular suits, overcoats, shoes and such were taken to be sold or cut up into other clothing. Silverware, dishes and other household items were put to immediate use by the Chinese. They certainly had a great time going through the Peak houses. They had never seen anything like it before and probably wouldn't ever again.

There was a purpose behind all this looting, and I will say that it was not entirely of a wanton or licentious nature. Remember that Hong Kong is an island. Everything must be imported, even firewood. The Chinese needed wood to cook their rice. A grand piano to the Chinese was more useful for firewood than for any other purpose. Mozart and Beethoven's Moonlight Sonata would not cook their rice, but the grand piano would. The Peak was looted by the Chinese, not by the Japanese.

There was some slight attempt on the part of the Japanese to stop this looting, but for the most part it was done with their full knowledge and sanction. The British and the Americans were the main people that the Japanese were fighting, and the Peak was occupied almost exclusively by them. The Hong Kong Government had refused to keep the police force going, so why should the Japanese detail soldiers protect their property when such men were needed elsewhere? They knew perfectly well what would happen if the Peak were not policed. They just let the Chinese go ahead.

On one or two occasions, they did tie up some Chinese looters and stationed them at the bottom of the Peak as an example. They also shot some and hung the bodies in a tree. My guess is that these Chinese had tried to get at some supplies in Japanese hands or had refused to turn over some of the loot that the Japanese asked for. I don't think any shooting was done with any real intention of stopping the looting on the Peak. It was open season on the Peak, and the Chinese did not need a license. None of the looters was armed, as the only people who could carry firearms were the Japanese.

At night we kept a patrol in the house and so did all the other occupants on the Peak. Two men would keep watch for two hours each, then others would take over. We rotated in this manner for the entire time that we lived on the Peak. We had only one visitation at night from the Chinese looters.

I was not on guard at the time, but about 2:30 AM a Chinese came up on the front porch and looked through the window. One man on guard flashed a light in his face. The Chinese called the rest of this gang, and off they went.

That is the last we ever saw of them.

We thought that they might be back, so the whole household was awakened. All that was seen by the guard were four men, but when everyone was awakened, one of the women came running downstairs saying that the house was surrounded by forty Chinese looters! How rumors get started!

This particular group of Chinese must have been very new at the game, because they generally would survey the place in the daytime, find out whether it was occupied or not. In the beginning there was certainly a choice, some houses having much more valuable things than others. In the end, all the houses were looted; the only safe insurance against looting was to have a house full of boiled shirts!

One of the saddest instances of looting happened much later. When we were all sent to internment camp, we asked the three Swedish officers, as third party nationals, if they would like to move into the house. They were living in one room downtown in very cramped quarters. The proposal was put to them that if they lived there and kept the property out of the hands of the Chinese looters, the Company would make a settlement with them for the expenses they had in holding on to the Company property. They moved in about two weeks before we left. On April 10th they were informed by the Japanese that they would have to get out on April 15th, as the Japanese governor of Hong Kong was coming there to live. The reason for this was that it was about the only livable house left on the Peak.

On the night of April 14, a gang of fifteen Chinese looters showed up, entered the house, murdered the three Swedish officers, and then went through the house and made a shambles of it. It was very sad, as we knew them quite well and knew they all had families at home in Sweden. The looters knew that it was their last night and, after the governor moved in, there would be an armed guard on the place. After the destruction, of course, the Japanese governor couldn't move in either.

Ruth Briggs, Pasadena, California

It's the end of January now and time drags on with no more news from Hong Kong. I contacted the Red Cross to see if they could give me any information. Even they have not heard from their Hong Kong contacts. I guess everything is in chaos there. I wonder if Norman is in the apartment he was staying in, or in another place. I hope the Japanese are letting the civilians stay in their houses. I hope the houses are still in one piece. I don't know how much bombing happened on Hong Kong Island. I hope they didn't target the residences on Victoria Peak. Aren't they supposed to only target military facilities? I try not to think of the saying, "All's fair in love and war."

I wonder how some of our friends in Japan are doing. I know most of the company men were no longer in Japan, but some of our missionary friends were probably still there. And I know Mr. Enikeieff is still there. Oleg and Nina came to Japan from Russia, but were not US citizens, so the company couldn't bring him back. Nina and their son are here in California. I certainly hope he's all right.

When I came back before Carol was born, I knew that families were not going to be allowed to return to Japan. I brought home all our wedding silver, and some other small items, but all our other household goods and other wedding presents are in Japan. We'll probably never see them again. But that's okay. I just want to see Norman again.

My project today was making oleo margarine. The girls enjoy mixing "the butter." I make them take turns on who gets to put the yellow coloring into the bowl. Kathie is a pretty good helper and really mixes it up fairly well. Carol thinks she's a good helper too. I try to praise them both.

Chapter IV
Atrocities and Brothel Hospitality

Before the Hong Kong Government "ceased resistance," it was understood on both sides that no prisoners would be taken. It so happened that this only worked one way, as the British never had a chance to take any. The Japanese did not want any prisoners; they did not want to be bothered with feeding them, guarding them, and, in general, looking after them.

There were many stories of atrocities about which you may have heard, but most of these happened, I believe, before the British surrendered. Personally, I did not see any, so therefore I am not going to tell of any. One I know to be true, however, is the bayoneting of the Canadian soldiers. The Japanese took these 25 or 30 Canadian soldiers, tied their hands behind them, and then just had live bayonet practice. It was cruel, but it was war, and that is no parlor game.

From a military standpoint, I can see nothing wrong with the way the Japanese took Hong Kong. The Japanese stood over in Kowloon with their army, and together with their navy, they just pounded the place. They had superior numbers and superior equipment and there could be only one result. The British did exactly the same thing 100 years earlier. They came alongside with the navy and blasted a bunch of Chinese pirates and citizens who had no defense whatsoever.

There was a considerable amount of face slapping, kicking around, and other humiliating incidents of that nature after the surrender, but I hardly think they could be classed as atrocities. There was no machine gunning, bayoneting, or mutilation of bodies after the Hong Kong Government surrendered, as far as I know. One had to be very careful when approaching or passing the Japanese, for you never knew what they would do. You had to take your hat off and stop and bow. People got slapped and pushed around for not doing that. In fact, some people got slapped for doing absolutely nothing. The Japanese sometimes just wanted to slap someone, and if you were around, it may be your turn, and that is about all there was to it. These incidents were very annoying and extremely undignified, but I hardly think they can be classed as atrocities.

There was a rumor about raping in the Kowloon Hotel. I was not there myself, but there were 80 Americans that were; all of these Americans came to Stanley, and not one of them said they saw any raping. The Kowloon Hotel is a big hotel, with something like 400 rooms. No one person could be in all the rooms at once. Maybe there was raping there, but I can't say.

The Japanese were not interested in any middleaged British or American women, and those women that were in Hong Kong were all this or older. There were plenty of young Chinese girls in whom the Japanese were interested. Anyone who knows the Orient knows that this kind of stuff goes on all the time anyway. About the only difference that the war made is that the Japanese did not have to pay for it.

I heard one story about the Japanese going into a hospital, taking advantage of the nurses, and then just going through the place, killing everyone in it. The following is what I heard from several different sources in the internment camp.

A Japanese officer went into a hospital and told a nurse there to throw back all the bed covers so he could see that the men actually in the beds were wounded, and not just a put-up job on the part of the British. The nurse started to do this. The Japanese either changed his mind or wanted to give further instructions, and he went after her with his arms extended out towards her. A British officer came in just then, saw the Japanese going for the nurse, pulled his revolver and shot the Japanese. There was a whole body of Japanese troops outside. When they heard the shot, they thought the British were making another fort out of the hospital, so they just went through the place and killed everyone there. The British had taken over the hotels and private houses on the Peak, making forts out of them. The Japanese thought this was another such trick.

When the Japanese took over Hong Kong, they immediately set up a newspaper in English called the Hong Kong News. This was their propaganda medium. At this stage, the Japanese weren't organized to put all the foreigners into internment. As long as we did not interfere with them, they were going to let us handle ourselves for the time being.

However, the Colonial Secretary wrote a letter to the Japanese commander saying that the Europeans were destitute, were without food, shelter and clothing, and that they must be cared for. I don't know the exact wording of the letter, but the tone was to the effect that all of the Europeans' troubles were the result of Japanese atrocities. The Japanese replied that the letter was an insult to the Emperor, and they promptly clamped the Colonial Secretary in jail. They then said that if the Europeans were not capable of looking after themselves, they will deal with it.

The Japanese put a notice in the paper that all British, Americans, and Dutch should report to the Murray Parade Ground by 10:00 AM on January 5th. Rumors had circulated that this would happen. The 23 of us in the house met to decide what to do. Al Bourne, the general manager, asked me what I thought, as I had more experience dealing with the Japanese with my previous years' living in Japan. The Japanese had been to our house four or five times every day since they had taken Hong Kong, and had never mentioned a word to us about reporting to Murray Parade Ground. I said the Japanese were very methodical, and they would come and get us later if we did not report. We had a month's supply of food at the house, and we did not know what would happen if we reported to the Parade Ground. If they asked us later why we didn't go, we could plead ignorance. We decided to stay, even though we knew we were running a risk by not reporting. It turned out we made the right decision.

The Japanese were prepared for around 500 Europeans, and when 2,000 showed up, they just didn't know what to do with them. They had tables set up with paper and pencils, probably to take a census of everyone. But the Japanese folded up the tables, dispensed with the paperwork, lined everyone up into four columns, and marched them down Queen's Road with all their baggage to the Chinese hotels nearby.

These hotels were all brothels. A Japanese officer went into the first hotel and told the Chinese owner to empty his hotel. All the prostitutes were pushed out onto the street. As soon as one hotel was empty, it was filled with Europeans, and then on to the next hotel, until five hotels were filled up with all 2,000 foreigners.

The conditions in these hotels were absolutely terrible. The rooms were very small, about five by seven feet, with no window and only one bed in each. Five or six people were in each room. It was impossible for everyone to lie down at the same time. People who were there told me that by lying perfectly straight, two people could be on the floor and two on the bed, and the other two had to remain in the corridor. The sanitary conditions were absolutely filthy. One small dirty toilet was on each floor. In fact, to give any adequate description of the life in these hotels is out of the question. Fortunately, I was not there, but I heard about it later.

The first forty-eight hours there was no food whatsoever. After that, the Japanese sent in food once a day. Although it was cooked, it was not adequately cooked. The food was rice, a few greens, and chickens and ducks taken from one of the large stores where the refrigerator system had broken down, so that the meat was completely spoiled. Diarrhea and dysentery started spreading throughout the hotels. There was no medical care at all.

They also had Indian guards who were very nasty. There was no exercise, and everyone was cramped up in the small rooms. I heard several people say that they didn't care whether they lived or not and, given the chance, would have committed suicide. While at Stanley, one man said several times that he wished he had jumped off the roof of the Meichow Hotel. I am very thankful that we decided to stay at the house and not go down to the Murray Parade Ground. Others can thank the Colonial Secretary for his hospitality!

Ruth Briggs, Pasadena, California

I have volunteered at the hospital group to help make bandages to send to our soldiers. Three times a week I meet with a group of ladies. We take old sheets or other material, rip them into strips, and roll them. We make different sizes, depending on the material. It makes me feel good to be doing something helpful. I only hope and pray that Norman doesn't need any of these bandages.

Ma and Pa Briggs help watch the children while I do this. Sometimes, though, we meet in our homes, so the children can come along. However, they like to go to their grandparents. Ma gives them treats. And Pa entertains them by funny drawings he calls feegle-fogles. They look like cartoon characters of different bugs. Carol one day came running into the house all excited, saying there was a feegle-fogel outside. I went out with her. She was prancing all around and finally pointed to a grasshopper, saying it was a feegle-fogel. I couldn't argue with her, as it did look like some of Pa's drawings. So I just said, yes, that was a grasshopper feegle-fogel. He's a good guy.

No good news. Singapore and Rangoon were bombed by Japanese aircraft, and Kuala Lumpur was captured by the Japanese 5th Division. No more news about Hong Kong, since the Japanese have already taken over there. I heard that Tom Nock got home safely out of Rangoon. And the news said Moscow was not under immediate peril as the Russian forces recaptured Mozhaisk, the last German stronghold near the Soviet capital. But US forces are withdrawing from Bataan. I haven't heard about the Company people in Manila.

I can keep busy during the day, but the nights sure are long. When we pull the blackout shades down in the evening, my mood also shifts into black. Although I think about Norman constantly, when we pull the shades down, the scary situation hits me in the face. After I put the girls to bed, I try to read awhile to keep my mind off thinking.

Chapter V
Life on the Peak

The Japanese published a second notice for all foreigners who did not report to the Murray Parade Ground before to please report now to military headquarters. Unofficially, however, the word was passed around to please not report. They only published the notice to comply with Tokyo regulations. If we did report, they would not know what to do with us, and it would just be another problem for them. They had run out of Chinese hotels, and they did not want to be bothered finding new quarters for a bunch of crazy Europeans who did not have enough sense to stay in their own country. If we were living in our houses on the Peak, please stay there. When they had a place ready for us, they would let us know.

This was what the Japanese had intended to do all along, and there was no need for the Chinese hotel business at all, if the British Colonial Secretary hadn't stirred up the issue. I don't think the British fully comprehended that they had lost Hong Kong. They still thought they had a say in the way things should be run. But the only people running Hong Kong after December 25th were the Japanese.

The 500 of us who remained on the Peak lived like kings in comparison to those in the hotels. We could not go downtown, but we could move around more or less freely. The Japanese had guards at all the roads at the bottom of the Peak, so they were seeing to it that we stayed there. When we heard about the Chinese hotels, you can bet your sweet life we had no desire to leave.

The (former) Chief Justice of Hong Kong appointed himself as the representative of the residents on the Peak in dealings with the Japanese. There was no opposition to this, as most of the residents left were British and agreed that he should be the one. After all, as far as they were concerned, it was still a Crown Colony, and the Chief Justice was number three in the local hierarchy. Sir Mark Young, the Governor, was being privately "entertained" by the Sons of Heaven, a.k.a. the Japanese. The Colonial Secretary, the number two person, was "enjoying" the fruits of his own efforts in the Chinese brothels.

The Chief Justice went down each day to meet with the Japanese commander. I believe I am correct when I say that the Chief Justice did the listening and the Japanese did the talking. A representative from each house on the Peak would go to number 151 The Peak, where the Chief Justice was housed, at 4:00 PM every afternoon to hear what instructions or comments the Japanese relayed to him.

One matter which did come up was in connection with policing the Peak. We were instructed to form a police corps, take regular patrols, and police the Peak to deal with the Chinese looters. The Japanese suggested that we were not to permit anyone to come up or go down the Peak unless they had a note saying who they were, the purpose of the trip, and for whom they worked. This was to apply to every nationality, but its main purpose was to keep a check on the Chinese servants. Foreigners could not leave the Peak, so naturally servants were sent on errands.

The whole idea was absolutely nuts. Suppose we stopped a Chinese. He would say that it was no longer British territory, so no foreigner could stop him from going anywhere in Hong Kong. We had no arms, absolutely nothing, so what could we enforce? We were also told that if the plan did go into effect, we should not stop the Japanese! Now just imagine the wisdom of that remark. Needless to say, the idea was voted down, as we all realized that the most effective policing force we could do was to look after our own houses, not leave them unoccupied, and to maintain a guard at night.

One of the leading British citizens of Hong Kong wanted a batman, which in the British army is a servant. I was at his house one afternoon shortly after the "cease resistance" order, and he said that his position in the Colony demanded a batman and, yes sir, he was going to ask the Japanese for a batman. Some more boiled shirt effort of the British and no real comprehension of who was in charge! I would have enjoyed to have been present when he asked the Japanese commander for one. I imagine the answer would have been, "Sa, big man one time, no account now." Anyway, our leading citizen never got his batman.

Every morning we would go to the War Memorial Hospital to get our food rations for the day. During the war this was one of the food distribution centers. It was well organized, and they had a record of the number of people in each house, including the servants, and we would get our rations on this basis. They were not always adequate as stocks were running low, but the Japanese would let sufficient supplies come in to keep us going.

Besides a food center, the War Memorial Hospital was a regular gossip and news factory. We would all gather there and exchange news. Boy, how the stories grew! There was also a radio which we operated secretly at night, with the news from this whispered around later. The stories that we heard from the radio were almost the exact opposite of what was published in the Japanese paper, the Hong Kong News.

With the supplies we had at the house plus what we had purchased downtown, and those supplied at the hospital, we managed to keep going. It was pretty thin at times, but we were to learn later what real hunger was. During the month of January we had two meals a day. If it was available, the children had a little Bovril and a cracker at noon. We had some flour at the house, and the cooks made biscuits which the British called Scones. We had some molasses which we put on the cereal in the morning, when we had any. The British called this treacle. We also had some jam, which was mostly lemon curd. Whenever the Americans would ask for the lemon curd, we would all laugh. However, the British could not see anything funny in it. Many of the incidents that month at Altadena were priceless and, I think, also helped keep our sanity.

The daily routine was about the same. We had been informed that Stanley was to be the place of our internment. The Japanese would inform the Peak Representative when we were to go. On Wednesday night, January 21st, a Japanese officer was sent to the Peak to inform the Representative that we should all assemble in downtown Hong Kong the following morning at 10:00 AM. The Japanese officer got drunk and could not find the Representative's house. I think he went to every house on the Peak except the right one, and then he could not remember what he was sent up for. The result was that the Representative did not know anything about assembling the next morning, nor did anyone else.

The Japanese had two ferries alongside Queen's Pier to take us out to Stanley. When only a very few showed up who had heard about the order, the

Japanese were greatly annoyed. Here they had soldiers to guard us, men to inspect the baggage, and very few British and Americans. They thought that if this is the way the Peak residents are going to act, we will show them a thing or two. Of course, they would never admit that the word was not passed on because their guy was drunk, but I think they eventually found out.

The next Friday morning Herbie Rea and I were coming back from the hospital with two suitcases full of food when a small Austin car pulled up in front of us and out got six Japanese officers. They stumbled out over their swords, got all tangled up, but finally managed to land upright on the pavement. One of them came up to me, and he was a nasty piece of work. I thought surely he was going to slap me as that was their favorite trick, but he didn't. He just looked at me and said, "You, why you no go Queen's Pier?" I replied that I knew nothing about it. "What! No information?" I said that I had no information, to which he said, "Why no information?" The situation was becoming very threatening, and I thought surely he was going to take some physical action.

Just at this time, around the corner came a truck full of Japanese soldiers. The officer stopped the truck, and I heard them talking back and forth. The Japanese officer wanted to put us right then and there into the truck and take us away. The Japanese in the truck would have none of it, as they had something else more important to do. While they were arguing back and forth, Herbie and I picked up the suitcases and beat it. We took a big chance, but we got away with it. We were right on a corner, so had only about 20 feet to go before we were out of sight. Maybe the argument got so hot that they never missed us, but we never heard anything from it.

Friday afternoon, January 23, we did get word from the Representative that we were all to be downtown at Queen's Pier at 10:00 AM on Saturday when we would go to Stanley. There was no drunk Japanese officer this time, so everybody got the word.

Saturday morning we got up early so we could leave as soon as it was light, about 7:00 AM. It would take an hour or so to get downtown, and we were not taking any chances of being late. We had the biggest breakfast we had ever had yet. It was to be the last good meal for many months. We did not expect the food at Stanley to be as bad as it was, but we knew that it would not be good, so we were having our last meal, so to speak. I ate entirely too much and felt the effects of it going down the Peak, but I didn't care.

We left the house at 7:45 Saturday morning and what a sight we were! A young army of 23 strong, bed rolls, blankets, suitcases, and everything else that we could possibly carry. One family of four even took mattresses with them. The three Swedish officers from the ship carried these down for them. They made several trips up and down the Peak that day. They were certainly fine men, and the end they came to can only be regretted.

Going down the Peak, I spied a wheelbarrow, so went and got this. Herbie Rea and I put our stuff in it and took turns wheeling it. One of our number was greatly concerned over this, saying it was Japanese property and we would probably get into trouble over it. Well, fortunately, we didn't, and when we got down to Queen's Pier, we abandoned it. We did not know at the time that we still had a lot of walking to do, but when we needed it the second time, it was too late.

The Japanese went through our baggage, hunting for fire arms, radios, cameras, and binoculars. There were several pairs of binoculars turned in voluntarily. I don't think the Japanese took anything themselves out of the baggage. The inspection was just a routine matter; they did not have sufficient men to go through it all thoroughly.

After several hours of waiting, they lined us up in four columns and marched us several miles along the Hong Kong waterfront. The Chinese were out, lining both sides of the street. I think the main idea was to show the Chinese what happened to the British and Americans. "Here they are, see? These are the people you have been following for the past 100 years and look at them now! If you continue to follow them, you will come to the same result; but if you turn and follow the forces of the Rising Sun, everything will be fine. You will have all that they have had, and under the co-prosperity sphere, everything will be peaceful and we will all be happy."

This was the idea that the Japanese tried to get across, but I don't think their propaganda worked. I recognized a few of the Chinese who worked in the office. They looked at me and just shook their heads as much as to say "What a mess this is." The Chinese were very solemn.

Walking along the waterfront, Chinese coolies would come up wanting to carry our bags for us. Of course, all for a price, generally about a dollar per bag. It was worth it. I had two suitcases, and after about thirty minutes of walking, I didn't know whether I would make it or not. I finally handed mine over to a coolie, but I made him walk right in front of me. I did not take my eyes off him for a single minute. Some of the people thought that they were in the Hong Kong of pre-war days when they could just hand their baggage over to a coolie and he would trot right along beside you. Those days were gone. The minute your eyes were off, the coolie would run up a side street. Many people lost their baggage this way.

The Japanese walked us through the main part of the city when they finally decided that was enough. They then put us on two old rickety ferry boats. We weren't sure whether we would get there or not. Stanley is on another part of Hong Kong Island, and we had about an hour and a half boat ride before we got there.

We passed under the guns guarding the Island which had never fired a shot through all the campaign, simply because they were pointed in the wrong direction. Hong Kong was amply defended from the sea, and if the Japanese had come from that direction, they would probably have had a tough time. There were practically no guns pointing in the direction of Kowloon. Bright boys, the Japanese! Hardly cricket, hey what? The Japanese were coming to a party, but it wasn't a British boiled shirt dinner party, so they were not going to use the front entrance. They put a couple of shots in the back yard, hammered down the back door, and came in to join the party uninvited. The British had ample guns, but they were useless, all pointing to sea. It convinces me more than ever that you don't have to be crazy to live in the Far East, but oh boy, does it help a lot!

We finally arrived at the little pier at Stanley. We unloaded our baggage and walked up the hill to find out where our quarters would be. This was to be our home for how long we did not know.

Ruth Briggs, Pasadena, California

I've now started another project to help the war effort. Besides making bandages, Ma and I knit socks to send overseas. It's comforting to get together with her while we're doing something that maybe might help Norman—maybe some of our socks will reach him! However, we still haven't heard any news about what's happened in Hong Kong. We are just keeping our spirits up by saying he's going to be all right.

Ma is a much better knitter than I am. I've done more sewing than knitting, but she gives me good pointers. I just try to keep both socks of the pair the same size.

While we were knitting, the children were playing in the sun room. Suddenly I heard a weird sound, something sprinkling on metal. I went to investigate, and Kathie was putting a whole box of the kitchen matches down the heat vent! She had discovered the vent in the floor, felt warm air coming out, and thought the matches would help heat the house! Although we don't need to have the heat on very much, that day was chilly, and I guess Kathie was cold. She thought she was helping, I suppose.

While I tore off the cover of the vent and tried to retrieve some of the matches, Ma turned the furnace down and called the furnace people to ask what we should do. They assured us that there was probably no real danger, but keep the heat off for awhile and do what we were doing—trying to get all the matches out.

Enough excitement for the day. After dinner and bath time for the girls, I was glad when story time was over, and I could also get to bed.

The Asama Maru

Standard Vacuum Oil Company employees aboard the Gripsholm

1st Row: 1. Folts, 2. Bill Costen, 3. ?, 4. Mal Southwick, 5. Ray Pidcock, 6. Chic Sprague, 7. Mills, 8. Erwin Kock, 9. Pete Kipp.
2nd Row: Jack Sindlinger, 2. Henry Durschmidt, 3. Mac Ulrick, 4. Elmer Nelson, 5. ?, 6. Jack Richmond, 7. Jones, 8. Dick Sanger, 9. Chief Meyers.
3rd Row: 1. Keemaham, 2. ?, 3. Myer, 4. Mac Corkle, 5. Charles Larson, 6. Fred Twogood, 7. Al Bourne, 8. Herb Rea, 9. Teitys, 10. **Norman Briggs**, 11. ?, 12. Austin Glass, 13. Frank Peters, 14. ?, 15. King Paget, 16. ?

The Gripsholm

Section 4:
Internment Camp

Chapter I
Arrival at Stanley

Stanley is a little peninsula of about one square mile and, with the exception of the little strip of land connecting it with Hong Kong Island, it is entirely surrounded by water. In 1942 it was a beautiful place with cliffs all around except for two small beaches. The area as a whole was about fifty feet above the ocean. Right where this little peninsula joined the Island, there was a little village called Stanley. This was the first foreign settlement on the Island. There was a cemetery where the first Europeans were buried with grave stones dating from the early 1840s. In the early 1860s there must have been some sort of an epidemic, because there were a number of graves bearing the dates 1861, 1862, and 1863, some of them infants. This cemetery had been kept up and a few trees had been planted, where otherwise there was practically no vegetation on the peninsula except for grass and scrub bushes. We buried the people there that passed on while we were in Stanley.

Speculation was finally at an end when the Japanese announced that we would be interned at Stanley, and they asked for ten volunteers from each community, that is, American, British and Dutch, to go out there and clean up the quarters. There had been intense hand-to-hand fighting at Stanley, with the last stand taking place on Christmas morning. A few shells had hit some of the buildings, but considering the group of buildings as a whole, there was very little structural damage.

The quarters, however, had been hurriedly evacuated by the occupants and some looting had taken place. They were filthy, disorderly, and generally cluttered up. A wholesale cleaning up job was needed to make the quarters livable, thus the purpose of the advance volunteer squads.

The American detail was promptly organized and they went right to work. All the rooms were swept, rubbish cleaned up both inside and out. Some of the rooms were knee-deep in filth, and dead bodies of English soldiers who had been bayoneted by the Japanese still remained in some buildings and on the grounds. They had been there since the siege, nearly a month before. Their faces had rotted out and they were covered with flies. Eighteen graves were made in the little cemetery where the bodies of our dead were placed.

Right outside the barbed wire which enclosed the camp were the bodies of other men. These the Japanese would not let us touch and they remained there for many weeks. One of the most heartbreaking experiences of the camp was that of a young girl whose brother's body was lying a few feet on the other side of the barbed wire. She knew it was there, but nothing could be done. It was some weeks before the Japanese gave permission to go outside the wire and bury him.

After the initial cleaning was done, the advance crew took the plan of the whole place where the Americans were assigned, specifically noting the number and size of rooms so that they would have some idea of the number of people that could be put into each room. With their good advance work, it was pretty well worked out where the American community would be billeted.

Each individual name was not assigned to a particular room, because all names were not available. But those that were available were tentatively assigned to rooms according to preferences that had been shown as to whom they wanted to live with. This was all worked out in the Chinese hotels with the result that there was very little confusion in getting settled as we arrived at Stanley. The volunteer committee deserved a considerable amount of thanks. The people in the hotels went out to Stanley on January 21st and 22nd; we on the Peak went out on January 24th.

The Stanley prison was completed around 1937 or 1938 so the buildings were comparatively new and in excellent condition, except for some damage done by shelling. It was built for 1,500 people, but it was always crowded since they generally had about 2,500 people in prison there. Known as one of the model prisons in the world at that time, it was general knowledge that many Chinese would rather be in prison than outside because they were better taken care of. They even would commit minor crimes just to get in.

The prison had a 20 foot wall around it. We were not in the prison itself, but were put in the European warden's quarters outside the wall, but within in the prison grounds. These quarters were modern reinforced concrete three-story apartment buildings. The individual apartments consisted of a living room, a dining room, bedroom, bath, kitchen, and servants' quarters. The American quarters consisted of what was known as the "Club" and three apartment buildings. Two of the buildings had six apartments each, and the other had three. The "Club" was the building used by the wardens as a club, hence its name.

The British had the same type of buildings with about thirty apartments. Another building of the same type housed the Dutch and the remaining British.

In addition to the European wardens' quarters, there were six apartment buildings in which the Indian wardens lived. These were also assigned to the British and referred to as the Indian quarters. The rooms here were smaller, the toilet facilities not as nice and were of the Chinese "squat" style. The buildings were just as new and built on the same general plan, but not as spacious. The location also was not as good as they were lower down in a small ravine.

St. Stephen's College, a private educational institution, also was located on the peninsula. For housing a large number of people, these buildings were really better than the apartments. The class rooms were used as sleeping quarters, and the laboratories were somewhat more adequate for large numbers of people. The three main buildings, known as the British Bachelor quarters, the Police quarters, and the Science building, housed the married people that could not be taken care of in the main block and the Indian quarters. Also on the campus grounds were several bungalows. Each of these took care of 10 to 15 people. There was also a long one-story building, formerly the Chinese coolies' quarters, which took care of 50 or 60 British men. There were also two private residences, one for the superintendent and one for the doctor. These were located on what was known as the "hill" and were used by the Japanese as headquarters.

The entire Stanley Internment Camp held 2,400 British, 340 Americans, and 60 Dutch. As far as housing goes, the Americans were far better off than anyone else. The quarters we were in were designed to hold around 400 people. We were smaller in numbers than the British, and the Dutch did not have enough to have a separate building by themselves. The group of buildings that the Japanese assigned to us was in a unit by themselves. We were lucky that our number adequately filled them. Where we would have five or six people in a room, the British would have from eight to ten in the same size room. We were very fortunate in this and it may have been done purposely by the Japanese, but in the main I think it was just good luck. If there were any advantages that could be given, I think the Americans were favored. But there were mighty few to be given; for all practical purposes, we were all treated alike.

One thing the Japanese did purposely with malice aforethought was in housing the Peak residents in the Indian quarters which were the most undesirable. The British Peak residents were the cream of the high-hat Hong Kong society, but were on the short end of the stick as far as quarters in the internment camp were concerned. The prominent citizen who wanted a batman was put into the Indian quarters, and he didn't have a batman either! The other British were quite amused about this. This would teach the Peak residents to stay at home, and it wasn't necessary to have "IN" or "OUT" marked on the mail boxes either!

One of the main reasons for internment was complete isolation. The Japanese wanted all the foreigners out of the Orient. For those of us who were there, they were going to attempt to break all connections that we had. No communication was allowed either in or out of Stanley that did not go through the Japanese. They wanted to break all contacts we had with the Chinese businessmen, missionaries, teachers, or any other groups. Had we been more or less free in the city itself, we would have made contacts with the Chinese and other third-country nationals and thus maintained some association with our former interests. The Japanese were taking over, and they wanted all influence of the foreigner eliminated.

The second reason for isolating us in Stanley was that the Japanese were going to use Hong Kong as a base. There were fortifying the Island and did not want us to see what was going on. Hong Kong was more or less the half way point between Japan proper and the new territories that they had conquered like Sumatra, Java, and Malaya. There would be a lot of traffic and the Japanese did not want us to see any of this. They could isolate us completely on the little peninsula at Stanley.

I arrived at Stanley on Saturday afternoon January 24, 1942. I was assigned to room with three other men, Henry Durrschmidt, Erwin Kock, and F. X. Lee. I did not take long to get settled, as I had only the two suitcases. As soon as they arrived, the Americans were taken care of. If they did not get a room assignment immediately, they at least had a temporary one before nightfall.

Unfortunately, the British were not as organized. When they arrived, they had absolutely no idea of where to go. The Japanese told them the buildings that were assigned to them. They would go into a building, walk into a room, find it taken, and then go on to the next one until they found one that was free. People tried to reserve rooms for families, some rooms having only a few in them and others very crowded. The result was that towards night there were people without any shelter at all. Some of the women and children were taken care of in the American quarters for the first night or two until the British got some semblance of an organization started. Some men slept in the hallways until they got regular accommodations.

The American quarters were in pretty good shape, clean and ready to move into because of the work of the volunteer squad. The British had the same opportunity, but did absolutely nothing about it. It took them a whole month after arrival to get the rubbish and dirt cleaned up in front of their buildings. There was a lot of dissension amongst the British, those who were government employees, those who weren't, those who previously had big jobs, and those who had not, those who lived on the right side of the track and so on. It was also much harder for them to adjust themselves than for us on account of their great number. They also had a fair number of Eurasians and people of all social classes. Although the Americans had a few such problems, as a group we were much more homogeneous and settled ourselves comparatively smoothly and quickly.

Ruth Briggs, Pasadena, California

The holidays are now long over. Not that they were that happy without Norman, especially not knowing where or how he is and what terrible things he must be going through. I still feel in my bones that he is all right. The holidays at least kept me busy, in addition to my volunteer activities.

I finally received more information from the New York office at the end of January, saying they didn't have advice on specific individuals in Tientsin, Tsingtao, Hanchow, Shanghai, Canton, or Hong Kong, but all "information indicated staff remaining where stationed and treatment reported reasonably good." They also forwarded information about censorship in correspondence, but that they could not act as an intermediary, as that was the job of the Red Cross. However, since we don't know where Norman is, I don't know what to do. I immediately wrote back, asking about a rumor I heard that the Hong Kong staff had been flown to Chungking. I got a nice letter back from a Mr. Ludlum, explaining that there was always the possibility that some of our Hong Kong staff escaped from Hong Kong, but it is almost certain that they were not flown out, as they are in communication with the Chungking office. He assured me that they are working with the State Department and the American Red Cross to do what they can about getting people out. Then, on January 28 I received a cable from New York, stating that the "State Department advises receipt following message dated January 23 that American Nationals Hong Kong are interned but all well." I've got to believe that Norman is okay.

I'm lucky to have Norman's parents close by to me. Pa Briggs is quite handy with his tools in the garage and made a child-sized desk for Kathie. It has little drawers and cubby-holes in the top as well as two bottom drawers, places for all her crayons, pencils, and little treasures. And a little stool to match! Kathie loves it, and keeps busy practicing her numbers and letters.

But Carol raised a fit—she wants a desk too! We thought the novelty would wear off, but Carol is constantly at the desk when Kathie is there. So, Pa is busy building another littler one. Now they can both have their own desk to do their "work" and hide their special things. Kathie's been very good at sharing with her little sister, but Carol always tries to sit with Kathie, which doesn't work very well. Kathie, at four and a half, is getting quite good at coloring and beginning to really learn her letters. Carol, at one and a half, scribbles just fine. So far, she has understood that her "drawings" must be on the paper and no where else. I am saving some of the girls handiwork to show Norman when he comes home.

Chapter II
Getting Organized

Immediately upon arriving at Stanley, we organized work details to take care of our needs: the Construction Detail, Water Boiling Detail, Sanitary Squad, Police Squad, Wood Cutters, Food Control, and Garden Squad. The first problem that occupied our attention was the building of the kitchen. The American bachelor quarters, or the "Club," already had a kitchen which took care of the 65 men living there, but could not take care of the 275 of us who lived in the other three buildings. For the first month the rest of us used one of the kitchens attached to one of the apartments. This was very small, so the main cooking had to be done outside, but it served the purpose.

Right across from the American quarters was a long, low garage with space for 28 cars. This structure was reinforced concrete, built in the form of a lean-to, open on the front and no doors. Divided into 14 sections with space for two cars each, the structure was open clear through with no partitions. The supports holding up the roof were flush with the front.

The first section was made into a tool room, the second a work room for the kitchen, the third section the actual kitchen itself with a range and fire boxes, and the fourth a store room. The rest of the space was left open, supposedly for a dining room, but was never used for that purpose.

The building of the kitchen took a month, and, if I say so myself, we did an excellent job. We were lucky to have men who knew how to do it. Amongst our number were 20 Maryknoll Priests and several Brothers who were masons, carpenters, and electricians. In addition, we had the supervising architect of the Seventh Day Adventist Mission, Mr. Wood, who was thoroughly familiar with all the details of construction work. We also had Henry Durrschmidt of Standard's engineering staff, so we really had competent leadership. They drew up a plan to scale on paper, then went to work to build it. With the materials we had, it would be hard to find a better kitchen anywhere.

F. X. Lee and I did the hard manual labor, such as carrying bricks, cement blocks, mixing cement, and hauling sand. We did all the work of common ordinary laborers, no high-powered executive stuff about us! The Japanese gave us cement, but we had to collect all of our other construction materials from what was available on the property. The doctor's house on the hill, which was now the Japanese headquarters, had received a direct bomb hit, completely demolishing one end of the house. Much of our material came from there. The bricks from the walls had to be separated, cleaned, and then hauled—up one hill and down another—over to the kitchen. The sand was in a different location. We used the bricks for the fire boxes and range. For the partition walls of the kitchen and store room we used cement blocks. They weighed in the vicinity of 75 pounds each, and lugging these blocks up the hill was no easy job. We would put a pole through the blocks and two of us would carry them up and down the hills to the kitchen.

One of the main places for congregating was on the banks of the road leading up the hill. While lugging blocks up the hill one day, I heard one of the British women say, "My, I think it is remarkable the number of the working classes amongst the Americans." What a sentiment to express in an internment camp! Here she was sitting on her rear end on a bench, and we were doing what we could to improve our situation. All of us were corporate executives, and we were certainly working!

The three bags of cement we were given were just enough to complete the range and fire boxes, but not sufficient for the walls of the store room and other enclosures. To close up the front exposure we used mud and clay, and I must say it worked fairly well. We had no typhoons while there, but we did have a lot of rainy weather, and the walls stood up okay.

The building of the kitchen was the most important and best job we did. However, if there was any rough work to do in connection with building or tearing down something, the construction crew did it. I was on the construction crew. I had not done any of this kind of work since college, when I worked for Santa Fe Railroad one summer building rail beds in the desert. And I thought that was hard work!

In front of each building a protecting wall of cement blocks, filled with sand bags, had been erected by the British during the invasion to give more protection to the main entrances and prevent shell splinters, bomb fragments, and bullets from entering. These obstructions were not only bothersome in going in and out of the buildings, but also prevented any breeze from going through. With the hot weather approaching, we would want all the circulation of air possible, so we tore them down.

We also made a drain for the kitchen which was extremely hard. All the roads in Stanley were paved, and we had to run this drain right across the street to connect it to the sewage system. We had to break up the road, lay the drain, and then fill in the road again.

There were all sorts of odd jobs to do. Although we gave a sigh of relief after we got the kitchen built, we always had plenty to do. The construction gang did all the odd and sundry jobs—carrying baggage, moving furniture (what little we had), taking people back and forth to the hospital, and so on. In fact, any job that they could not get anyone else to do fell to the construction gang who invariably did it.

The water boiling detail was very important work, and it was well done. The minute we arrived at camp, instructions were issued that no water should be used for drinking purposes that was not boiled. We were very careful about this, and saw that everyone understood that the water must be really boiled and not just heated. As a result, the American community had very few cases of dysentery.

For the British with eight times as many people, it was much more difficult. Many of them could not wait for it to be boiled; of course, there was only one result, dysentery. In the first few weeks of the camp, we boiled a considerable amount of water for the British and continued doing so right up to the end. Their facilities were not as good for the number of people they had to take care of as compared to ours.

In the former servants' quarters was a laundry with copper kettles set in concrete over fire boxes for boiling clothes. These kettles would hold about 25 gallons. They were thoroughly cleaned and used for boiling water. We had a few electric clothes boilers of about the same capacity which were also used for the same purpose. These we used as much as possible to save fuel.

The water boiling patrol had to get up at five in the morning to start the fires, as it took a little over an hour to bring the water to a boil. Three hundred people drink a good deal of water, especially in the tropics. In addition, we were also boiling for the British. A 68-year-old sea captain was in charge of the water boiling, and a more conscientious person would be hard to find. When you got water boiled from him, you knew it was boiled, no doubt about it. He got up at 5:00 AM and didn't quit until 8:00 PM. Although he was relieved several times during the day, he kept an eye on the operation. If everyone at Stanley had been as conscientious and careful as this old China hand, all operations would have gone much more smoothly.

Everyone had their own water bottle, generally a beer bottle or some kind of liquor bottle. We had all kinds—Haig & Haig, White Horse, Johnnie Walker and so on. Some of the British had small canteens and thermos bottles, or rather, as they called them, vacuum flasks. The British can think up the oddest names for articles of common ordinary use!

The use of liquor bottles for water was one thing I didn't hear the missionaries complain about. They actually used them themselves. I think a few might have demurred at first, but most of them came right along with their Canadian Club bottles and had them filled right up. There were many wisecracks going back and forth about it, but everyone took it all in good spirit. It was at least one source of amusement. Imagine an old missionary of 60 years, coming along with a couple of bottles of Four Roses and having them filled up for the people in the room. "Say, Brother, where did you get hold of that stuff and what did you do with it before the bottles were empty? Got any more? I bet you have a couple of cases hidden away somewhere. Come clean now, be a sport and tell us where you've got 'em." And so on without end.

Our other amusement was pointing to someone when we passed them, yelling "SING."

The job of the sanitary squad was to keep all the outside drains, sidewalks, street and back entrances of each building clean. They also burned all the trash, buried the tin cans, and took care of the refuse from the kitchen. There was precious little of the latter, but still there was some, and it was important to dispose of it safely.

We had fire hoses connected to the main water pipe. The sanitary squad would get up at 6:00 AM to wash down the street, the sidewalks, back stairways, and generally clean up the grounds around the buildings. This would take several hours every morning. The American grounds not only looked clean, but were clean.

It was essential to keep the outside drains and down pipes on the buildings clean because otherwise mosquitoes would use them to breed. For the first month at Stanley, the flies were absolutely terrible, especially around the kitchen. After all the refuse and rubbish had been cleaned up and the grounds generally policed, these disappeared. We realized that flies spread dysentery and kept all food and utensils under cover as much as possible. We screened in the kitchen with cheese cloth and anything else we could find. Most of the British kitchens were right out in the open, making it impossible to keep the flies away. Towards the end of May they finally got their kitchen inside.

Believe it or not, we had to have policemen in Stanley, not only to protect us against members of our own community, but also against the British. Every piece of property was at a premium. Money amounted to very little, but a knife, a fork, and a good dish to eat out of, well, there was just no price on it. A box of matches? Hardly such a thing to be had. If you laid down a box and took your eyes off it a few seconds, the chances are ten to one that you would never see it again.

The police detail was organized by the older men in the camp and by others who could not do hard physical work. Imagine a missionary being a policeman? Well, many of them came out and did this work, and they didn't make a fuss about it either.

For the first three months the patrol was on a 24-hour basis with shifts of four hours each. Every Britisher who went in and out of the buildings was closely watched to see that he did not take anything away. The British had the same system, and they were watching us just as closely. There is no honor amongst thieves, but there is to a certain extent as far as nationality goes.

An American could not swipe a chair from another American, because we had to live too close together; besides, it would be swiped back. But if a Britisher could sneak into the American quarters and get a chair and get it back to his room, that was okay. This worked both ways. It was life at its lowest. How we managed to live through it without being at swords point with every other individual is something of a miracle.

In my room four of us were living together. One of us walked into the room one day and found a British policeman there. When asked what he wanted, he said he was looking for one of us. He was obviously taken by surprise and had not had a chance to get to work. There is no question that he was on a private looting job. Later questioning proved that even the British had him marked and were following his activities closely.

Whenever we had community meetings, it would mean that the living quarters were largely vacant. It would be an excellent time for one or two members of our own community, as well as the British, to go through the rooms and help themselves. We were always careful to have a guard of at least two men who constantly protected the American quarters. Several times I was on guard while the meetings were going on. I bolted all the front doors from the inside, and then policed the back entrances. The Japanese would not permit us to have anything locked because of their suspicion that we were hiding things from them.

We had to air our blankets frequently, and washing was done almost daily. We had to keep an eye on all of these things. If you hung your clothes out to dry or the blankets to air, you had better not go very far away. It was impossible for the police force to watch all such individual items. If you had to go away to do some work while your things were drying, it generally worked to ask someone to watch your things for you. This system worked pretty well. Although there was some stealing going on, most of the time all things of real value were "exchanged" during the first month or so. By that time our mutual policing system was pretty effective. If anyone acquired anything new, you were immediately under suspicion.

After the first three months, we dispensed with the night patrol. Later we gave up the day patrol for a little while, but had to put it in force again. The mutual system would guard purely personal belongings, but there was certain community property that it did not take care of like brooms, fire hoses, wheelbarrows and such, so the missionary police force had to come back into being.

All our cooking was done with wood. The British had prepared for a blockade for six months. Not only had they stored food to feed a million and a half people, they also brought wood in from Malaya, Java, and Sumatra since Hong Kong did not have much supply. This wood was hard and in long logs about six feet long and eight inches in diameter.

In the first days of the camp the Japanese would bring the wood in on a truck and dump it at camp headquarters. Each community would have to go there to get it. This was quite a job as it was very heavy. All we had were wheelbarrows which did not work very well for carrying logs of this size. Later on the Japanese regularly delivered a ten-day supply right up to the American quarters. This made it much easier.

The logs, however, still had to be sawed and split into kindling wood as our fire boxes were not very large. We had to have wood for the kitchen and also for boiling water. It took a large amount to keep a community of over 300 going. There were six men on this detail. There was no question that this was hard work, but there was one advantage. They were considered part of the kitchen crew; therefore, they were the first in the food line.

There was some criticism of this as there was no real reason why they should get fed before the construction gang or any other unit of workers. The people that worked were all doing their share, and why some should get special privileges could not be justified. Well, anyway, they did not get much extra, because there was nothing extra to give, so the privilege to get there first was all it amounted to. But there were many moans of contention about it. Mountains certainly can be made out of mole hills when you get in an internment camp.

Food control was a problem, especially at first. The Japanese distributed the food in bulk at their headquarters for both the American and British. Representatives of each community would pick it up to distribute proportionally to the various kitchens. However, graft ran rampant. After a couple of months, we discovered there was a shortage of 500 pounds of rice as well as several other discrepancies between the quantity of food received from the Japanese and that actually used by the Americans.

After getting the food from the Japanese, the first kitchen passed was the "Club." However, all the food was supposed to be taken to the main kitchen, where it would be weighed with approximately 17% sent to the "Club" for their use. However, it seemed a few choice items had been dropped off earlier for private consumption.

This was a favorite racket over the entire camp, not just confined to the Americans. The food details of the various kitchens would go get the goods, then "accidentally" lose some of it on the way back, such as letting it roll off the wheelbarrow into the bushes. After they had arrived at the kitchen, they would go back and pick this up for themselves. Men with families would get themselves on the food detail, and then the wife or children would follow behind and pick up the things that had been "accidentally" lost. After the first two months, most of these rackets were stopped.

The total supplies for the camp came in around 10:00 AM. For the Americans, there was one man in charge and three of us to push the wheelbarrows. The meat and vegetables were weighed out and divided up on a percentage basis. The Americans were roughly 11% of the camp, so we got 11% of the total food brought in. Each community signed receipts to the Japanese who kept a record of all expenses, showing both the quantity and monetary value. Two of us would take a wheelbarrow and go up the "hill" for the food; generally we were back by 11:30 AM. As there were three assigned to this detail and only two required for the wheelbarrows, it meant that one man would have a holiday.

The main American kitchen fed about 260 people. We called it the galley, because it was manned entirely by eleven men from the crew of the American vessel Admiral Williams, which was in dry-dock in Hong Kong when the war broke out. This part of the crew had been taken as civilians and included the first and second cook as well as other members of the galley crew. The balance of the crew, including officers and men, were unfortunately caught with some of the British military and interned in a military camp. Some effort was made to get them out of the military camp as they were unquestionably civilians. But our appeals were unsuccessful. The captain was 65 years old, but it was impossible to get him out. As we understood, the military were interned in worse conditions. It was surely tough luck, but we could do nothing about it.

We were very fortunate to have these men cooking for us as they were used to cooking for a large number. After the first week at Stanley, every meal was served on time and the food was cooked, not half done. We ate regularly at 9:30 AM and 5:00 PM. In contrast to this, the British were always changing their kitchen staffs and it took time for each crew to get acquainted with the routine. When you are serving a large group of people, to have what there is thoroughly cooked and served on time is a big advantage. I have lived in construction camps, building railroad beds summers to put myself through college, so I know whereof I speak. There were many people at Stanley who never appreciated this point.

If there was ever one group at Stanley that was constantly under criticism, it was the eleven-man galley crew. Nothing was ever right. Gripes were that the food was the worst possible, the cooks were keeping all the good food for themselves, the British food was far better than ours, it didn't take a real cook to throw together the swill they gave us, anyone could cook the stuff and get far better results than our cooks, and so on without end, A-men.

I have never eaten with a large group of people yet for any length of time but what the food was complained about. Construction camps, college dining halls, army camps, no matter what the place was, and even if the food was the best that could be purchased, there would still be some who would complain and say the stuff was no good and who did they have for cooks—garage mechanics, cement mixers, or what? Wherever I have been there have been complaints, but I think Stanley surpasses them all.

However, with all these accusations, no other group volunteered to come forward to do the cooking. No, they were not going to get up at six in the morning and stand over a hot kitchen range all day. These complainers said they took into consideration that the Japanese gave us only swill to start with, but surely something better could be made out of it. Miracle men come forth!

In fact, that was one name for the kitchen, "Miracle Room, Keep Out."

The kitchen was run as a "closed corporation." No question that the cooks secured certain advantages. In the first few months, we had no meat. When it did come in later in small quantities, it would have to be cut up and the bones taken out before it could be made into stew. Probably the cooks cut off some meat for themselves. In the first days at Stanley, we had only a little flour, not sufficient to make bread, but only enough to thicken the soup or stew. Our main diet, however, consisted of a half cup of boiled rice and lettuce. We had to pick out the wiggly pieces first, although the cooks tried to get most of the maggots out before they cooked it. If they missed some, we just chalked it up to adding a little protein to our diet. Occasionally we did have biscuits. But the cooks made themselves pancakes. Well, why not? They probably got a little more to eat, and maybe a grade slightly better than what we got. Food was the one main problem at Stanley, and anyone who had anything to do with it was not letting that job go in preference of some other work. There were many advantages to working in the kitchen. In my opinion, the cooks were more than welcome to what they got. They did good work and I don't believe anyone else could have done any better. The galley crew of the Admiral Williams did okay, and the community owes them quite a bit, even in spite of the unquestioned advantages that they had and the sentiments expressed against them.

With all this work going on, you might wonder where we got the equipment to do it. Stanley was in the prison area, and all the work done about the place had been done by the prisoners. There were shovels, picks, poles, lawn mowers, rollers, hammers, and many other odds and ends. We had many items to makeshift, such as trowels for laying bricks. There were other things of which we were short, but everything considered, we had access to quite a few tools. We could have used more, but we were fortunate to have what we did.

We never had access to the actual prison itself, as the Japanese were using this for some kind of headquarters. I think we would have been far better off if we had as it was a complete operating unit to house 2,500 people. It had a bakery, a hospital, and numerous work shops which would have come in mighty useful. According to the Japanese, the Geneva Convention stated that civilians could not be put behind bars, that the greatest physical restriction that could be placed on us would be barbed wire. Actually, I think the Japanese wanted the prison for other purposes. It was certainly full of supplies. Furthermore, from an international standpoint, I don't think the

Japanese would want it around that we were in a prison.

The Japanese gave us a section of land to make a garden. Several of our number had brought in quite a few seeds, so at least we had something to start with. Gardening had been a hobby in Hong Kong, so there were a few people who knew something about local conditions. The head of the garden detail was an agricultural professor who was on loan for a couple of years to one of the universities in China. We planted tomatoes, beets, and lettuce, but the main crop was alfalfa. The alfalfa would be thrown in with the lettuce and the stew. Although it did not taste very good, it at least gave us something green. In fact, there wasn't any taste to it at all, but I guess there never is to hay. Anyway, I think it gave us a little extra in our diet that was needed. The Americans were the only ones who grew alfalfa; the rest of the community could not see much sense to it.

One of the greatest lacks in the garden was fertilizer. In connection with the prison building were two big cesspools to which nothing had been added for six months. Our agricultural professor assured us that it was perfectly okay to use the contents of these cesspools anytime after six months. So, we organized a detail, emptied the cesspools, and used the fertilizer on the garden.

We got several batches of lettuce. A few times we took the beets, lettuce, and a few tomatoes and made a green salad. Although it was thoroughly washed with potassium permanganate, many people were very cautious. I admit that I was myself, as I did not want to get dysentery. I did not like the idea of eating raw vegetables in our circumstances, but I knew they were just what we needed dietary wise, so I ate them. Most people did and not a single person got sick from this, so it shows that the permanganate was effective.

We did not have much success with the tomatoes. As soon as one got anywhere near ripe, it would be picked. Anything in the garden that could be eaten was stolen right and left. We could not keep a guard on it 24 hours a day. We had to be in our quarters at night, but individuals would sneak out and get what there was. The Indian and Chinese guards also would help themselves at night.

Stuff was also stolen in broad daylight. We caught several people red-handed and what do you suppose the excuse was? "Oh, we didn't know it was anyone's garden in particular; we just thought it was there for the use of all!" There was not much we could do. We had no means of enforcing any punishment, and if people wanted to steal, they stole and that was about all there was to it. Some fairly prominent members of the British community were caught in the American garden, but was anything done to them? Because the Americans were so much smaller in number and because the culprits were quite "important" people, we did not dare advertise the fact that our honorable British friends were thieves.

Ruth Briggs, Pasadena, California

It's now feeling like spring, although it's not quite March yet. The New York office cabled that they received word from Macao that the Hong Kong staff is safe. Then another letter later said they received word from the Chungking office: "Friend departed Hong Kong February 12th reports all staff interned at Stanley. Food inadequate and quarters unsatisfactory, but conditions better than interned soldiers. Know staff is all well, but no contact possible with interned nationals." The letter also said that Mr. Parker was in Washington a few days ago to talk to the State Department. He was again assured that everything possible was being done to arrange an exchange of nationals. He was told that there were definite plans, the details of which cannot be released, for the repatriation of Americans from Hong Kong and other areas. Some real hope! I sure wish we would get some definite word from the Red Cross soon. I wrote a letter last month addressed to him at Standard Vacuum Oil in Hong Kong, but it was returned. I sure wish we could have some contact. I continue to "feel" that he is safe, and I know Norman is strong. I know he'll make it. I keep telling myself that. Oh, how I long for him to be here with us.

I have started my Victory garden in the backyard. The gardener is advising me as I'm a real novice. Since it has warmed up, I've turned the soil in the sunniest part to get it ready for planting. And I've order seeds from my "long, lost relative" (or so my mother tells me) Mr. Burpee. I don't know much about planting, but I guess I can learn. Pa has had a garden in back for several years, so he's given me some pointers too. I've been fairly successful with flowers in the past, so maybe I can get vegetables to grow too.

The real "victory" will be when the war is over and Norman is home. Kathie can write her name now and colors pictures with her crayons very nicely. She voiced our sentiments the other day when she said she wished "the bad men would go away and let Daddy come home."

Chapter III
The Food Line

The one major problem that we had to deal with at Stanley was food. It was far different from being turned loose in the wilderness to forage for oneself, for we were hemmed in by bayonets. There was no choice of taking or leaving it; we just had to take what was sent in. I never want to spend a leaner two months in my life than that February and March. I went to bed hungry every night, and more than my stomach was doing flip-flops all night long, simply because there was not sufficient substance there.

Everyone else in the entire camp was practically the same. Some had a little more than others from what was being smuggled in, but even these people did not eat all they needed. The food situation at Stanley was a very serious one. The average weight loss was about 20 pounds, but some lost as much as 40 or 50 pounds. I was on the high end—my 6' 2" bodyweight dropped to about 90 pounds. Whatever the effect was on various individuals, the camp as a whole was not only improperly fed, but also underfed. The official Japanese rations were all we had for the first two months at Stanley, and this was during the time we were doing much of the hard labor cleaning up the place.

These ration figures are per person per day:

Rice: 6.5 ounces
Sugar: 0.42 ounces

Salt: 0.21 ounces
Peanut oil: 0.21 ounces
Flour: 2.00 ounces

This totals 9.34 ounces of food per person, per day!

The only food we saw was rice. We never saw sugar for the first two months, and our salt intake insufficient. We asked the Japanese if we could use sea water for cooking the rice, and they said no. A whole ocean full of salt, but we could not have it! There were only two beaches on the place where we could get down to the water, and these were fenced off by barbed wire. No one wanted to be caught on the wrong side of that, because the only answer would be a rifle shot.

We were the prisoners of the Japanese, thus could get nothing for ourselves. If they permitted us to go down to the beach for water, they knew it would not be long before someone would hide out, make contacts with the Chinese fishermen, and hence get additional supplies or arrange an escape. All through our life at Stanley, people could not believe that they themselves were prisoners. The British and Americans as communities were prisoners, but the individual thought that he should be allowed more freedom. As individuals, few of us had ever been in prison before, and mentally and psychologically the status of prisoner was refused as unacceptable. Instead of saying the Japanese can't do this to us, I think our own outlook would have been far better if we had just accepted it.

Peanut oil was issued regularly and was used for general purposes in the kitchen. We had chow-fan, which for all practical purposes is fried rice. The rice we received from the Japanese had been stored for some time and was full of weevils and worms. It was quite a job to get it clean. In fact, sometimes there was not much left after the vermin had been cleaned out. Not all of it was this way, but a lot of it was. Whether or not the food value was lessened, I am sure I don't know. There was some opinion expressed that the worms and weevils got most of the nourishment, and that possibly might be so. Or, if we had just left them all in, maybe we would have gotten more nourishment.

We did get some flour, also full of weevils and worms, but it did not come in sufficient quantities to do anything with it. By saving it, we managed to have pancakes twice during the first two months, and biscuits a couple of times.

In addition to the rations listed, we did get a little meat and a few vegetables, but precious little for the first two months. During February we were given fish several times. The weather was cold enough then so that the fish was okay. After February, whenever we got fish, it was spoiled.

Just what the meat was, we didn't know. The general opinion was that it was water buffalo. For the American community of over 300 people, we would get about 75 pounds of meat, when we got it. This works out to roughly 4 ounces per person. This was the bulk meat, including bone. After it had been trimmed up, the part left fit to eat was probably about 2 ounces per person, if that much.

The main vegetable they gave us was lettuce. Once in a while we would get a few carrots and beets, but not much. All the food, of course, had to be cooked. When you have nothing to eat but boiled rice and lettuce, it is not a very attractive diet. I can assure you, one does not gain weight on it.

This was all we had for the first two months. It was the hardest two months at Stanley, because all the hard physical work had to be done when we first arrived. We built the kitchen, mixed concrete, tore down air raid shelters, pushed wheelbarrows—all on less than a pound of food per day, and that pound was rice and lettuce! On good days, we figured we may be getting about 1,200 calories per day, when the minimum one should have is 3,000. It is very difficult to give an adequate description of the life of those first two months, but they were extremely grim, with no outlook for improvement. In fact, we thought things would probably get worse, although we could not see how.

For our two daily meals, the main kitchen cooked for approximately 270 people. The Catholic Fathers and Sisters, about 30 of each, ate in their own separate groups; they always got their food in one big lot first.

The rest of us formed in line, passing through and getting ours individually. There were sometimes two dishes, one was rice and the other stew, if we were lucky. We would pass by, get our share of rice and then have the stew poured over it. The dishing out was done by the kitchen staff, and it was done fairly equally.

Although there was some comment about the helpings, some getting more than others, there was very little justification for it. However, the racket developed in getting into line first, as it was first come, first served. When cooking for such a large number of people, it is impossible to have the last bit of rice and stew finished as the last person passed in line. There was always some left over. In that climate, food could not be kept over night, as it would go bad in no time. Several people tried to keep some of their rice from the evening meal so that they would have a little in the morning and not have to wait until 9:30. That is where some of the dysentery started. Flies would get on it over night, and the dysentery would spread.

People who were not on work details would start standing in line at 3:30 PM for the 5:00 PM meal. As soon as they got their first helping, they would dash back to their room and eat, they dash out again to get in line for seconds. Sometimes a person would get food for all the four or five people in his room. The rest would wait in their rooms until the person came in with the first helping for all, empty their dishes, then dash out and get in line for seconds. This meant that the people who were doing the heavy work were getting less to eat than those who were doing nothing.

To get around this racket, everyone was given a number. The system was so arranged that those living together had consecutive numbers. When everyone had passed through the line once, and there was perhaps sufficient food left for another 20 people, those with numbers 1 through 20 would get seconds. The next meal, the seconds number would start at 21, and so on. When all had received seconds, the rotation would start over again. We had a checker, and everyone's name was marked as they went through the line. This system worked miracles. The line did not form then until right before 5:00 PM as there was nothing to be gained by getting into line early.

The food line was some sight, especially when you saw our utensils. Knives and forks were at a very high premium. If you let them out of your sight for 30 seconds, that would be the last you would ever see of them. A few people had dishes of one sort or another, but most of us had tin cans. We would take these tins, make the edges smooth, keep them clean, and they would serve the purpose very well. The best tins were the five pound jam tins, as these could be used for stew pans, for making coffee (when we had any), making tea, which we did have, and in general heating things over for all sorts of purposes.

Some people had army mess kits. There had been a lot of hand-to-hand fighting the last day at Stanley and a lot of this kind of equipment was left lying around. The first people who arrived had picked these up. They were mighty useful and one did not dare let these out of your sight. It would be gone in no time. Quite a few did change hands in this way, but as all the equipment was the same, it was very difficult for any individual to say absolutely that any particular mess kit was theirs.

I myself had a tin jelly mold and one spoon. Boy, did that jelly mold get hot! I will say one thing about our food; it was always steaming hot when served. When the rice was put into the jelly mold, it was almost impossible to hold it. I had this jelly mold for about three months, and then I got hold of a regular British Army plate made of China. I will not say how I got hold of it.

TAKEN IN HONG KONG
DECEMBER 8, 1941

The food line was the place to get acquainted and also hear rumors. A story would start at the front end of the line; you would not recognize it by the time it got to the end of the line. If there ever was a place for rumors, Stanley was it. I wish I could remember them all, as there were some absurd ones. By the end of February, Tokyo had been in flames several times. One rumor had the American Fleet was right outside Hong Kong, blockading the port. (Of course, we could see the Japanese ships going in and out every day.) The Americans had retaken Wake, Guam, and were back in full possession of Manila. Americans had landed in Formosa. And so on, rumors without end and with absolutely no basis. How they got started, I am sure I don't know. Many believed them, but many of us didn't.

The ship traffic did produce rumors. We could not see Hong Kong harbor, but we could see the ships going in and out. Ships would come in convoys of four or five or sometimes alone. Whenever we saw ships, rumors had the American Navy all over the place. We would be out of Stanley within a week. The American Navy was massing outside for the retaking of Hong Kong. They had already taken Manila and were on their way over. So we wished.

We saw many times the ships being towed. These ships were always very dirty, in fact muddy. We could not see them very well as they were at least two miles away. But as far as looks go, they were in very bad condition. I only saw one or two that looked damaged by shell fire. Most of the ships looked to me as though they had been scuttled, the Japanese had raised them, and were bringing them in for repairs. The dark, dirty, muddy color certainly indicated to me that they indeed had been scuttled, rather than damaged by shell fire, especially when they were being towed with no evident structural damage.

The British had scuttled their ships, but did not damage them as they hoped to raise them themselves. They just opened the sea cocks and down they went. Along came the Japanese, sent divers down, closed the sea cocks, set the pumps to working, and up they came. Marvelous, say what! The Japanese are using them now instead of the British.

I remember one evening standing in the food line talking to one of the missionaries. He told me the reason he had lived through the attack and had not been hurt was because there was an angel guarding both the front and back entrances to his house. Therefore, the Japanese never came anywhere near him. The angels kept the shells and bombs away too. How about the 20 Chinese coolies on a truck in front of the lower Peak Tram station who got a direct hit? No angels guarding over them!

Sometime toward the latter part of April the food rations materially increased. We got some sweet potatoes, some Chinese spinach, and a few more carrots and beets. They also gave us more meat. From the first of May we got meat every day, about 100 pounds. This was still not sufficient, but as we got it every day, it was a vast improvement.

At this time we also received more flour, about 8 ounces per person per day. After picking out the maggots, we made bread and, boy, did that make a difference! I don't mean to say that things were good, but it was such a vast improvement over what we had been getting that it seemed almost enough. Rice is the Oriental's food, but wheat is surely the European's. After we began to get flour, everyone picked up some weight, even if it were just a few pounds. People began to look and feel better, both physically and mentally. There was a vast improvement in the entire camp after the flour supply was increased.

The flour was issued one morning without any notice by the Japanese. Of course, it took no time for the word to spread. At the 5:00 PM meal, people wanted to know why we didn't get bread. The next day when we didn't get any, there was real trouble. What were we doing with the flour? Was it being made the basis of another political racket? That last question was quite in order as there were more dirty politics in Stanley than I had ever seen before. Even the missionaries, and they were 60 percent of the camp, were howling over this flour. What did they think we could do, perform miracles? Just look at the flour and turn it into bread? How about yeast? That had to be made. We also had no bread pans. These had to be made out of anything we could find, mostly old tins. Outside of the galley crew, I doubt if anyone in camp had ever made bread before. Knowing nothing about it, they clamored an immediate demand for it.

When we made the kitchen range, we did not make any ovens. We had the huge Chinese kettles and made places for these for cooking rice and the stew. We did have two small electric stoves with ovens. These we thought would be ample for any baking that we might do. Now that we had flour, we could make bread. But how would we bake it? The two small electric stoves in the kitchen were not sufficient.

In each of the apartments there had been one small electric stove. Most of these had been taken out, given to the hospital or to the British. The Maryknoll Fathers and Sisters quarters had one stove, the clinic had one, and two were left in the American quarters. The question was, should those two stoves now be moved to the kitchen? What a fight there was over this!

Some people who had gotten extra tinned goods would open them up at odd hours and heat them up on these stoves. Having them removed to the kitchen where individuals could not get at them whenever they wanted to? Nothing doing. Much controversy arose over whether the bread should be brought to the stoves or the stoves to the bread. One of the Maryknoll Fathers calculated mathematically that all our bread, say 100 pounds per day, could be baked in the two stoves already in the kitchen, but he declined to take over the job of doing it.

To make a long story short, some bread was baked in the kitchen and some on the other stoves in the apartments. Believe it or not, the system worked, but it was the hard way.

It took us about three days before we got the bread going. Then people wanted to be sure that they were getting their full quantity. The Japanese gave us eight ounces of flour daily, but two ounces were used for general purposes in the kitchen, such as thickening soup and stew. This left six ounces, less the weevils, for bread. Some people actually weighed their bread! We had some home made scales in the kitchen. This got to be such a sore point that people were finally told they could have their six ounces of flour and do with it as they wanted which, of course, no one wanted. We were not going to weigh out each and every loaf to the exact ounce. Distribution was made as fair as possible, but of course, all the loaves were not the same size. If you got a small loaf one day, you would hope for a bigger one the next. You just had to take your run of luck.

After the bread baking was on a systematic basis and baked every day, I will say that I never ate any better bread anywhere, anytime. There is no question that our restricted diet had much to do with our liking the bread, but I think that bread would have taken prizes anywhere.

Most of the camp never knew the work that went into baking it. The bakers were up a couple of times each night to see that the dough was rising. Then it had to be kneaded and baked. All in all, there was a lot of work to it. After a while, a few men besides the regular galley crew took over most of the work of preparing the bread up to the baking point; then the regular kitchen crew took over from there. But at the very start the kitchen crew did the whole thing. They did not want anyone else to get in that kitchen! The kitchen had too many advantages, and the fewer people in there, the better off the galley crew running it were. The sign was up, "Miracle Room Keep Out." And it was a miracle room. To see the stuff going in, you would never think that a community of over 300 people could live on it, but we did. The cooks were welcome to all the advantages that the kitchen afforded.

Can you imagine a diet kitchen in an internment camp, especially after all

I have said about the food? What could a diet kitchen do with rice and boiled lettuce that the main kitchen could not do? But we had a diet kitchen which fed around thirty people, mostly children. Some people cannot eat rice; it simply will not stay on their stomachs. And people who had just come back from the hospital, and others who were ill, would eat in the diet kitchen until they recovered enough to go on the regular diet. I think it developed into somewhat of a racket of some feigning illness, but in the main it was necessary and many people benefited from it. We nicknamed it the Riot Kitchen.

We had twenty children in the camp, and we tried to feed them a little better. They got three meals a day instead of two. Some of the tinned foods available in limited quantities were assigned to the diet kitchen, including tins of milk. The Japanese also gave us a regular supply of fresh milk for the children. All in all, the diet kitchen food was much better simply because they had a very small quantity of better food to deal with. Expectant mothers and those with small babies were fed from the diet kitchen. This was a great help to the main kitchen, as it took a load off them. Just feeding the children was quite an undertaking. The woman in charge of the diet kitchen, who had six children in Stanley, ran it well.

I think about six or eight times the Japanese gave us Soya beans. Boy, were they good! It surely was a red letter day when we got beans. They were soaked and then baked in the big Chinese kettles. When we had beans, we did not have rice as we were not going to spoil the beans. Baked Soya beans! Try them sometime; you will be surprised!

When we complained to the Japanese, it was about food, food, and more food. The Japanese were getting annoyed at our continual complaints, so they decided to do something about it. They told us that all individuals who had bank accounts in their own names could take this money to buy food for the American community. Company money could not be used. Any money that Standard Oil, General Motors, or any other American firm had was completely taken over by the Japanese.

In addition, our individual accounts must be used for community benefit. That is, if I had $100 in a Hong Kong bank, I could take this and buy food for the American community, but I could not buy it for myself. Well, this was good news, as it at least showed that they were willing to do something.

We formed a committee and went around to every individual, asking how much money they had in the bank, the name of the bank, and whether it was a savings or checking account. We finally got all the details and handed them over to the Japanese, but never heard another word about it.

We kept after them, but the Japanese in charge of the camp said they handed the details over to the Army, then the Army had to get the understanding of the Navy, and finally the Japanese military police, the Gendarmes, had to pass on it. The same old government red tape you see everywhere. Nothing ever came of it, but please bear this story in mind, because it has a very interesting connection with our departure. Just remember that we took a census of the amount of money available to feed the community. Later on in this story you will see a very interesting sidelight on human nature.

As I mentioned before, the British had stored enough food to feed a million and a half people for six months. In Stanley there were twelve godowns full of food. Of course, the Japanese immediately put barbed wire around these and declared them out-of-bounds as far as the internment area was concerned. They put up a notice that anyone found near the godowns would be shot.

One day the Japanese came to us and said that if you people are so hungry, we will give you a chance to work for food. The next day they were having thirty trucks come from town. They were planning to unload the godowns. If we could supply the labor of thirty men to carry the food from the godowns and load the trucks, they would pay us in food. They only wanted thirty men because they said they could not handle any more.

My, what a howl went up both in the American and British communities! "What, help the enemy? Nothing doing! Let the food sit there in the godowns. We would see it in hell before we would work for the Japanese. There will be no cooperation with the enemy in this internment camp!"

Such were the opinions expressed. I said if the Japanese want those godowns unloaded and will pay in food, I for one am willing to work. Here was a chance to get more food. My stomach was empty and I did not give a damn what the British or anyone else thought about it. The Japanese had asked us to supply the labor, and if we didn't do it, they would go right into town and get a bunch of Chinese coolies to unload the godowns. The Japanese weren't going to leave the food there. Given the chance to get more food, I was going to take it regardless of the opinions expressed.

There were other men in camp who thought the same as I did, so there was no trouble in getting thirty of us. We were called scabs and other worse things, but that did not bother any of us. We went down and worked all day. At noon the Japanese fed us. They opened up tins of milk, margarine, and hard tack, even heating the milk for us. We had free access to all the dried fruit that we could eat, such as figs, raisins, apricots, and apples. There was syrup by the case, and we helped ourselves with no interference from the Japanese, even though they were standing guard over us.

When the end of the day came, they gave us several tins of corned beef, packages of hard tack, and a couple of tins of milk. Besides this, I had managed to stuff my pockets full of dried fruit, and I got it back to the room without being caught. Everyone else did the same thing. For once, at least thirty men in camp were full. When I went to sleep that night, I could not have eaten another bite. The Japanese held to their promise; they paid us, and paid us well. They could have given us much less, and they could easily have prevented us from helping ourselves at noon, but they did not.

The Japanese told us to come back the next day, saying we had done good work, and there was more to do. They wanted 100 men, but said the rest would have to be British, as we already had more than our proportion. The Americans were twelve percent of the total people in the internment camp, so on this basis, we should have only twelve men. But as we had volunteered first, they would let us all remain. Seeing that we did not get thirty men without a lot of remarks, we thought it would be difficult to get 100 men, especially from the British community as they were more against this type of manual work than the Americans were.

When the rest of the camp saw us getting paid off, they changed their minds. Instead of refusing to work, everyone wanted to work. We asked them why they changed their minds so quickly. Well, they said they didn't think the Japanese would pay off. They thought they would get the trucks loaded and then tell us to breeze off. So, nothing to do with helping the enemy, eh?

Well, anyway, we had plenty of workers now that everyone wanted work. So then they said that this kind of work should be rotated so that everyone would get a chance to have a little extra food. We agreed to this in principle, but all thirty of us said we were going to work the next day anyway; after that we would rotate the jobs. There was at least ten days worth of work if not more before these godowns would be emptied. We finally arranged that there would be the same thirty Americans, five Dutch, and sixty-five British to make up the detail for the next day.

The next morning the thirty of us lined up to report to the godowns; the five Dutchmen joined us as there were not a sufficient number of them to make an extra unit. When we got to the godowns, there were a couple of Japanese officers and several soldiers. Lining one side of the street was the entire British Hong Kong police force of 250 strong who were interned. We reported to the Japanese officer that we were the previous day's work detail, and he showed us where to wait for further orders.

He asked where the British detail was. The British evidently had agreed that the first 65 men to report to the Japanese would be the ones to be chosen; their organization did not go any further than this.

When the Japanese opened up the gates, the entire Hong Kong police force pushed in like madmen, jamming us Americans and Dutch right out. A near panic almost broke out, and I thought the Japanese were going to use force. We resented this on the part of the British police very much, but we did not want to start a fight in the internment camp. If we had it would have been a free-for-all. The Japanese would surely have turned the machine guns on us to bring it to an end. We realized this, so kept our heads. Although we tried to get in, we were just too greatly outnumbered by the British Hong Kong police force. We Americans did not break ranks at all. When we saw that our case was hopeless, we turned around to a man and walked away. The British got the point. Some of them were ashamed, but not the British police force.

The Japanese took the first 100 men through the gates, got everything under control, and turned everyone else away. The Japanese should have seen that we thirty Americans got in, but they did not seem to care. So the British would not work, huh? When they saw us getting paid, the part about cooperating with the enemy did not bother them any.

After this incident, we got the word around the camp that there was only one sure way of winning the war and, believe it or not, the British were going to do it for us. The idea was to get a godown full of jam in Berlin, tell the British, or preferably the Hong Kong police force, that it was there. The British would march on Berlin in no time! If the Hong Kong police had fought half as hard during the fighting as they did trying to get the Americans from getting from unloading the godowns, the British would still be in possession of Hong Kong! As time went, the story would get better. We had British parachute troops dropping tins of jam behind the German lines, the British using barrage shells full of jam, and then the main might and force of the British Empire would come into being and go right after that jam. The way to win the war: send jam over and let the British go after it!

The British, of course, did not like our cynical remarks, and I don't know as I blame them. But it was surely a dirty piece of work they did on us. Some of the Americans did not like our remarks about the British jam tactics and said we should not make such remarks against a nation that had stood up so magnificently in London. Now, all together boys!

We did have a canteen in camp. The first one was started by the Japanese themselves, but it was not very successful. I don't think it was open more then four or five days. They only had a few tins of this and that which were sold out in no time. They did have some women's silk stockings! For some reason, Stanley society decided to go on strike and not buy silk stockings. Imagine silk stockings in an internment camp!

There was some opposition to this canteen, mainly by the British. The three communities had asked the Japanese for a canteen to be run by us. If we now patronized this canteen, the British thought the Japanese would not permit the community to operate their own. They never thought of the fact that if the Japanese canteen was not patronized, the Japanese could say that there was no need for a canteen, because they did little business. I would like to know one single thing started at Stanley that the British did not oppose at first.

The community finally got its own canteen, and I will say that it helped out quite a bit. With 2,800 people in camp, there was never sufficient stock to go around. Certain things like jam, oatmeal, and chocolate would be gone in no time. Even when it was organized at its best, open about once every ten days, there was no system except for first come, first served. People would get up at 5:00 AM and line up for the canteen which opened about 9:00 AM. By the time the canteen was ready to open, there would be a line of 500 people. They would bring chairs and books with them and sit down for an all-day siege.

The canteen could only serve about 200 a day, so to get in at all you had to be there early. People would trade off their place with each other. One member of a family would go and get a place in line, then be relieved by another member. People who were living together would also relieve each other, then who ever got in would divide up the purchases with the rest. The rackets that developed over that!

We needed to get the thing down to a system, because the same people were getting into the canteen all the time, never giving others a chance. Those of us who were doing work about the camp could not get anything. Finally we devised a system. Everyone in camp got a ticket; these tickets were in three groups: A, B, and C tickets. The B tickets could not be used until the major part of the A's had passed through, likewise for the C tickets. One person could purchase for three others, making a total of four purchases in all. When you gave up your A ticket with a purchase, you were given a B ticket, then a C ticket. Hence, the cycle would start over again. This meant that everyone in camp at some time or other got a chance to go to the canteen. Although there was still a lot of competition as to who should get in first, the system as a whole worked fairly well.

Towards the end, the tickets were allotted to the buildings. Then we drew lots to see who would get preference. The person who got the preference would go to the canteen, make his purchases. He would not get another chance until all others in the building had made their purchases. The preference tickets were in addition to the A, B, and C tickets and were limited to 200 per time, as that was all that could be taken care of in one day.

I will just mention a few of the articles that were sold at the canteen: jam, shredded wheat, raisins, dried apples and apricots, chocolate, rolled oats, corned beef and corned mutton. There were other items, but never in sufficient quantity of any one item. For that matter, all items put together did not meet the demand of the camp. The canteen was made a part of the political racket. There appeared a shortage in the American section alone of $500. It could not possibly be that the politicians were handing out food for voting favors, could it? No, of course not, not from the cream of Hong Kong Society!

The canteen was a racket in more ways than one. The men who worked there could stand behind the counter and help themselves to all the dried fruit they wanted, and the chocolate and various other things that came in bulk. When they wanted to buy things, they had the first choice of all. It was hard work in the canteen, there is no two ways about that. But it carried with it very distinct advantages. Even with all the monkey business that went on both within and without the canteen, I think the community as a whole was better off than if we had none at all.

We were successful in getting practically all of the food supplies that were in the American Club out to Stanley and this was a considerable quantity. One-half was given to the British, mainly for use in the hospital. The British had arranged for the transportation, and one-half of the supplies was the payment. There were about thirty members of the American Club at Stanley, of whom I was one. We decided that we would take the balance that was left and divide it equally amongst all the Americans. This included about 500 packages of Camels cigarettes. The thirty members of the Club had already paid for these things, but we did not want any comments going around saying that we had more than the rest, so everything was taken and divided equally. Each person received about four tins each of canned goods plus the cigarettes. All did not get the same thing—some got canned peas, others corn, soup, and so on—but all got approximately the same quantity.

This went over very well and everyone was pleased with the way it was done. What do you think happened to the cigarettes and our missionary friends? Did they refuse the cigarettes, or did they smoke them? No. They sold them for $4.00-$5.00 a package. The market price was around $4.00 at the time. I heard one missionary woman say that she was going to hold hers until she could get $5.00 for it. She certainly never would have bought a package of cigarettes, but in an internment camp would accept them as a gift, then turn around and sell them for money. I heard one missionary offer to trade one cigarette for one piece of bread. To smoke a cigarette himself was a crime, but he had no scruples about taking legitimate food away from someone else and let that person smoke his way to perdition!

I will say in fairness that all the missionaries did not do this. Everyone accepted the cigarettes, including the women, but many immediately gave them away to people who did smoke and did not sell them. We had thirty or so Catholic Fathers. Most of them smoked, so the Catholic Sisters accepted the cigarettes and immediately gave them to the Fathers. Some of the Protestants also gave them away, the women taking them and giving them to their friends who did smoke. That is perfectly okay, but in my way of thinking, for missionaries to accept cigarettes free, then go and sell them is something else again.

Ruth Briggs, Pasadena, California

Finally, more word from New York. They said while American nationals are being assembled at Stanley, they are not in the prison, but in various houses and guard barracks there. The Americans have been able to band together and pool their resources. In addition, it was said that the Japanese are reported to be supplying rice, pork, fish, and fresh vegetables daily, and that general conditions, while not normal, are not too bad. That certainly is good news!

Boy, did I have a scare today. I was busy planting vegetables in my Victory garden. Kathie was at nursery school and Carol was "helping" me from time to time, in between playing with her toys in the back yard.

Suddenly I became aware that she was very quiet. I looked around and couldn't see her in the back yard! I quickly searched the house and the garage, but no Carol! Then I went to a neighbor's house where she and Kathie sometimes played with their children, but she was not there. I ran down the street, looking in around each house for any sign of her. At the end of the second block, I saw a woman working in her garden. I asked her if she had seen a little blond girl, almost two years old. She said yes, she saw this little girl walking all by herself. She watched her stop at the corner, and look both ways before she crossed the street, so she figured that she must know where she's going. She pointed in the direction of the school, another two blocks away.

I rushed to the school, and thank goodness, there was Carol in Kathie's nursery class! The teacher said she thought I had dropped Carol off so I could do some shopping! I would never do that, but was so glad to see Carol I just grabbed her and hugged her. When we got home, I explained to her to never go by herself again. Carol is always trying to keep up with her big sister!

Chapter IV
Politics and the Black Market

If anyone wants to know the ins and outs of dirty politics, how the machine is started, kept going, and operated purely for the distinct advantage of an exclusive few, I suggest an internment camp. Stanley offered the best laboratory possible for the observance of this phenomenon. As an outside cover, the form of civilization was still trying to be enforced. Here was a group of over 300 Americans, hemmed in by bayonets, underfed, with everything of a material nature at a premium. The veneer on top of all this was that each was trying to be his brother's keeper. Here we all were in a predicament which we could not help; now that we were all together, we had to help each other, with the welfare of the community the important thing.

It was an opportunity for a first rate politician to get himself into control by playing upon the sentiments of individuals for the supposed benefit of the community, then direct everything into their own advantage! The stage was set for just such a scene, and a person emerged as a politician of the first rank. I will refer to him as the "Brain."

Neither his organizing ability nor his intelligence is to be underrated, but the purpose, methods, and results achieved are something entirely different. The "Brain" was from Shanghai. He was on a trip, so it was just pure accident that he was caught in Hong Kong. The "Brain" was interned in the Chinese hotels, and the basis of his organization started there.

He got himself appointed as the head of the volunteer squad that went out to Stanley ten days ahead of the rest. That squad did good work, and the "Brain" deserves the credit for organizing the work efficiently. He and his associates were responsible also for getting a good part of the American Club supplies, including food, cigarettes, and a library of 1,000 volumes out to Stanley.

As I mentioned, the "Club" was set a little apart from the other buildings. I don't believe that the Japanese meant to give us this building, but the "Brain" argued with them, saying we really needed the space for men, as the apartments were to be used for families. As the volunteer squad was staying there during their clean-up period, and possession is nine-tenths of the law, the Japanese agreed to the Americans keeping it. The British were sore about this, as they were cramped in their quarters and could have used this extra space. Anyway, we got the quarters and were therefore that much better off.

The work details that were immediately started when we arrived at Stanley were done under the "Brain's" guidance, or at least at his suggestion. When we arrived at the camp, the "Brain" was the only man known to all and the only person who had done anything for the community as a whole, organizing and negotiating with the Japanese. Most everyone was busy doing some kind of work; those who were not were laying the groundwork for the first community meeting to get the "Brain" elected as leader.

The first meeting was held, and the "Brain" was elected, just as he had planned. Then the real underhanded work started. I will give a few instances of some of the things that were done, and you can judge for yourself. Many of these things I did not get the full details of until we were on our way home, which shows how efficient his organization was in keeping them under cover. The community as a whole did not know about them either, but we did know that something was rotten in Denmark, and the "Brain" was just about to be kicked out of power when the Japanese took him up to Shanghai to explain some of his funny work there.

There were several members of the British-American Tobacco Company, and they managed to get into Stanley 20,000 Chesterfields. It was decided that these would be sold to men only, with the price of one Hong Kong dollar a package. The proceeds of the sale were to be turned over to the International Welfare Committee, which was composed of members of the three communities with the purpose of taking care of special needy cases. There were some people in camp who needed special supplies in the way of medicines, clothes and so forth. The cases were studied by the committee who then submitted requests to the Japanese if special supplies had to be purchased.

There was a very acute shortage of small money in camp, that is, $10 notes or less. For any notes over $10 a discount of about 40% was taken. If you had a hundred dollar bill, all you could get for it in small money was $60, so you could only purchase $60 of goods.

The proceeds of the sale of these cigarettes amounted to about $3,800 which was all paid in one dollar notes. This money was handed over to the officials of the camp, i.e. the "Brain" and his gang, who then turned it over to the International Welfare Committee in five hundred and one hundred dollar notes, in reality worth much less than $3,800. This was one of the rawest deals that the "Brain" pulled, or tried to pull, because he did not get away with it. The International Welfare Committee insisted on getting the $3,800 as it was originally paid in by the people who bought the cigarettes, in small notes.

In another instance, there was a group of four or five Americans who were driving trucks before the Japanese victory. They continued to drive them for the Japanese when they took over. They expected to be interned any day, but this never happened. They continued to drive the trucks for the Japanese until we were repatriated.

While the fighting was going on, one of the truck drivers got $2,000 in cash and converted this into food supplies. For the first month or so at Stanley, the trucks came out from town once a day. There was a room reserved for these truck drivers as it was expected that they would be relieved of their jobs and join us.

This room held their personal belongings and was also used as a general storage room. The truck drivers managed to get the $2,000 worth of food out to Stanley and put it in this room, but this fact was not known to the community as a whole. Only the "Brain" and his gang had any knowledge that there was such a quantity of food in Stanley. The "Brain" arranged with the Japanese to have this room locked, but as far as the community knew, it just contained the few personal belongings of the truck drivers.

There were also two representatives of the American Red Cross in camp who were on the "Brain's" staff. A loan of $25,000 US dollars had been arranged in America, with the deal completed through a wealthy Iranian ship owner in Hong Kong by the name of Namazee. This loan amounted to $100,000 in Hong Kong dollars. These two representatives got hold of some of this money. I think the amount was $5,000 because this was the shortage that showed up.

Sometime during the month of April one of the truck drivers came out to Stanley and wanted to get into the room reserved for them. When he did, he found that all of the food was gone! A little investigation on his part proved that the "Brain's" gang had been using it. He, of course, made a fuss about this. To keep him quiet, the Red Cross man immediately paid the truck driver $2,000 with the Red Cross money! They also paid themselves $1,000 each as salary, with the other $1,000 thrown in to cover unaccountable expenses.

Some of the other Red Cross money was used for the benefit of the community, however. About the first of June (why it took so long, I do not know) supplies were delivered to us from this money: clothes, tooth brushes, soap and other personal items that were more or less essential for carrying on our existence. Our eating equipment was also greatly improved with the arrival of some plates, knives, forks and spoons.

The "Brain" kept his control for the first two months by the well-known political method of personal favoritism. He would go to people with families and give them a couple of tins of milk. They, of course, would say nothing, as they thought they were the only ones being so treated. Naturally, they would vote for the "Brain" and any motion that he would put forth. That was where some of the $2,000 worth of food went.

The "Brain" knew what he was doing, and he planned it well. There were over thirty Standard Oil men in camp. He got the word started around the rest of the community that Standard Oil was trying to run the camp and "you know what Standard Oil is—so we need to break up that combination!" This was not a difficult point to put across. Standard was the biggest single group in camp. The fact that it was Standard did not make so much difference. If it had been Singer Sewing Machine, General Motors, or any other corporation that had this many people in camp, it would have been the same. With food it was not difficult to get a good part of the community against one big corporation, so the votes all swung in favor of the "Brain."

There was always some kind of row going on in camp, which was another way the "Brain" worked. Keep something going for the people to talk about and vote about. Keep them divided and thus maintain control. After about two months when most of the heavy work was done, people had more time and they began to look into things a little closer and compare notes. They found that everything was not on the level, that there was entirely too much commotion for a community of 300 plus people. The ground work was just being laid to throw the "Brain" out when the Japanese took him to Shanghai. Apparently there were several deals there that could not be explained, and the "Brain" seemed to be in on every one of them. After he left, things went much better. The crooked work was eliminated. Even with all the talk against Standard Oil, several Standard men were put on the camp committee. Things finally began to function on an orderly basis.

One of the "functions" was a black market. Yes, we even had a black market in Stanley, a thoroughly up-to-date community! This black market dealt in everything, but the main item was food. How did excess supplies of food get into Stanley? There were two methods: one, the right honorable Hong Kong Police force, and the other the Chinese guards.

Remember, the Hong Kong Police force took our jobs of unloading the godowns away from the thirty Americans. At the start of that shemozzle the Japanese had said that if we did not supply the labor, they would just go into town and get some Chinese coolies to do it. Well, this is eventually what they did because they found that the Hong Kong Police force was not thoroughly honest. Imagine that, the Hong Kong Police force questioned on a moral basis!

The Japanese did not have sufficient guards when they let the Hong Kong Police in. A little gang of them organized in the back of the godown, with others of them keeping the guards very busy. This little gang would sneak cases of food out and throw them down an embankment. Then at night when the place was all closed up, they would sneak back to get them. Some of the police coming out the regular way from the godown would also purposely fall with a case of, say, corned beef, in such a way that the case would break, always right on the edge of an embankment. Tins would roll down to the bottom into the tall grass and weeds. The Japanese would not waste any time sending men down to hunt for them, so the tins just stayed there. At night, the police would go and get them.

It took the Japanese about four days to catch on to this little racket. When they did, they fired the Hong Kong Police force and brought in Chinese coolies to do the job. However, the Hong Kong Police force had collected quite a bit of loot by that time.

These raids by the Hong Kong Police Force were not limited entirely to daylight attacks. The Japanese had put barbed wire around these godowns and a sign in English that any one caught there would be shot. This kept most people out, but not the Hong Kong Police Force. Other than the barbed wire, the Japanese had no guard on the place. The Hong Kong Police broke in at night and helped themselves.

The Japanese noticed this and knew just about where to look. They went up to the police building, emptied it of every person, and then inspected the place. They found cases of corned beef, 25 pound tins of margarine, cases of jam, and other items under the beds. Of course, it was pretty hard to explain where it all came from. The Japanese locked up about 15 policemen in the prison. They had a trial of some sort, let the majority go, and held several in the prison. Later, they finally let them go too.

The police, however, were not so dumb. They did not hide all of their loot under their beds. They had buried most of it in various parts of the grounds. I don't know whether the Japanese caught on to this little caper or not. The police managed to keep most of it.

The police would sell the loot around the camp at outrageous prices, but those that had the money were not arguing much about the price. The police seemed to have more cases of tinned cheese than anything else and this was their big stock in trade. They were selling these 12 ounce tins for the equivalent of US $2.00 or more. I bought a couple. Corned beef they were selling for less. They had sufficient stock to set them up in a profitable business.

The other suppliers on the black market were the guards. These guards would go in and out of camp with stuff that was not too bulky, such as bars of chocolate, concealed in their clothes. A bar of chocolate that normally would sell for five cents went for 60 cents in Stanley. Sugar is one thing you crave if denied it for any great length of time. Occasionally, a few eggs would also come in the black market.

In addition to the guards, each group of buildings had a Chinese superintendent. After you got to know them, they would also bring in supplies for you. Every ten days they got a couple of vacation days in town. When they came back, they would be pretty well loaded. They also had methods of getting things in by truck and used this to their best advantage. I think all the Chinese guards and superintendents were making a pretty fair income on their black market sales.

The police, however, had the thing pretty well tied up. Before the war Hong Kong was full of rackets; it was well known that the police were accepting "squeeze" money all over town. It was very hard for some of them to explain how they were keeping their level of living on the salary they were paid. By the sale of goods they had stolen from the godowns, they had sufficient money to finance the Chinese guards. The Chinese would bring the stuff in and hand it over to the police, who would sell it around the camp. In this way several profits were made.

The main problem at Stanley was food, food, and more food. That was all we thought about. Even in view of the extra supplies, food was not sufficient in any sense for a balanced diet. For the first two months, no extras were coming in at all. All we got was six and a half ounces of rice and a little boiled lettuce. To my dying breath I never want to spend a leaner two months than what existed at Stanley in February and March.

Ruth Briggs, Pasadena, California

On my birthday, April 9, I tried to count my blessings and not harp on how much I miss Norman and how worried I am about where and how he is. At thirty-seven years old, I'm healthy and have two wonderful little girls. And a wonderful, supportive family. But it's been nine long months since he left us last summer to go back to work after his home leave.

Everyone is coming over here for my party, each bringing a potluck dish. Pa helped to set up tables in the back yard so we could have a nice picnic. Brother Don is bringing my parents in from Pomona, and my brother Walter is coming from Santa Barbara with Edith and their two daughters, Lynette and Marcia. Lynette is a year younger than Kathie, and Marcia is just two weeks older than Carol.

It was fun having everyone here as they really helped to buoy my spirits. So, on May 9, Norman's birthday, they all came back again for another potluck. And on his birthday, I received another cable from New York: "Glad to advise message from Macao states all Hong Kong staff well." So we really celebrated!

The war news, however, was not good. At the beginning of April, the government started evacuating Japanese-Americans and putting them in internment camps! I feel so sorry for them having to leave their homes and businesses. It doesn't seem fair, as most are American citizens; some have never even been to Japan! I should think that there would be a better solution for security.

Later in the month I heard that Bataan had fallen to the Japanese. Then we started bombing Japan. That made me think of our friends who are still there. When will this all end?

Chapter V
Community Living

We had one formal meeting a month at which minutes were kept, and two other informal meetings. In these meetings the "Brain" submitted a long report, telling all that he had done, how hard he had worked, emphasizing the few benefits that we did receive were purely the result of his work. We just sat there and listened to it. It was good rhetoric, and most of us realized that no matter what was done, our position was not going to be greatly improved anyway. The Japanese were going to let us live, and beyond that there would be no extras. The "Brain" kidded himself quite a lot that he was the one who could save the American community, but I don't think he kidded the community much.

Every major issue was voted on by the community as a whole, a perfect example of democracy. Although everything was done by popular vote, the "Brain" had everything well lined up beforehand. We had around twenty Catholic Fathers in camp that had the whole top floor of one of the apartment buildings. It was one of the best locations in Stanley, and they all ate together. The "Brain" had the Fathers lined up solidly in back of him. As the Fathers voted, so did the twenty Sisters. In addition to the private deals he made with his own gang, the "Brain" knew exactly where he stood.

One of the smartest tricks I saw him do was at one of the meetings concerning his leadership. He gave a long speech about the things he had heard that were said against him. If the community thought that such things were true, certainly he was not the man to lead them. Accordingly, he submitted his resignation. A great howl of protest immediately went up. If he resigned, what would the Japanese think? He had been conducting all the talks with them. If we changed horses in the middle of the stream, we would lose face not only before the Japanese but also before the British. No, we could not change leaders right now. Very well done, "Mr. Brain." He knew exactly how it would go. Of course, he was retained in office, conducting his affairs even in a more high-handed way.

When the "Brain" finally departed for Shanghai under the protective custody of the Japanese, the Fathers conducted a little orchestra to lead the singing of "He Is a Jolly Good Fellow" and "Aloha." It was very pathetic, as there was no real sincerity shown by anyone. No one was greatly elated or downcast by his departure.

No community of 2,800 people could get along without a hospital. Although Stanley was exceptional as communities go, it did establish a hospital in one of the Indian Warden's Quarters. As it was located away from all other buildings, it was ideal. Also, because it was used as a barracks before and had larger rooms, the structure was good for hospital wards.

The hospital was for the entire community, but run and operated entirely by the British. It was a complete unit in itself; they got their own percentage of food and cooked in the hospital kitchen. Including staff and patients, there were between 150 and 175 people living in the hospital. Most of the patients were British, and most of the cases were dysentery. It surely showed the difference in the care of food in the American and British communities. The Americans boiled their water, but not all the British did. In addition, all the British kitchens were not screened, so flies collected. And, more British apparently kept food overnight during which it would go bad. Granted, a community of 340 is much easier to control than one of 2,400. Eventually, the British gained more control over the food management, and the dysentery cases dropped considerably.

There was an adequate staff of doctors and nurses, all British, and operations were performed at Stanley. The Japanese gave us an operating table from the prison. Most of the medical supplies were obtained from the British store houses and set aside before we were interned, but if anything was absolutely necessary, the Japanese would send it in. There was no sterilizer, so after every operation, the Japanese would take the instruments into town, have them sterilized at the French Hospital, and then return them to us. There were several appendicitis and hernia operations performed and three births, one in the American community and two British, while we were there. If anyone was so sick that they could not be adequately cared for at Stanley, the Japanese would permit them to be taken into town to one of the hospitals there.

There were twelve deaths while we were at Stanley, all amongst the British community. The average age of the British was much higher than in the American community, and this alone accounted for the deaths. All who died were in their late 60s or early 70s. Internment probably hastened these deaths, but I do not think that one single death could be directly attributed to the conditions existing in the internment camp.

In addition to the hospital, we had a clinic for the entire community, located in the American Quarters. The clinic was for all minor cuts and bruises and other small ailments. Anything that could not be taken care of in the clinic was, of course, referred to the hospital.

A British doctor who was formerly the prison doctor was in charge of the clinic and lived in the American quarters where an American doctor was formerly living. Boy, what a row that caused! The whole proposition was aired at one of the community meetings. Personal incriminations were let go and for about ten minutes, I thought the bombs were dropping again in Hong Kong. There was no mincing of any words—people were called liars, a few damns were heard here and there. If there had not been so many women present, I am certain the language would have been stronger.

The issue was between two doctors and their living quarters. In the American community there was an M.D. who was of Eurasian heritage. He was a graduate of the Hong Kong University, but had never been to America, although he was an American citizen. He had a practice in Hong Kong.

Living in the Indian Quarters was the British prison doctor and his wife, who was expecting a baby the latter part of May. The Indian Quarters were very crowded. The doctor in the American quarters had a good sized room next to the bathroom. The "Brain" had put over some kind of a deal with the doctor formerly in charge of the public health of the Colony. This doctor was not in Stanley, but living in town doing special work for the Japanese. I do not know exactly what it was, but it was very evident that the "Brain" was under obligation to the doctor of the ex-colony, who was a close friend of the prison doctor, so he was going to get the prison doctor better quarters.

The doctor of the ex-colony went to the "Brain" and said that the community could not have a doctor whose principal practice was venereal disease, referring to the American Eurasian doctor. Therefore, could not the

American doctor be put out of his present quarters, and the prison doctor moved in to take charge of the clinic? Well, the "Brain" arranged that. One day without any notice, a couple of the "Brain's" gang appeared at the American doctor's door and said he would have to move, that they had another room ready for him. I don't know how many questions the American doctor asked, but anyway the change was railroaded through, the American doctor moved out, the British prison doctor moved in, and the pay-off was complete.

The American doctor's wife had no grass growing under her feet; she was not going to have her husband slighted in any way. The flag waving started by someone getting up, asking why an American doctor was put out, and a British doctor put in charge of the clinic, also living in the American quarters. The first broadside had been fired and the battle was on.

The "Brain" handled most situations, but this was beyond him. The American doctor's wife got up and read the riot act to him. It was certainly washing one's linen in public. The British prison doctor was mixed up with the police in some way with the supplies that they were selling. It seems that the "Brain" had made a deal with him for the purchase of supplies, and the better room in the American quarters was a part of the deal.

Well, the upshot of it was that there was no change. The community as a whole did not care much for either doctor and, although the American doctor had been pushed out, no one was going to bat for a Eurasian. After this meeting, the "Brain" diminished in power as the whole community saw for the first time the sort of things he was up to. He lost his temper and showed his hand. If the Japanese had not taken him away, he would have been out of power soon anyway.

Another uproar entailed trying to invoke the Geneva Convention, a great subject amongst our missionary friends. I guess several of them had made a study of it. All I can say is that it did not do them or anyone else any good. If the Geneva Convention had never been mentioned at Stanley, there is no question in my mind but what we would have been better off. Many things that came up with the Japanese we opposed, citing the Geneva Convention.

What did the Japanese care about the Geneva Convention? The Americans were as bad as the British in insisting on compliance with the Geneva Convention. Didn't we realize there was a war on? We were at the complete mercy of the Japanese. The theoretical bunk about the Geneva Convention just complicated the situation. The missionaries, of course, were in their element, with the human equation, the attributes of life, and surging of the spirit to sustain us in our difficulties. Yes, the Geneva Convention was the answer, and the Japanese must recognize it.

Well, this is how it worked in one instance in connection with the canteen. According to the Geneva Convention (so the experts said), civilians interned were entitled to a canteen. It was put to the Japanese more on this basis, with the actual need of it by the people put secondary. Well, we got the canteen, but the supplies were not adequate. I sometimes wonder if we would have had more supplies if nothing had been said about the Geneva Convention. After we once got it, the Japanese had complied with the Geneva Convention; whether or not the supplies were adequate was of no concern to them. If we had left the Geneva Convention out of it and based our request purely on the needs of the camp, I think we would have been better off. Anyway, the scholarly people had a nice time with their academic discussions.

The Geneva Convention, again according to the experts, also says that civilians should have access to their money in the bank. This was put to the Japanese before and nothing happened. The full details were submitted of the money available to each, but they just thumbed their nose. This was a slight rebuff to our theorists.

The Geneva Convention also said that we could not be punished, so we said the face slapping must stop. The Japanese then published rules, and said only the people who broke those rules would get their face slapped. However, after one old doctor was slapped and kicked around by one of the Indian guards, such a protest was made to the Japanese that there was no more face slapping of any kind. In our appeal, we emphasized not the Geneva Convention but the physical harm done to the recipient and the fact that he was perfectly innocent of breaking the published rules. The Japanese accepted this logic, and the face slapping ceased.

So much for the Geneva Convention. In my opinion it never amounted to anything in the first place. Although it probably did not do us any harm at Stanley, I am just as positive that it did not help us any. A large amount of time in the meetings was taken up discussing the Geneva Convention. It was something to talk about and maybe gave some of us some hope. It did give a few of the boys a chance to show their education.

I have always heard stories about people who could not get along without tobacco, but it took Stanley to show me what people will do to get it. From my experience there, I would say that tobacco is a far greater drug than liquor. There were many people in camp who were known as "bottle a day" men who had no chance to taper off when they were shoved into Stanley. With liquor done away with, they certainly looked much better—thin, but sturdy. Tobacco, however, was a far different matter.

The American community as a whole had more tobacco than any other community. Hence, all the tobacco addicts came around the American quarters to see what they could find. They would pick up butts; when they had enough, they would tear them apart and make a new cigarette. It certainly is a dirty, filthy habit, but you would be surprised at the so-called respectable people who would pick up butts.

We called it the "Stanley neck." A man would be walking along with his head down, going from side to side, scrutinizing very carefully the ground in his immediate vicinity. When he spied a butt, he would lean over, his hand would go out, and in a flash, his body would be erect with the prize safely tucked away in his pocket. People who had children would send them out on scouting expeditions for cigarette butts. The first thing every morning there would be a regular patrol around the American Quarters picking up butts. Some would also come around several times during the day. The morning, however, was the best time because they could get all the butts from the previous evening.

The Japanese supplied the camp with some cigarettes. For the time we were there, each person probably got about 100 cigarettes from them. These were issued free twice, once celebrating the fall of Singapore on February 15th, and the other on the Emperor's birthday on April 29th. The other times we had to pay for them for the nominal price of 50 cents a package. They were, of course, looted from stocks in Hong Kong.

The main source of cigarettes was from the Hong Kong police and Chinese guard black market operations. They were mainly Chinese cigarettes, selling around $2 for a package of ten. These same cigarettes sold in town for 25 cents Hong Kong currency. This cigarette business was a racket pure and simple. There must have been a concession on it, because with large quantities coming in, no one could not be seen doing it. Most likely the Japanese were accepting bribes from the Chinese for the privilege of getting them through.

There were stories that some Chinese had been caught trying to get tobacco in and were beheaded. If it were true, they were probably trying to sneak the tobacco through and not paying the squeeze. Nice atrocity stories are made out of this, but I don't believe a single one of them as far as beheading the Chinese in Stanley.

We also had small cigars from Macao. The price depended on the market and how great the supply and demand was. They were the Double Horse Brand and were pretty terrible. I don't believe I ever smoked any worse in my life, nor do I ever hope to. It was impossible to get used to them, so I just gave them up.

If you saw people going around the camp with small wicker baskets or a package all done up, you knew they were selling something, probably either cigarettes or candy. Both were racket businesses and people were making a lot of money. The Hong Kong Police were in with the Chinese guards, coolies were getting the stuff, and all were making money.

We had no means of punishment or any way of restraining people who did not behave themselves. The British, I believe, did have a couple of trials, but they could enforce nothing. What the British did do, however, was keep a list of names of the individuals who were taking advantage of people. When the war was over, they intended that such individuals would be dealt with by law. The people selling cigarettes and candy were probably not listed for trouble, but some members of the Hong Kong Police Force I am certain were asked a few questions. There were certain people who were taking advantage of the situation and were making more than legitimate profits; these were the people that were marked.

The camp did try to provide education for the children. We had about twenty American children, some Dutch, and around 150 British children. A school was attempted, but it was impracticable. The food problem alone was against it. Everyone did not eat at the same time, and school would have to be conducted on a definite schedule. With 2,800 people to be fed twice a day, it was just out of the question to formally instruct children. Furthermore, the food was far from sufficient for conducive studying. It was far better that the children use up what energy they did have in play.

We had no text books, no pencils, no paper, or supplies of any kind to carry on even the groundwork of education. For the first two months, some sort of a school was kept up, but then the effort was disbanded. Parents took on the work individually which was the best that could be done under the circumstances.

One little incident is worth mentioning. On Washington's Birthday, the American community gave a party for the American children only. We got hold of a couple of sacks of flour and made doughnuts with coffee for the adults and cocoa for the children. Never mind how we got these supplies, but the black market proved its value.

The Catholic Fathers took charge of the children and put on a little pageant about Mount Vernon and George Washington. The play started off with a little country school of the time, and a boy of about five or six years old, who lisped a little, got up and recited the following lines:

> In fourteen hundred and ninety-two,
> Columbus sailed the ocean blue,
> Which is more than you can do,
> In nineteen hundred and forty-two.

This, of course, went over big as it was all too true. Some thought we would be repatriated, but the majority in camp thought we were there until the finish.

The children had a relatively good time in camp. It was more like America than anything else they had seen before. Most of the children had been in interior points in China where they never saw any American children. They had been brought up mostly by Chinese servants. Here they were absolutely free with a chance to express oneself. Even with those that had spent most of their time in Hong Kong, the education had been pretty formal. They never had a chance to mix freely with each other as they would have done at home in America. In the Hong Kong schools, I imagine the social distinctions were pretty sharp, reflecting the Hong Kong society, so they never had a chance to play and roughhouse as they did at Stanley. Even so, it was not worth the experience for them. I think the children will always feel the effects of it from the lack of food alone. The food was not sufficient for adults, and for growing children it was just that much worse. I certainly was thankful that my family was not with me.

Two or three times a week groups of about thirty children would meet, each led by two women who would supervise the play. These "classes" would last about an hour and was the only form of what might be called a school that was maintained throughout our stay.

We tried to do a little in the way of adult education, but we had the same conditions to deal with as for the children. There was one class started in the Chinese language for about 25 people. This kept up for a little while, but finally petered out. There was no chance to do any real concentrated work and nothing to do it with. There was an old piece of cardboard painted black on one side which was used as a blackboard. What was used for chalk I am sure I don't know. When hemmed in by bayonets, there is not much that one can do in the way of advancing your education, nor is there much incentive to do so.

But we did have entertainment, not only for the camp at large, but also individually in small groups. Among 2,800 people you are bound to find some talent and Stanley was no exception. Of course, part of the "entertainment" was to point to someone when you walked past them and yell "SING."

In the American bachelor quarters, the "Club," was an assembly hall used by the whole camp. Sunday nights were a favorite for camp entertainment. There were quite a few who could give monologues, and some singers and piano and violin players. For the months of February, March and April, when the weather was cooler, the assembly hall was packed every Sunday night. Very little of this entertainment was on the serious side. It was all horse play, which is what we needed. If the truth were known, that is about all we were capable of too. As the warmer weather came, these entertainments fell by the wayside, as people would congregate in smaller groups outside to pass the time away. Yet these Sunday night affairs were not purely spontaneous and impromptu; there was a little planning necessary. It was not only more pleasant outside, but soon we had reached the place where our repertoire became exhausted.

There were a few dances during the cooler weather, but these also were given up. The programs in the Club usually closed with a dance. A couple of times the assembly hall in St. Stephen's was used, but special permission had to be obtained from the Japanese for it. The Japanese came out and took pictures so they could offer this proof in their propaganda that we were not being mistreated and life at Stanley was very pleasant. Why, the internees even hold dances! Kind Japaneseu!

Every night during the week the jazz piano players gave the community the benefit of their art. It was good entertainment and everyone enjoyed it, except those who lived in the building who could not get away from it. It was mostly noise, but it was fun. People would wander in and out of the assembly hall. One could not stand it for too long, but the players always had some sort of an audience for an hour or so every evening.

Card games were also a big pastime. We had a bridge tournament and also a poker school. A small group of us played poker every evening from 6:00 to 7:30 without fail. It was not really poker at all, just a small game with a five cent limit, just really a case of showdown. Thinking back over it, I don't see how we did keep it up night after night, the same gang, the same game. We had no arguments, and it was friendly and certainly helped to shorten the evenings. Sure it got monotonous, but what activity at Stanley didn't? For an hour and a half ever day, we were taken entirely out of Stanley and transported ourselves elsewhere. All transactions were on the cuff. Believe it or not, no one backed out; we all settled up when we got to New York. How is that for a game of five months standing?

The British had lawn bowls. No British community would be complete without them. There was a regular green at Stanley which was used by the wardens before the war. The British worked on this green, kept the grass cut, watered, and rolled. There were quite a number of things around their quarters that needed cleaning up which were not touched, but the bowling green was kept in first-class shape.

During the cooler weather there was some interest in softball, but this was also when we had the hardest work to do. It was too much with the little food we were getting to take great interest in softball. There were several games between the Americans and the British, and a few games within the communities themselves. The Catholic Fathers had the nucleus of a team, as did the Hong Kong Police. When the real hot weather came, the interest disappeared entirely.

The teenage boys and girls, however, spent quite a lot of time at softball. They had a couple of teams and were out throwing the ball around a lot regardless of the weather.

What, no cricket? Nope, no cricket. You know that old saying that all of England's battles are won on the playing field of Eton. Well, I guess that just could be correct, because they haven't won any anywhere else. France, Norway, Greece, Crete, Africa, Hong Kong, Malaya, and Singapore—very poor cricket fields, all of them. Then there's that old line: England loses every battle except the last one! Well, by that time she has gotten someone else to do the fighting for her.

Religion was another aspect of the Stanley community, and did we have religion! The American community was 60 percent missionary, so we had plenty of religion. The Catholic Fathers would say mass first thing in the morning, and every other religious denomination had some kind of doings throughout the day. Sunday was, as elsewhere, Sunday. The Catholic Fathers would walk up and down in front of the apartments in the early morning and late evening reading their breviaries. Both they and the Sisters would hold week-day services in their own quarters, but on Sundays they used the assembly hall in the Club. As soon as the Catholics finished their service in the assembly hall, the rest of the denominations would hold services: the Lutherans, Presbyterians, Baptist, Seventh Day Adventist, Christian Scientists, in fact almost any denomination you might think of. The missionaries held meetings and sessions all the time. They would put up notices on the bulletin boards inviting all to attend. One of them had a story hour at 3:00 every afternoon.

They did have a united service for the entire community. This was held in St. Stephen's and was the most popular service of all. It would be impossible to get to all of them, but I did go to the service several times. There were no benches or chairs. We just stood up for the opening of the service and the hymns, and then sat down on the floor. The Church of England had Vespers in the afternoon and also held several other services, but the percentage of missionaries amongst the British was far less than the American community.

One thing we did have an adequate supply of at Stanley was Bibles. Before we got the number system organized in the food line, the missionaries, as well as others, would start lining up at 3:30, bringing their Bibles to read in line. They would underscore them with red, green, and other colored pencils. Right after breakfast, a few of them would take their Bibles and go off some place alone to read. There was work to be done, but not for them; they had to read their Bibles. By no means did all of the missionaries do this; some missionaries did a lot of work. There were also others besides the missionaries who did absolutely nothing, but I expected the missionaries to all pitch in to do what was needed. Those who are always talking about working for the Lord, self sacrifice and so on, it would seem that in a place like Stanley, they should pitch in one hundred percent to participate in the work of the camp.

I know I am cynical, but here is another little incident of the missionary outlook. We kept our own rooms clean, but took turns keeping the hallways and bathrooms clean, rotating week by week. One Sunday morning we noticed that the hallway had not been swept, so we went to the person whose turn it was. Yes, he said it was his turn, but it was Sunday, and he was not going to work on Sunday. You've got it, he was a missionary. Can you guess who did sweep the hall? His wife came out and did it.

The best service of all was the Sunday school for the children. This was held in the American Quarters, and it was well attended, averaging around thirty children. They had a little organ to lead their singing and different leaders each Sunday. They presented Bible facts and stories to the children in a very interesting way. Many adults also wandered in and out. To hear the children singing every Sunday morning was pleasant and took you, for a brief few minutes, out of the atmosphere of Stanley.

Sunday night from six to seven was the real climax—an outdoor revival service. If there was any really pitiful sight in Stanley, this Sunday night revival service was it. Here we were hemmed in by bayonets and all the hatred in the world. People got up and talked about the love of Christ, the redemption of sins, and how far we had fallen. All this from a group who would not clean their rooms on Sunday, who evaded questions about the amount of money they had, and who rushed the food line. Their actions seemed to me that their line of endeavor had not been successful.

Taken all in all, however, Sunday was a different day. The dress at Stanley wasn't much anyway, but on Sundays people did try to dress a little better, for some very much better. In fact, we saw people on Sundays that we never saw before. The big service of the day was the Catholic Mass in the morning and most of the "brain trust gang" went to that. There was one businessman and his wife who would get all dressed up. I think he had the only whole suit in camp, and I am certain she had more clothes than any other woman. She never did a thing all week except to toady to the "Brain" and his outfit. She never left her room except on Sunday. A great help to the camp she was! But, Sunday was beneficial. We saw new faces and new clothes, and everyone felt a little better because it was different.

The missionaries did try a few times to win converts. By and large, however, the missionaries minded their own business. Unless you went to them, they did not come to you and try to improve your moral status. The cleavage was pretty distinct between the missionaries and the business people, and even between the various denominations themselves. The Catholics were a closed corporation and operated as a unit, as did the Protestants.

Money was another issue to deal with. What does one do for money in an internment camp? We had the canteen and the black market of goods (in addition to the racket of the discount on large notes) and a couple of other ways that money could be used, but where did the money come from?

Most of the money, and there was a considerable amount of it, was brought in, all in cash, by the people when they came to Stanley. I myself did, and it is probably a fair indication as to how the average person operated. When the war broke out on Monday, December 8, I went to the bank and got out $1,000 Hong Kong in cash, equivalent to $250 US dollars. In retrospect, I should have taken more, but I didn't. Of that, four hundred was in large notes. The $600 in small notes made quite a wad, but if I had been wise, I would have taken it all in small notes. Of this, I had $300 taken away from me by the Sons of Heaven, so maybe it was just as well I did not take any more out of the bank. I would have probably had more on me, even though I did have the sense not to have it all in one place. Well, anyway, I arrived at Stanley on January 24th with $380 in cash, and that is every cent I had.

Some people arrived with a lot more cash, and others with practically none. The camp as a whole, I think, was pretty well supplied with money, particularly amongst the British community. Those people who were operating their own personal businesses had taken what money they had in cash in their stores and offices in addition to taking cash out of their bank accounts. Some of the British Government officials had large sums of money, as they had access to Government money. I am not hinting at all at any dishonesty; what they did was perfectly proper and legitimate. They saw, or at least suspected, what might happen; there was the cash, so they took it. As far as I know, they took it as Government money, not their own personal means. I think they distributed some of this money around after they got into camp for payment to some government employees and such. Those who were not Government employees also got some of this money by signing notes or making other promises to pay it back when the war was over.

Money also came into camp by various and devious methods. Not interned were the several Europeans driving trucks and a couple others who worked for the Japanese. Their actions were always supervised, and wherever they went, a Japanese was always with them. However, they did make trips from Hong Kong to Stanley on an average of two or three times a week, sometimes bringing money with them. I think the rich Chinese in Hong Kong advanced considerable sums to people who they knew were financially sound and who would pay them back when the war was over. Also, the Chinese agents of some of the big companies got money smuggled into Stanley one way or another. I don't know how much was taken out by the various hands it passed through, but you can bet every Chinese whose hands it touched got his rake-off. Considering this and the lawless conditions that were prevalent in Hong Kong, it is a wonder that any money got into Stanley at all.

The large note discount was a big racket. You could turn your big notes over to a committee. When several notes had been handed to them, they would turn them over to the head Chinese superintendent of the camp. On his next trip to town, he would get them cashed and bring back the small money, a process which took about ten days. Whether this was done with the knowledge of the Japanese, I do not know. If they did know of it, officially they just closed their eyes.

But you can bet that the Chinese superintendent took his share; on everything that went in and out of the camp, he got his rake-off percentage.

He was the supreme man in camp. For the first two months, he was running Stanley for the Japanese. Things got so bad that all three communities complained to the Japanese directly that this Chinese was taking entirely too much. I don't know whether or not the Chinese was not paying the Japanese their share or what, but in any event, shortly after this complaint, the Chinese superintendent became very sick and had to have several months' vacation. He was relieved, and we never saw him again. A Japanese who had previously been the barber in the Hong Kong Hotel was put in charge.

As in all communities, some people had a lot of money and others had very little, in some cases none. As far as the American community goes, I think most of the men had some. A few of the women were completely without means, but were taken care of by other members of the camp. One could make a little money by selling your canteen ticket. Everyone got a ticket, so those who did not have any money to buy anything with would either sell their ticket outright or turn it over to someone else who would buy the food at the canteen and, as payment, give the owner of the ticket part of the food that was purchased.

Money, however, was a hush-hush subject in camp. If anyone asked about money, no one had any at all.

Ruth Briggs, Pasadena, California

I got a notice from the Red Cross that Norman's name was on the roster of civilians interned in Stanley, Hong Kong. I knew he was alive! And they said they would try to get letters to him through the Red Cross channels! They said they would be unable to get any of the internees' letters out, but thought they could get some delivered. They suggested, however, that we write only about personal family items, as the Japanese would undoubtedly read all letters and confiscate any with pertinent information. They also gave instructions on how to address the letter, with the internees' name, place of internment, in care of the International Red Cross Committee in Geneva, Switzerland.

I immediately told Ma and Pa, and we sat down to write Norman letters. I feel better already knowing that I can reach out to him, even if it's in a letter.

Earlier in the month I had heard from New York again. They had received an encouraging report from the Chungking office that a person arriving from Hong Kong talked with Bourne, Sanger, and Peters on March 18, and all were in very good health. He also stated that other members of the staff were known to be well. Even though that was old news—it apparently took almost two months to reach New York—it certainly was good news. Then, with the Red Cross confirmation, and being able to write a letter to Norman, I really feel elated!

The news I hear on the radio, however, is not encouraging. Things are not going well for the United States in the Philippines. I worry about our friends who I think were stuck there. And Japanese forces are taking over Burma.

Chapter VI
Inspection and Escapes

On Saturday morning, February 14th, when we had been at Stanley only two weeks, the order came at 7:45 AM that the entire camp should assemble on the vacant lot by the side of the prison. Everyone had to go. It made no difference whether one was sick, old or infirm, including men, women, and children.

Of course, everyone wondered what it was all about. Going down to the field, someone made the bright suggestion that it was going to be a massacre, that the Japanese were going to get us all there and then "let us have it." I don't think he was serious, but in our frame of mind, it sounded entirely within the realm of possibility.

Another fellow, however, had a slightly better idea and a sense of humor. Oh yes, he knew that this was a Saturday, so it must be pay day. There was no question about it; the Japanese were going to line us up and pay us off!

You would be surprised what a small space 2,800 people can get into. I did not think we could all get on the field, but we did. It took about an hour for everyone to assemble. Some were brought on stretchers, others were carried, and, with women with small children, it took time before all were accounted for. Each building was numbered, and we lined up according to the number of our building.

There were soldiers with fixed bayonets all around. It started to rain and, I will say, it was very uncomfortable. No one had any proper clothes anyway, let alone rain coats, rubbers, umbrellas and so forth. The ground was wet and muddy, so we could not sit down. Two women fainted and had to be taken to the hospital.

Finally, after we had been there around two hours, no one having the slightest idea what it was all about, three Japanese officers and three Indian guards arrived. They took up positions at the end of the field, and we were told to form six lines. Each person went along in one of these lines, and each was inspected by the guard. The inspection was quite casual. They ran their hands over our bodies, feeling us all over to see if we had any firearms. We emptied our pockets as we approached the guard and held the contents in our hands with arms stretched out sideways. The main thing in our pockets was money, but they did not look at this nor did they take any away from us. It was an inspection for firearms only as far as I could make out. When they had satisfied themselves that we had none, they did not molest us further.

When the individual inspection started, we really got nervous. There was a lot of adjusting of clothing, as quite a few people still had watches, rings and, of course, money. One person had a diary with him on which he had written his experiences in Hong Kong during the attack. It was on ruled paper, and he had written two lines to a space on both sides of the paper. He had 35 pages with him. I don't know what he had written, but he decided it was for his own good health that it had better not fall into Japanese hands. He did not dare tear it up, as there was no place he could throw it without the Japanese seeing it. So, what do you suppose he did with it? He tore it up into small pieces and ate it! Actually, that was not so dumb; it was probably one of the best meals he ever had at Stanley. At least it was a little variety and, in some ways, preferable to rice and boiled lettuce day after day. Good bond paper is not so bad, even if it wasn't boiled. Maybe what he had written had even warmed it up a bit!

When the inspection was over, we found out the real reason for it was to inspect our rooms. Every building was entirely empty and they went through every single room. The main thing they were hunting for was a radio, as the Japanese had heard that there may be several in camp. In some rooms they opened up every suitcase and made a thorough inspection. In other rooms, they just looked around.

In my room they opened my bag under the cot, but did not touch the one on top of the clothes closet. Some people missed a few things, like razors. They did take a few things officially like binoculars and a couple of portable phonographs, which they evidently thought were radios. In spite of the fact that we were told not to bring in any binoculars, and if we did to hand them over, there were still a few wise guys who thought that it did not apply to them.

It was noon before they would let us back into our quarters. By that time the rain had ceased and the sun was out. This was our first and only lunch at Stanley. We had missed our breakfast, so we had it at 2:00 PM. It took two hours to get the fires going and the stuff ready. Anyway, after standing all morning in the rain, even rice and boiled lettuce was good. I guess this was dessert for the guy who ate his diary.

There were two escapes at Stanley. I do not remember the exact dates, but I think the first was toward the end of March. There were nine people in all, seven British and two Americans. Rumor had it that these two Americans were included because they had found out about the plans and went to the people concerned, saying you take us with you or we will inform the Japanese of your plans. How true this is I don't know, but it makes a good story anyway. Personally, I think it was true, because they were just the type of fellows to put the pressure on, and it does seem strange that two Americans would be included, especially these two. There was at least one, and I think two, women included in the nine who got away.

This escape was planned down to the last detail. There was a small boat on one of the beaches. Sometime after midnight, they got this through the barbed wire along the beach and got away from Stanley where a junk was waiting for them outside. They were passed through the Japanese lines by the Chinese, got to free China and hence to Chunking. Rumor had it that it took them about ten days from Stanley to Chunking. Several of these people could speak excellent Chinese, and they also had plenty of money. Getting out of Stanley was a fairly simple thing to do, but what to do after that? That was the important question, and these people had it all worked out and hence were successful.

It may be just pure coincidence, but the improvement in our food rations started about the time that these people arrived in Chunking. As soon as they got there, they broadcast the conditions at Stanley. Whether this had any effect on the Japanese, I don't know; maybe they simply got themselves better organized and were going to give us more food anyway. Our meat and vegetable rations were increased and flour added to our diet about the middle or latter part of April, which was about the time of these broadcasts from Chunking.

Some rumors had these people taken out of Stanley in a motor car and handed over to the Chinese in Hong Kong. Maybe they did get out this way,

I don't know. But I do know that this boat was beached behind an old swimming shack at Stanley. The day after their escape, it was gone, and you could see where the barbed wire had been broken down and the boat pushed through.

After this escape, we were checked on once a day. The Chinese superintendent in charge of each building handed in a list of everyone in his building each day. No further restrictions were imposed; the Geneva Convention said they couldn't, you know!

The second escape was not as well planned. Four men decided that they had enough of Stanley, so thought they would go elsewhere. One night they just decided to leave. They got out of Stanley okay and walked to Hong Kong. They thought they would look up some Chinese friends whom they hoped would hide them out until news of the escape had subsided. They were picked up by the Japanese before 8:00 AM. It shows the results between plans and no plans. Whatever happened to them I don't know. There were all sorts of rumors, such as they were taken to Hong Kong, hands tied behind them, put on a truck and paraded around as an exhibition. Still others said they were shot, beheaded, and so on. The one fact we do know is that several weeks later, the Japanese brought them to Stanley and put them in the prison. What happened after that, your guess is as good as mine. The Geneva Convention says that you can't punish civilians who escape from internment camps. Well, now isn't it peculiar that the gracious Sons of Heaven were not impressed by a ruling drawn up by such an august body?

After this second escape, we were checked on twice a day. We had to be in our quarters at 8:00 PM and could not leave before 8:00 AM. The quarters where these four men lived were a separate unit, removed from the rest of the buildings. I think there were 34 men living there. The Japanese immediately emptied the house and declared the area out of bounds. The rest were billeted elsewhere, mostly in the Indian quarters. This did inflict a hardship, because they were already crowded.

The Chinese guards were greatly increased; I think about fifty men were added to the guard detail in camp. We could see them change the guard every evening. Around the shore line they put up electric lights. They were very flimsy poles, and the first typhoon that would have come along would have taken them down. However, the entire shoreline around the camp was lit up every night after this.

Everyone thought that the restrictions would be much more severe, such as cutting down our food, but other than the few things mentioned here, there was no change in our ordinary daily routine. I heard several people say that it was bad for people to escape because the rest of us might have to suffer for it. The opinion of most of the camp was that anyone who could get out, more power to him. We all hoped if people tried, they would be successful and not get caught. We were in such a predicament anyway, a few more restrictions would not hurt us.

At the same time, people began missing things out of their rooms, particularly food. The canteen had been broken into twice. It got to a point that something had to be done. We had our suspicions and thought we knew who was doing it. There was a gang of two or three, they would break into the canteen, take as much as they could get, and then go and hide it. We found one night's haul in the corner of a small building back of the Indian shrine. We were quite sure that it was Americans and not British. For once, we were to blame for something that happened in Stanley.

Several of us took turns sleeping in the canteen. We tried to not get that word out, but just the same it did. I spent a couple of nights in there, but nothing happened. However, I did help myself to dried fruit and chocolate, so I did get something out of it!

Well, one night the guy was caught, and it was just who we thought. He was an American sailor off the Admiral Williams. A more worthless American would be difficult to find. He did not do one single thing in camp and bragged about it. In America he said he never worked, so why should he in Stanley? In America he was on the bum all the time, spending his winters in California and Florida. He also spent quite a lot of time in jail, but he got out once in a while to see the country. He was tried and found guilty of robbing the canteen. As a punishment, he was to keep the dining hall clean, cut the grass in front of the American quarters, and clean up the bathroom and hallway in the apartment where he lived.

Do you think he did any of these things? No sir! Was there anything we could do about it? Yes, but we didn't want to go that far. We could have handed him over to the Japanese, saying that he was a tough character which we had no means of dealing with, and would they take him? They would have done so, I am quite sure, and he would not have pulled any funny business with them. But we did not do this, because he was a member of the crew. Half the crew was in the civilian camp with us and the other half in the military camp. If we took this one sailor to the Japanese, it would bring to their attention that there were other sailors in the camp. They would probably take them from Stanley and put them in the military camp. The rest of the crew in

Stanley was doing the cooking. Every one of them was working; it was just this one that was a slacker. We did not want to jeopardize the rest for the sake of one man. I think the Japanese knew the sailors were in camp, but as long as no one did anything to bring it to their direct attention, they were going to overlook it. At the end, justice was done. When we arrived in New York, he went to Ellis Island.

When we first went to Stanley, the little fishing village was full of Chinese junks. The Japanese took over supervision, but the junks still went in and out to fish. Each had an identification flag on them, and some also flew the Japanese flag. The Japanese had a small gun boat at the entrance to the little bay, which we named the "Murder Boat." It was a small diesel-engine boat, around forty feet, with a couple of machine guns on it. The Japanese also had sentry posts on shore that were manned by machine guns right outside the internment area. Whenever junks not belonging to Stanley would come too near the shore, the machine guns would open up. Also, if some of the junks left Stanley without proper permission, they would be fired upon. This firing happened mostly in the early morning.

One afternoon, however, around five large junks were fired on by the "Murder Boat." These junks burned to the water line and then immediately sank, probably meaning that they were loaded with something pretty heavy. We surmised that they were trying to run some sort of a blockade and get supplies either in or out of Stanley. The actual firing and sinking of the junks only happened this once, but it was by no means unusual to hear machine gunning in the direction of the junks.

The Japanese made official inspections of the camp. Top military officers, the governor of the ex-colony, big shots from Tokyo and such would come and walk around the grounds. Sometimes they just drove through in cars. Whenever one of them came, we were all confined to quarters for several hours. The whole work of the camp had to stop, making it very inconvenient at times. Sometimes we would be just getting food when one of these big boobs came out. Then we would just have to wait until he had gone. This would throw the kitchen staff and everyone else off, but of course that made no difference to the Japanese. These were nuisance visits pure and simple.

When they walked around the camp, they would sometimes bring candy and give it to the children. They had photographers with them to document how "kind" the soldiers were by giving candy to the children. Of course, it was all for propaganda. After one of these candy visits, an account came out in the Hong Kong News, the Japanese paper, saying how good the conditions were at Stanley, how well fed and happy we all were, as could be seen by the pictures of the laughing children being given candy by the kind Japanese.

What do you suppose the Colonial Secretary's office did when they read about the kind treatment in the paper? I will give you 1,000 guesses, and then I bet you couldn't get it. They made an official protest. They sent a letter to the Japanese saying the conditions outlined in the paper were not so, that we did not have sufficient food and other essentials. What good did such a protest do? All it did was just antagonize the Japanese further.

The English set-up was a little different from the American. When the British held their elections and put people in office to run the camp, they saw to it that no government official had anything to say about the running of the camp. The officers of the British community were purely from the civilian ranks. The British community saw how completely sold down the river they had been by the Hong Kong Government, and they were not going to let that government have anything to say about how things would be done in Stanley. That is one thing I will say for the British; they kicked their own people down the stairs after they had seen what a mess the Government had made of the defense of Hong Kong.

However, the Hong Kong Government still operated as regards to British affairs outside of Stanley. The Japanese would go to the elected committee for matters within Stanley, but in anything to do with the British government outside the internment area, they would go to the representatives of the Hong Kong Government as they were before the war. This meant that the Colonial Secretary's Office was still functioning. They made recommendations about Stanley to the British and American communities. In fact, they wanted to set up a little Hong Kong Government in Stanley, but the community board did not allow this. There was some friction between the two British organizations, but they kept separately for the most part.

Several times we had visits in camp from drunken Japanese officers. Although they were menacing, no harm, fortunately, came from them. One night shortly after 9:00 PM a drunk Japanese officer came to the American Quarters, having just come from a party in the prison. He wandered into one of the passageways and opened a door to the room of a woman and her seven-year-old son. The mother was visiting on one of the floors above playing bridge, but the son was sleeping in his bed. The Japanese noticed only the small boy. He wanted to know where the mother was, so opened the door to the next room which was occupied by two women. They were asleep, but awoke when the drunk Japanese barged in. They screamed, alerting the whole building.

The officer spoke crude English and tried several other doors, one of which was locked. We used that room for boiling water and had firewood in there, so kept it locked. He insisted on us opening this door. He was very threatening and had his revolver drawn, waving it around. The real harm, I think, was in the revolver going off accidentally, as he was too drunk to fire deliberately. In fact, if we had knocked him out, he would probably not have remembered a single thing the next morning. Of course, we didn't dare do this. He was finally satisfied and went reeling off down the hill. Visits such as this by drunk Japanese happened about once a month.

The following letter from Ruth Briggs was returned as undeliverable:

405 S. Craig Ave.
Pasadena, Calif.
May 17, 1942

Dearest Norman,

Since we have just been told that at last we may be allowed to write letters, I hardly know what to write. It has been so long. There are so many things concerning the world situation that we would like to discuss, but of course that would be unwise. We know each other's viewpoints enough, I think, without writing about that, and we'll just have to have patience and endurance till we can get together again.

The children are developing nicely. Carol still keeps me hopping, keeping her out of mischief. But I don't have the big washings I used to have, so in one way it is easier. She is quick in catching on to sounds and says a lot of words already. She is always on the go—never at a loss for something to do. She surprises us once in awhile by something unusual, like pointing to your picture and saying "Daddy." And she was barely a year old when you left! Also, one day she dug out my ancient walking shoes (golf shoes) which have flat heels like a man's. She brought them out from the back of the closet and said "Daddy's shoes." She thinks she is too big for a high chair now so she sits at the table with Kathie and me. Of course she has the little "Junior Chair" on the breakfast-room bench to make her high enough. Or sometimes I put the high chair down as a little chair and table, and they enjoy eating down there for a change. Her good appetite is helping improve Kathie's appetite.

Kathie has developed a lot since last summer too. She feels most grown up when she answers the telephone for me. If I happen to be busy when it rings, she runs and answers it and says "Mother will be here in just a moment." She is getting to be more and more of a help to me. She does a fair job of keeping her room "picked up" and making her bed. And once in awhile she washes or dries the dishes for me, but I usually have to do some of them over again when she is out. If I criticize her work too much in the beginning, I'm afraid she will lose her enthusiasm and feeling of importance in doing it. Often it would be much easier and quicker for me to do it all myself, but I want her to learn. She does pretty well for her age, I think. She is eagerly looking forward to her fifth birthday, and to "going to school next September!" I'm glad the school is so near.

You ought to see our yard now. I keep flowers planted in season. The gardener gives me tips on the things I don't know—which is plenty. But I'm learning. I also have a small "Victory garden" with carrots, beets, and lettuce. It's fun watching things grow. With my ignorance along farming lines, if anything turns out to be edible I'll be real proud of myself.

Gene Bolar called up the other day and invited us down to their place on the beach. So we went yesterday and had a wonderful time. Your mother went with us. We got there a little before lunch, had lunch on the patio, then got into our suits and went down to the beach. "Bill" is a nice, easy, natural hostess, so we all felt at home and had a good time. Their little girl Tony was three years old yesterday so there was a birthday cake and ice cream, too. Kathie and Carol had such a good time on the beach they didn't want to come home. Even Carol hung back and said "No bye-bye."

Perhaps I shouldn't write any more. The censors might not want to take time to go through a long letter and might scrap it all. Well, I'll just say a few words about the relatives.

Your parents are fine, as usual. My parents are well, too, and still making more and more improvements on their place. We run down to see them every two or three weeks. Your mother usually goes, too, and once in a great while your dad goes. Don still lives there, but commutes to a factory on the other side of L.A. He used to live near his work, but felt that my parents would be lonely by themselves and at their age ought to have someone around to do the heavier work, so although it is harder on him, he commutes—chips in his share with three other men who also live fairly near and also commute by car to the same place.

Clara and family (that is, my brother Percy and their son Don) are in Washington. Walter and his family are busy and popular in their church work in Santa Barbara. Ed and his family are still in Riverside. May and Bill are still in Texas with only Shirley with them now. Billy is a pre-med student in college, and Vivien is out working. May and Bill celebrate their silver wedding anniversary this summer. Twenty-five years for my big sister! Imagine that!

Malcolm is kept awfully busy now, and Eleanor, too, of course. They are still in Boston. Uncle Tom has had a stroke or two but has recovered enough to take short walks by himself again. I hear from Margaret and the others occasionally, too. All are well. The chief concern, of course, is about you.

Somehow I feel that you are comparatively safe. Of course, things are not very wonderful for you, perhaps; but from all reports you are being taken care of, more or less. So it could be a lot worse. I imagine you might be bored at times, being so cooped up. But your pet game of poker will help wile away the time. I am trying to be sensible about all this, and not let myself get tragic. I am taking care of everything—even your college alumni contribution. So you don't need to worry about anything over here—unless it is something I don't know about. I'll tell you one thing, though,—I'm saving everything for you.

I guess that is all I had better write this time. Oh, Kathie speaks of you often, and as she asks questions I have explained your situation as simply as possible. I think she understands pretty well. However, I'll be glad when it is all over. And I'm sure you will be too.

All my love, Ruth

P.S. - I got a letter from Vic recently in answer to a note I wrote last fall thinking Kathy was already there. Of course he was worried about her since she is stuck in Manila. There is no communication so all we can do is hope for the best.

Chapter VII
Rumors & Release

One day at Stanley was about like every other day, very little change, just the same routine over and over again. Although life got very monotonous, I must say that time slipped by fairly swiftly. We would get up in the morning about 7:00 AM, have a cup of tea and a piece of bread. (This was after the first couple of months, of course, when we had bread.) Then we would clean up our quarters, the room, hallway, and bathroom. By then it would be around 8:30 AM, so we would sit around until 9:30 AM when we got our rice and boiled lettuce.

The work details would then start which would keep most of us busy the rest of the morning. Around noon we would either have tea or sometimes coffee, when available, and a piece of bread. In the afternoon, we might get a bridge game going, breaking up before our 5:00 PM boiled lettuce and rice. After cleaning up the tins and dishes, we would sit around until 6:00 PM when my poker game started. We would play poker until about 7:30 PM.

For about an hour after that we would go and sit in front of the apartments with our backs up against the iron fence. We would talk for an hour or so, listening to all the rumors, then go back into our room for a little tea before going to bed about 10:00 or a little after.

Such was the general routine, with very little variation. If we were not playing bridge or poker, we were reading, visiting friends, or taking a walk around the camp. We had one square mile in area, and it would take about 25 minutes to make the complete circuit. As I said, Stanley was naturally a beautiful place. It was a very pretty walk indeed, especially as you looked out to sea.

After we had been at Stanley a little over a month, a rumor started about a loan of $300,000 Hong Kong dollars. This amounted to a little over $100 per person. Where this money came from no one knew—advanced by the Red Cross, the British or American Governments, or the Japanese? One guess was just as good as another. Anyway, it was a loan of some sort from somebody that will probably figure in the final peace settlement. The talk about this had been going on for a couple of months. Finally, the Japanese came and said the money was ready.

For all practical purposes, we will deal with the figure of $100 per person. The American community decided that $25 should be collected from each person for general community expense. I think there was some dirty political work here to cover up some unexplained deficits, especially in connection with the canteen. I cannot prove this, and have no definite information about it, but I imagine the "Brain" knew all the ins and outs of this deal. Well, anyway, that meant that we could have $75 to do with as we saw fit. We referred to this money as the 75 dollar purchase. As the loan was in large notes and everything has to be paid for in small notes, the actual purchasing value for commodities was $50.

Everyone quickly made up a list of the food they wanted to purchase. We had prices, and everyone ordered what they wanted, up to a value of $75. Two people were appointed from each community to form the purchasing committee. The Japanese permitted them to go into Hong Kong to make arrangements for the purchase. I think the whole business was placed with one of the big department stores, either Sincere's or Wing On's. In any event, sometime about the 10th of June the packages arrived at Stanley, marked with each individual's name and listing the contents.

We went and got our packages, checking the purchases with the list we sent. All items requested could not be filled, but some other food was purchased in its place. The American community got their packages first, as our number was smaller. It is much easier to handle 300 than 2,400 packages. The British packages had not yet arrived at the end of June, but we understood all orders had been filled, and the packages were in Hong Kong, waiting transportation to Stanley.

After these packages arrived, we certainly lived well as compared to before. We got flour about the first of May, but now we had tinned butter, dried fruit, cocoa, jam and a few other such staples. Of course, these could not last forever, and when the $75 worth was gone, the chances of getting any more were pretty small. But with careful planning, this food would last about two months.

We had one distraction—tigers! Yes, sir, we had tigers at Stanley, and that was no rumor. Just before the war broke out, a circus had come to town. They set up their tents, establishing headquarters in Wanchi, a part of Hong Kong. Sometime during the shemozzle, the animals got loose and headed for the hills. As Hong Kong is basically a barren rock island with very little vegetation, the animal's foraging for something to eat did not result in much. At night the tigers would sneak down towards civilization, and, of all places, they chose Stanley.

The Japanese were quite concerned about this. Whenever the tigers were reported in the vicinity, they sent a body of soldiers to hunt them down. When they showed up at night, people beat on pans and other objects to attract attention. Twice during the daytime, we were confined to our quarters when tigers were reported within the internment area. There were four tigers in all. The Japanese got every one of them within five days, publishing a picture of the biggest one caught in Stanley village.

One of the great topics of conversation during the month of June was repatriation. It had been talked of ever since we arrived at Stanley, but more or less it was rumors and expectations rather than facts. We really did not have any facts, but we did have reason for a little hope. In their daily propaganda sheet, the Hong Kong News, the Japanese told us negotiations were going on between the governments for repatriation. The United States had chartered the Swedish vessel Gripsholm to take the people out of the Far East. They said the Gripsholm left Goteborg on May 21st and was expected in New York the end of the month. Other than this, we had no further detail, but rumors without end continued…we were going across the Pacific; we were going to Lourenco Marques; we were going to South America; only women and children and men over 45 years were going; men of military age must remain behind. And so on without end.

One day the Japanese came around and made a list of those who wanted to go home and those who wished to stay in Stanley. Most of us expected that there would be only one choice: that the entire 300 of us down to the last man would elect to go home. Surprisingly, this was not true; about 40 Americans stayed behind. These were largely Catholic Fathers and Sisters, who were continually shifting back and forth. One day they were all going, the next day there were staying. They finally decided twelve Fathers would stay, leaving eighteen to be repatriated. All the Sisters left, except for the five who had been allowed out of Stanley before to either return to free China or work in Hong Kong. Some Protestant missionaries also stayed to carry on their work as soon as the war was over.

In addition, there were several people who were married to Chinese; their wives were in Hong Kong and they did not want to leave. A few others had all of their business interests in Hong Kong and were staying behind in the hopes of salvaging something when the war was over. They said they had no relatives, friends, or business interests in America and also no money in America, so why should they leave? And who would support them if they did go? In addition, there were one or two who had been wanted by the US Government for the past several years and they decided they had better stay behind the barbed wire at Stanley rather than look out from behind bars at home.

Rumors continued as did preparations, so it was looking more hopeful all the time. The Japanese told us that those who had $500 in the bank could have it in cash. Anyone who had more than $500 could have twenty percent of the balance. All payments would be in Hong Kong currency.

Back in February the Japanese said we could use our private funds to buy food for the American community. At that time we made a complete list of all funds available and gave it to the Japanese. Nothing came of it, however.

Now the Japanese wanted another list. We went through the community again, asking each one what bank he dealt with and how much money he had in the bank. Do you think this list agreed with the one made up in February? It did not! In June there were fifty more accounts declared than there were in February!

When people could get their money in actual cash, they declared their accounts in full. But when the money was to be used to buy food for the American community, they declared only part of their deposits. Our group was sixty percent missionary, and a good number of those fifty accounts were missionaries'. One missionary had a personal account of $20,000. It was mission funds, but as far as the records went, it was in his personal name. We asked him why he did not declare it in February. Oh, "he forgot; he did not recall that he had the account then." Of course.

The Japanese paid us this money in Hong Kong currency. Well, what good was Hong Kong currency? It was no good in New York. Of the few Americans who were staying, some gave us checks on New York banks for our Hong Kong money. The Catholic Fathers took all they could get. In the British community there were quite a few who had American traveler's checks; they were more than willing to dispose of these, as they were no good to them, whereas Hong Kong money could still be used in Stanley. There were also some British who had funds in the US who gave us checks or a letter against them. We also gave money to some friends who had no US funds available, but promised to pay us at the end of the war.

There was some discussion about the rates of exchange, but that was a secondary matter. In spite of all these opportunities, some Americans did not get rid of the money. What do you suppose they did with it? They brought it home with the expectation that they could go to the Hong Kong & Shanghai Bank in New York and get American dollars at the four to one rate, which was the rate when the war was declared. Imagine taking money out of Stanley that could be of absolutely no use elsewhere, but could buy greatly needed necessities for those who remained behind!

Rumor had it that after the Americans left, the Japanese would let the British have money from their personal accounts on exactly the same basis. What do you suppose the advice of the Colonial Secretary's office was? They recommended that no one accept the offer of the Japanese, because if they did, it would prejudice their interests for a full settlement after the war was over! Here were people who badly needed money to buy food, but the Colonial Secretary's Office recommended that it should not be accepted. The money that they got now would help to keep them alive. A lot of good a hundred percent settlement would do them when the war was over if they were not there to accept it.

June was a hot month. We stayed inside during the daytime and outside at night as much as possible. There was always some breeze. At night several of us would take our canvas cots outside and sleep on the lawn. Before morning, a blanket was necessary. Several times we were driven in by rain, but otherwise it was good sleeping in the open. Stars were out by the million, and I would lay there watching the various constellations, gradually dropping off to sleep. You can see the Southern Cross from Hong Kong. I also saw another sight that I had never seen before—my first rainbow in the moonlight. It was beautiful!

Stanley was a beautiful place, and with moonlight on the sea, it was just that much more so. Occasionally we would see a few fishing boats go by. It made a very charming scene. The incongruity of it all—hatred spread far and wide throughout the world, we hemmed in by bayonets, yet sitting in comparative safety, watching a small Chinese fishing fleet go by in the moonlight. Maybe we will learn someday what utter foolishness the whole business of war is.

On these moonlit nights several people in camp who were knowledgeable about the subject gave us classes in astronomy. I really enjoyed these lessons on the position of the stars. In spite of all I have said, it shows that we still had a little human understanding left. These moonlit nights are one of the few pleasant recollections of Stanley.

The cooks finally got tired of the complaints on the food and quit. I do not blame them at all. They gave us a week's notice so we could get a new kitchen crew and said they would be willing to help out anytime. They had been on the job ever since we got into camp, and they wanted a few days relief before going home, if there was anything at all to this repatriation rumor.

They had been greatly criticized. When the $75 worth of food arrived, it looked pretty certain that we were getting out, so the advantages of working in the kitchen were not such a premium. They also thought that no one else in camp could do the cooking. So they wanted to turn the job over to a bunch of novices to turn the food the Japanese gave us into something edible. They imagined burned rice and more, thinking it would not be long before the community would be asking them to cook again. Then they would be appreciated.

But were they, and everyone else, surprised. We got some men to do the heavy work, but the women did the supervising. There was a vast improvement! We did not have much seasoning, but what little there was, they did much better with it. I think we also got more because there was less waste. I am not saying that the crew wasted supplies. But our new cooks had only cooked in small lots before, so I think they were a little more careful with what was available.

Anyway, whatever the reason was, there was a general all-around improvement in the food, so much so that the galley crew did not have much to say after the new gang had been in a week or so. It was hard work, and the women had to have frequent changes. If we had continued on at Stanley much longer, I think we would have taken turns in the kitchen, rotating crews every two weeks. The community owed a lot to the original crew. I don't think they were appreciated as much as they should have been, but that was the way at Stanley.

One amusing incident happened around this time, or rather it was amusing after it was over. In the "club" there was a room in which seven men lived. On one of the walls they had drawn a map of the world. It showed every country in the world except Japan. They had purposely left Japan out because they thought it might cause trouble. There was a lot of college horseplay on this map, with all sorts of names for various countries, such as the Los Angeles city limits right outside of Rio de Janeiro.

When the repatriation began to be talked about, they put the route of the ships on the map, the Asama Maru from Hong Kong to Singapore and then to Lourenco Marques, then the Gripsholm from there to New York.

On the right hand edge of the wall there was a bullet hole which the boys designated as the "geographical center of Stanley." No one knows exactly how the Japanese found out about this, but they did. One day several Japanese officers came in, took a look at the map and said: "Where is Japan? No Japan on map!" The explanation given to them was that the map was not completed yet, and they were just going to put in Japan. This made no impression. The officer took a crayon from his pocket. All over east Asia on the map he drew a huge circle which included Hong Kong, The Philippines, Malaya, Sumatra, Java, Australia, the Hawaiian Islands, and, of course, all of China. Over all this he wrote in big letters, JAPAN. Then he said: "Everything Japan now, all else finish."

He spied the bullet hole, "the geographical center of Stanley." He had no idea what this was all about. He read it and just stood there looking at it, saying "Meaning wa, meaning, geographical center, geographical center Stanley, meaning wa?" Well, no one could explain it to him, so he thought it was some military code. He was waving his hands around and getting excited. The boys thought he wanted the map erased, so they went and got some water and started to wipe it off.

I do not know exactly how it started, but there was confusion. The Japanese thought the boys were not doing as they should, so they started to slap faces. One officer took the broad side of his sword and hit one of the men several times on the back. As far as I know, the sword was sheathed, but it caused welts on the man's back. The marks were there for several days. The situation got very nasty, but it could have become much more serious. After they slapped faces and used the sword, they departed.

Rumors and facts kept increasing, repatriation, repatriation. It was just like a mirage, something in the distance, but you could not touch it. The Japanese told us the Asama Maru would arrive on June 15th and would sail on the 16th. About the 12th they informed us there had been a delay, and we would sail on the 23rd. On June 19th we were informed that the delay would be indefinite, that we would not sail on the 23rd. No other date was mentioned. Well, there was quite a lot of hope lost, and the community was pretty depressed.

The Hong Kong Government thought we were making a great mistake on this repatriation move. One Britisher asked me when the war was over, who was going to start up our business. I replied that if and when the war was over, and there was any business in Hong Kong, there would be plenty of planes coming out. We could be back in Hong Kong within a week, if necessary. Furthermore, the people who stayed in Stanley would be in no condition to go back to work, even if the war was over shortly.

Well, they could not see this point; they thought we were making great mistake, and were more or less like rats leaving a ship. As far as the Hong Kong Government was concerned, there would be no mass evacuation of the British subjects from Stanley. This was British territory, and they were going to remain there. No government employees would be permitted to leave Stanley. The sun never sets on the British empire; as long as there is a sun, there will be a Hong Kong. So, therefore, in Stanley they would stay.

Rumors became stronger and stronger that we were going home. The British community thought it would be a nice gesture for them to give the Americans a farewell party. They put on an excellent show for us. The music was good, they had a lot of originality, the stage dancing and costumes were marvelous for a place like Stanley and the conditions under which we were living. Everyone enjoyed it. It was a good evening's fun and entertainment, thoroughly appreciated by all the Americans.

As the month's end approached, we had several meetings in the hope of making definite preparations for departure. What do you suppose were the questions asked? Several people got up and asked if we should take our $75 worth of food with us! Imagine taking food out of a place like Stanley! The food on the ship could be no worse than we had been eating for five months. At the very most, we would only be three weeks on the Japanese ship. Wouldn't it be worth taking a chance and leaving the food behind for the British? But no, some people were going to take theirs, and they did!

The next thing was Bibles. The missionaries had marked their Bibles with all sorts of colored pencils. The Japanese said that no printed matter could be taken out, and certainly not books that had been marked, as such might be some kind of a code. The Japanese were perfectly right, as a lot of information got out of Europe by just exactly this method. Well, the missionaries could not see why they should not be permitted to take their Bibles and papers. Here was a war on, we had a chance to get out, and then to kick up a fuss about papers. Most of this commotion was made by the Protestants.

On Friday, June 26, we read in the paper that the Asama Maru had left Yokohama on Thursday for Hong Kong, and the Conte Verde had sailed from Shanghai for Singapore. The Asama Maru would arrive on Monday, June 29, the date on which we would embark, and sail on June 30th. We really believed it now. This was the first definite announcement, and the dates confirmed in the paper. The Japanese told us that our baggage would be picked up and inspected on Sunday, then put on the ship on Monday. We could keep one small overnight bag to carry ourselves, but all other baggage would be put on for us.

On Sunday morning we put all our baggage out in front of our quarters, and they inspected it and took it away. They did not go through it very thoroughly, as they did not have sufficient men to do so. They might have taken some things away, but as far as I know, very little was taken out of the suitcases. I saw some food packed. If I had been the Japanese, I would have certainly taken that out. Just think of the situation at Stanley to even think about taking food out!

We cooked our last meal of rice and lettuce on Sunday night. Who do you suppose cooked our breakfast for us? The forty Americans who were staying behind? No. The British cooked it for us. As the American kitchen was the best kitchen in Stanley, I hope they kept it for their use. If the forty Americans could not cook for us, the British were more than welcome to the kitchen. It was nice for them to cook our departing meal and was thoroughly appreciated by us.

We were all up early on Monday with the excitement of leaving. We saw the Asama Maru come into the harbor about 2:00 PM and anchor off Repulse Bay. This was the one and only time that we were completely certain that we were going. We were confined to our quarters until 3:00 PM when the Japanese sent word that we should go down to the little pier where we had landed five months ago.

The British were all lined up to bid us farewell. I never have seen, I never again want to see, and I never expect to see a sadder or more depressing sight than that departure from Stanley. There were quite a few British women who had married American men. They were permitted to go. However, they were leaving behind brothers, sisters, and parents. There were also American women who had married British men; these women could go, but not the men. Most of the husbands were in the military internment camp, but just the same it made the parting pretty hard for those concerned.

Everyone tried to put on a bold front, but it could not last; the pressure and sentiments were too great. They were leaving their loved ones behind and to what? Starvation, greed, and lust, or just plain existence on the lowest level. You can't blame those for leaving, because they could do nothing in Stanley to help anyone, and those who left made that much more room for those who must stay. It was a sad sight indeed, and it gave you an inner feeling that you were doing something wrong in departing for a land of plenty and leaving those behind in such deplorable conditions. I wonder how those Americans felt who were taking food and money with them? I did not have that on my conscience anyway. Everything I owned was in my one suitcase, except a few clothes I had left behind with friends at Stanley. It was a terrible sight, and that is about all that can be said.

We went down to the little pier and lined up in alphabetical order. We went through one by one between two tables with the Japanese checking our names off the list. A member of the American community was also there to identify us as our name was called. We got aboard a small launch which took us out to one of the Star ferries. Each of the two launches made several trips. Finally the ferry was full. In fact, it was so crowded we had to rearrange ourselves. As many of us were on the upper deck, some had to go below to give it better balance so that it would not capsize.

We came up on the starboard side of the Asama, but the sea was too rough to tie up. We went around on the port side with no better results. They finally got a couple of barges to put between the ferry and the Asama to make it safe. This took a couple of hours before we were finally tied up to safely transfer. Our names were again checked in alphabetical order by both the American and Japanese at the hatchway.

We were aboard! Miracles do happen, and this was certainly one. We now started our two month journey home.

The following letters from Ma and Pa Briggs were also returned:

410 S. Mentor Ave.
Pasadena, Calif.
May 17, 1942

Dear Norman,

   Word came from 26 Broadway yesterday that we could get letters through to you and we are hoping it can work the other way too. It has been a long, long time.

   Things go on about the same here as when you left. Carol Irene and Katherine have grown a lot. Kathie is almost a young lady. She will be ready for school for the fall term. Carol has grown a lot and is a real person, beginning to talk and as full of mischief as an egg of meat. She is going to be the wit of the family. She has a very happy disposition. She pulled an old pair of shoes out of the closet the other day and said, "Daddy's shoes." And she has said a number of things about Daddy. She does remember you.

   Pa has done over the paint in the living room and dining room. Walls and all. There is a paint made to put on over the paper and it worked fine. The rooms look very nice now.

   I have had the two front rooms rented for two months to two women. One came Feb. 4 and one March 12. The first one leaves to go back east this week and the second one hopes to be here a year. She is at Caltech. The first one hopes to come back next October. She is a widow and lives on her income.

   The Mossmans came back last week later than usual. Everyone asks about you and if you can get letters. I imagine you may hear from some of the family later.

   Eddie Edmondson is coming right along. Had a paper to read before the medical convention on tumors last week. Norman P. is still at Stanford. It takes a long time to educate him. He wrote the senior play for Pomona this year. We all went down to see it. It was simply terrible. Too much language if you know what I mean.

   Betsy Ross is to be married in June at her home in Escondido. We are asked to be present. Ruth will write you of the family doings. You don't realize what a blessing that car of hers is. It is so far to stores from her house. It is a splendid neighborhood for them. Mostly young people with children who have the same interests. Very nice people all around them. If you could only be with them!

A letter I wrote November 9 has just returned. Hope this one reaches you.

Love, Ma

Pasadena
May 18, 1942

Dear Norman,

We have just got word that it may be possible to get a letter through to you via Red Cross. The subject matter must be strictly limited to family affairs, but fortunately in that particular there is nothing but good news to report as everybody is well and has been, except for minor upsets which are always in evidence, ever since you last heard from us. Ruth and the children are OK and we are all living as far as we can in the usual way. We, of course, think of you not only every day but all the time.

All the other folks are "pretty tolerable" as we used to say back east. Just had a letter from Malcolm. Tom is failing right along but still gets about and has his walks, though shorter. Bertha is in Boston and getting along all right considering her disabilities. All "the folks" are here now, Paul and Emma having arrived ten days ago.

We have been down to Pomona a couple of times lately for an overnight stay. The last time was in celebration of your birthday a week ago. The folks down there are OK and we really had a very enjoyable time. We had a cake for your birthday and the children blew out the candles. Had a letter from Arthur Mason. They contemplate going to Munsonville soon for the summer.

I know that Ruth will write about herself and the children, so I am using my space to tell a bit about the others. So far as Ruth and Kathie and Carol are concerned, we are, of course, in touch daily or oftener at least by phone and mostly by visits. Pretty generally we have Sunday dinner together at one house or the other. I guess that's about all the space I ought to use. We are all full of hope for the best.

Affectionately, Pa

P.S. This doesn't read like much of a letter, but it's mostly due to the limitations on what can be said. I expected to mail my letter with Ruth's and your mother's, but there was some misunderstanding, so mine comes separately.

Section 5: Repatriation

Chapter I
Boarding the Asama Maru

After being checked off, we boarded the Asama Maru on D deck and proceeded right in line to the purser's desk that had tables set up in the passageway. He had the complete passenger list before him. We gave him our name, he checked the list, and then we were handed a slip of paper giving our cabin number and berth assignment. This paper also served as the ticket from Hong Kong to Lourenco Marques in Portuguese East Africa, now known as Maputo, Mozambique.

In the course of my existence I have purchased several railroad and steamship tickets, but never before had I completed a transaction as simple as this. There was nothing to sign, no carbon copies, such as a green copy to the traffic department in charge of a vice-president who was probably an ex-street car conductor, the yellow copy to Mr. Quinby in the shoe department, a pink copy to the janitor on the 5th floor, and finally the blue tissue copy to the accounting division who would use it as a basis to make lengthy statistical reports to the board chairman showing the costs per ton mile in carrying custard pies from Yokohama to Watts, California. No long set of conditions in small print and legal phrases which no one understands, no perforated tickets from one division point to another. It was all very simple, just one piece of paper from Hong Kong to Lourenco Marques.

My cabin was on D deck, number 367. There were fifteen of us in it. However, we were fortunate, as we had a porthole. As it was just above the water line, we did have it open most of the time. There were one or two rough days when we had to close it, but for all practical purposes, it remained open. The boys down on E deck did not even have a porthole. The D and E decks were all third class accommodations, but there was very little complaining as everyone was so glad to get out of Stanley. We were not going to complain about the methods or conditions of getting out. Every inch that we moved forward was a vast improvement.

The billeting of the ship was done on the basis that all of the diplomats were given their choice of the first-class accommodations. Next came the people who had actually been in prison and in solitary confinement. We had all been prisoners, but there were only a very few who had been in solitary confinement. When these were taken care of, the women and children were put in the rest of the first- and second-class cabins. What was left in the rest of the ship was assigned to the men, with most of us in third class. Some of the consular boys gave up their first-class accommodations to the women and came down in third class with us. Regardless of what may be said to the contrary, as far as assigning space in the Asama Maru, I think this was the best way to do it.

As we were sailing in the tropics in July practically all the way to Lourenco Marques—Saigon, Singapore, and across the Indian Ocean, the voyage was very hot. Regardless of where our cabin was, we had complete freedom of the ship. It was a one-class ship apart from the actual sleeping quarters, so during the daytime most of us were in the public rooms or on the promenade or boat decks. I understand the Japanese were not agreeable to this at first, that they wanted to make it a regular passenger ship, enforcing restrictions for second- and third-class passengers. If this had happened, what a howl there would have been! However, Ambassador Grew, the US ambassador to Japan, absolutely refused to listen to the Japanese on this, so they finally relented to making it a one-class ship.

By the time we got our tickets and found our berths, it was supper time. We sat at long tables with ten on each side. The food was put on, and we helped ourselves to coffee, bread and margarine. To control the quantity, the main dish and the dessert were served to us. From ordinary standards, the food was not very good, but from the standard we had been living on at Stanley, the Asama's food was so far superior that we considered it first class.

We could always have eaten more of the main dish, but we had all of the bread, coffee and margarine that we wanted. Everyone said the coffee was colored pine leaves, but it was hot and had some taste to it, so it was okay by me. I forgot exactly what we had for the first meal, but it was good and it was the first time we had had any meat, served separately as meat, for many, many months. The little meat we had at Stanley was always in a stew, but on the Asama, we had pieces of meat. There is a vast difference. If you don't believe it, just try living on rice, stew, and boiled lettuce for nearly six months. Then you'll appreciate a piece of meat!

I felt really comfortably full for the first time in months. I went up on deck to meet some old friends. I had known quite a few people who were in Japan at the time war was declared, and they were all on board. They had been in Japan on December 8, and boarded the Asama Maru there before she proceeded to Hong Kong to pick us up. I spent an hour going around, speaking to everyone I knew. We did not have any lengthy talks, as there would be plenty of time for that later, so we just shook hands, asked a few personal questions such as where each other's families were. For the first time in months, you really felt that you were a human being again. Although none of us had any information about our families, as we had not heard a word since December 7th, nevertheless it was reassuring to ask about them and to know, once more, that you were a part of the world.

All the baggage that had been inspected the previous day by the Japanese was dumped on the promenade deck. Everyone was familiar with Stanley habits, so people were not going to leave it around for someone else to take away in the dark. Furthermore, many people thought that the Japanese might have more or less looted the baggage, so they wanted to see what was missing, if anything. For about two hours it was one mad scramble trying to locate your luggage, as where they dumped it was not well lighted. Then you had to get it to your room. Everyone was running this way and that, hands full of suitcases, stumbling over other people's baggage, in the passage ways, bumping into people backing out of staterooms and corridors. I do not believe the four Marx Brothers could have made a better picture than getting located on the Asama Maru that first night.

I helped other people, particularly the women, find their baggage and get it to their rooms. The most general remark that I heard all through the ship that night was, "My, isn't this fine! This is the first time I have ever traveled first class!" In my opinion, the women saying this had no business being on the boat anyway. They should have gone home when our families went home. However, we got all the baggage down. I don't think one single piece had been tampered with. I think some people were rather disappointed at this, as it did not give them a chance to enlarge on some more Japanese atrocities.

That first night I got to bed about midnight. I can't say it was a bed at all; it was a place to lie down, that is about all. There were double bunks, all too short for most Americans. Fortunately, I had an upper one. There were three of these double deckers in a row, and I had a middle one. We slept head to head and feet to feet.

The bunk had some kind of a mattress, stuffed with old tatami, and a sheet and blanket for each bunk. Sleeping down on D deck in the tropics was almost the same as being in a Turkish bath, only not as comfortable. I just laid there and perspired all night long, shifting from one pool of sweat to another, while the tatami soaked it up. Fortunately, I got through the entire trip without catching a cold, but I cannot say this for all.

I was up at daylight on deck, looking over at Stanley and thanking my lucky stars that I was aboard a ship, even if it was a Japanese ship. I was not still behind the barbed wire of the camp. I had seen many sunrises over Stanley, but this was the best one I had ever seen, because it was to be the last.

Smoke was coming from the American kitchen, which the British had taken over. They were getting ready to cook their rice and boiled lettuce. I didn't know what I would have for breakfast, but whatever it was it was bound to be better than the boys in Stanley would have. As I stood at the rail, looking at Stanley, it was a sad sight from just the thought alone of leaving those people there.

The breakfast bell rang at 7:30 AM! No argument about that. Down we all rushed, and those who were not up got up mighty quickly. The people who had gotten on in Japan had been better fed than we had been. You could tell by just looking at a person whether he was from Stanley or not. If he was thin and drawn, he was from Stanley. If you had any doubt, just wait until the meal bell sounded and all doubt was removed. Those who rushed, got there first, ate the fastest, asked for more bread, margarine and coffee; yes, no doubt about it, those people were from Stanley.

No one knew when we were supposed to sail. Some rumors were 10:00 AM, others at noon, then all sorts of other time, up to midnight. We from Stanley did not care. We had heard so many rumors that a few more did not bother us anymore. We were actually out of that place and on our way somewhere, but where we did not much care. All day Tuesday we spent walking around talking to people, looking at Stanley, and finding our way about the ship.

In the middle of the morning the Japanese brought a couple of water boats alongside and started to pump water aboard. These, of course, were former

British barges as were all the launches that towed them were British equipment that had been taken over when Hong Kong "ceased resistance." We knew we would not leave until the water was pumped aboard anyway. Noon came, the lunch bell rang, and there was another wild dash for food. We were still in sight of Stanley with the water pumps working when we were served cold tea at 3:00 PM.

The water barges pushed off at 5:00 PM and forty-five minutes later there was one long blast on the whistle; something was going to happen. For the last couple of hours, the sailors had been batting down the hatches, so we knew that the time for leaving was drawing near. At 6:00 PM there were three long blasts on the whistle, we heard the propellers turning over, and we were finally moving. We were off!

Everyone was on the port side, waving towards Stanley. We were too far out to see anyone, but we were all waving. Suddenly from St. Stephen's came a flash. Someone had gotten a mirror and was signaling us good-bye. The last signal was a V for Victory. I have often wondered if anyone got into trouble over that. Signaling from an internment camp would certainly be a military offense.

When the Japanese gave three blasts of the whistle, it was the only time they did it. I am certain it was done for our farewell to Stanley. When we left Saigon and Singapore, we just pulled out without any ceremony at all, but when we left Stanley, the Japanese pulled on the cord three times, just as if we had been leaving under normal peace-time conditions. I think the Japanese also thought it was a momentous departure. I will say this: it was far better than leaving with no final acknowledgment at all. The whole ship appreciated it, and I am certain the people in Stanley did too.

It was a thrill leaving, but at the same time a very sad sight with Stanley dropping behind us. We saw a few houses on the top of the Peak fade in the distance, and gradually the Island of Hong Kong merged into the haze and disappeared. There was much sobbing and crying amongst the women, many of whom were leaving husbands, brothers, sisters, and close friends behind. Some were crying who were not leaving anyone behind, but had spent all their lives in Hong Kong. Now the past memories of their childhood and many happy gatherings were coming before them as they stood and watched Hong Kong recede in the distance. Sympathy and understanding were extended, as we all knew exactly how everyone felt.

Ruth Briggs, Pasadena, California

A wonderful cable arrived June 5 from New York: "State Department today advises your husband definitely listed to be repatriated by Asama Maru sailing shortly." Hallelujah! A couple of weeks ago they informed me that the Swedish ship Gripsholm was scheduled to sail from the United States about June 10 for exchanging Japanese and American diplomats and civilians. The State Department did not know who, as yet, would be on board besides the diplomatic personnel, but indicated that probably Americans in Hong Kong would make up the first shipload returning from the Far East. That really gave me hope. And, they told us that we could write letters, addressed to the Postmaster of New York City, to American internees returning on the Gripsholm. I immediately told all our relatives and friends.

I hope our letters will reach him. What a relief to know that he is actually on a ship coming home! The Company did not know the exact sailing dates, but estimated the entire trip would take two to three months. How I worry about what he's going through! I wish I could do something to help him, but all I can do is pray that he is all right.

I took the girls to Riverside to celebrate my younger brother's birthday on June 13. Ed and Jane are wonderful, and their two girls, Kay and Judy, are just a year younger each than Kathie and Carol. We all had a wonderful time. They have a couch swing on their front porch, and the girls had a glorious time climbing up on it and swinging. Kathie and Kay took turns riding the tricycle, while Carol and Judy toddled along behind, not wanting to be left out.

These trips out-of-town to visit my family are a life-saver for my sanity. I am careful in my driving around town to save my gas rations so I can visit Riverside, Pomona, and Santa Barbara occasionally. It means so much to me. I try to take some snapshots with my Brownie camera so I can show Norman how the girls have grown and the activities they have done.

Chapter II
From Hong Kong to Singapore

Our first night at sea! We not only had full running lights, but all the decks and every public room was lit. No blackouts for us! In addition to the running lights, there was an illuminated electric cross about ten feet square on each side and also one on the stern. This was our identification, and it was very clear. The hull of the ship was black, and on each side, both fore and aft, white crosses were painted which would show up much better in the daytime than the electric lights would. No one feared being torpedoed; our greatest cause for worry, "Was the repatriation going to go through?" It had all been so vague, postponed twice, and we were still within Japanese territory. No one could feel completely easy until we got out from under their grasp. We worried that anything could upset the whole business, and we could turn around and find ourselves right back in Stanley. This was our one and only fear, much more real in our minds than being torpedoed. However, this first night out, everyone was in pretty good spirits. We were actually moving and headed in the right direction for home!

We were at sea now, and all 934 of us settled down pretty much into a routine. There were two sittings for every meal, breakfast, lunch, and dinner. I think the best meal of the day was breakfast, because we generally had some fresh fruit. There were also eggs, with one pancake served last. This was the best of the whole lot. If you could manage to eat your pancake quickly enough and push the dirty dish under another one so it wouldn't be seen, the chances are you could get a second one. There were so many to serve that the boys could not keep track except by the dirty dishes. For the three plus weeks we were on the Asama I think I pulled this trick about four times. I don't know whether the boy ever got suspicious or not, but at Lourenco Marques I gave him ten Yen; he thanked me very much and gave a rather knowing smile, so I don't think I fooled him.

The food all through the ship was basically the same. The only difference was that first- and second-class got a few extras and the surroundings were a little better as they had table linen. The temperature was also much better higher up on the water line. D deck in the tropics was hot and sticky. However, after six months in an internment camp, the improvement is so great that it seemed just like first class. At least, that is how most of us felt about it.

The first- and second-class dining rooms were run just as if it were a regular passenger trip. They had printed menus, smaller tables, and regular waiter service. I think they also had a choice in the main dish, and the little extras they got were in the way of a little fancier desserts, nuts, and appetizer first course. We did not suffer any down in third class, nor did we go hungry, as the main food was basically the same. First class might have had a choice of chicken or beef whereas we would only get one. And we were waited on by the boy in his undershirt rather than someone in a white coat, but this didn't make much difference to us.

The one big problem on the ship was fresh water for bathing and washing. The Japanese purposely put water restrictions on us which made no sense whatsoever. We had fresh running water in the wash rooms twice a day from 7:00 to 7:30 AM and from 5:00 to 5:30 PM. To us these restrictions appeared unnecessary, as they put on sufficient water in Hong Kong. We should have been able to have had water at least one hour, if not two hours at a time every day.

On D deck there were two wash rooms, one forward and the other aft. With only fifteen wash bowls on each side, these wash rooms were some sight! For the thirty men in each room, there were twice that number outside waiting their turn to wash. Men would line up at 6:30 in the morning and just go in and stand in front of the bowl to wait for the water to come on. The favorite method was to have a bottle and fill it up. When you were finished, you could then take this in early the next morning before the water came on. A quart bottle was sufficient to shave and wash up with, saving a long wait in line.

Traveling in the tropics, perspiring all day and all night long, only a half an hour of running water twice a day was not sufficient. If there had been some real reason for it, I don't think there would have been any comments, but there wasn't. It was just pure cussedness on the part of the Sons of Heaven.

From 2:00 to 5:00 PM you could always get a hot water salt bath, and I took advantage of this. About 3:30 or 4:00 PM the place was generally entirely free, so you had plenty of room, time, and salt water. The difficulty was in getting a little fresh water to rinse off with. Sometimes this was available in the small tub, but generally it wasn't. The tub was regular Japanese style, about six foot square, and you could get in and soak if you so desired.

Another main problem was laundry. Some people did manage to get a little done, but it was next to impossible. Most everyone did their own laundry when they could get water to do it. If you watched your chance, you could manage now and then to get a bowl full of fresh water. I did a little washing twice for the several weeks we were on the Asama. There seemed to be no sense at all to this business of restricted water, because there was a swimming pool full of water. The swimming pool was a reserve supply, and we could not go near it. We arrived at each port with it still full. Particularly across the Indian Ocean, the water situation was bad. We certainly thought that within several days of Lourenco Marques they would ease the restrictions a bit, but they did not. When we arrived in Laurenco Marques, the swimming pool was still full.

On Friday morning, July 3rd, we arrived at the mouth of the Mekong River. We surely thought that we would anchor there and not go to Saigon, 80 miles up the river. We knew we were going to pick up Americans interned there and in Bangkok, but we thought they would be brought down, rather than the Asama going up for them. But up the river we went, and it was quite a sight. I would say the river from bank to bank was not more than 200 feet. There were lots of turns in the river. Several times it surely looked as though we would touch one bank or the other, but we didn't. The river was very deep and had a strong current. It was tropical, marshy country, and we could see native huts and some well cared for plantations in the distance. There were many canals and irrigation ditches running into the river. The main crop, of course, was rice, but there was also a lot of cattle as well as tropical fruits grown on a commercial basis. As the ship wound its way up to Saigon, we also saw a lot of bird life; the parrots with their bright colors were particularly interesting.

We arrived at Saigon shortly before noon, anchoring about five miles below the city. As soon as we dropped anchor, the boat was completely surrounded by small sampans. They had native fruits to sell—bananas, mangoes, pomelos, pineapples, and coconuts. They certainly did a roaring business. They could not come aboard, and we could not go down to them. We transacted business by getting a basket, lowering it down by rope with money in it. Then, by means of a rudimentary sign language, hollering and pointing to the various articles they had for sale, your basket would be filled up. I suppose the prices were several times what they could get in their ordinary market, but they made change for us. We had very little small money, as most of our money was in 5 and 10 Yen notes. We would send a ten Yen note down in the basket, and up would come fruits and change. I imagine there was about 1000 percent profit on the merchandise with an additional profit on the money exchange. By the way the sampans fought for position, I presume the profit was very good, but no one complained. Although we had a little fresh fruit on the ship, we did not have much, so we just loaded up.

In the afternoon a small Thailand steamer arrived with the people from Bangkok. "Diplomat" or rather the French version of it was written on the side of the boat. Just as the exchange was taking place, it started to rain. It would. About 80 people were transferred to the Asama in an open barge. Now we were really full.

All night long it was hot and sultry, by far the worst night on the Asama. It was hot in Singapore, but there we were out in the open. Here we were hemmed in by the riverbanks. Just take my word for it, it was good and hot.

The next morning we pulled anchor at 10:00 AM and went down the river. At 3:00 PM we got to the mouth of the river, but it was low tide. We could not get over the sand bar, so turned around and went back up stream to anchor. This turning around was not a comfortable feeling. We were not certain of the exact reason; we only surmised it. What was going to happen now? Had negotiations broken down? Were we going to be put back and thrown into a concentration camp again? Such a possibility was very real to us. There was quite a lot of speculation on this for the few hours that we were anchored. We heard the anchor being pulled up around 6:00 PM and the propellers turned. When we went over the sand bar and headed out to the open sea, a sigh of relief went through the entire ship.

There was no epidemic on the ship, but after we left Saigon, most of the children and a good number of the adults had some kind of a cold. Some blamed the people who got on at Saigon of bringing the cold germs, but I think the main cause for the colds was just the close quarters that we had through the tropics.

Five days later we reached Singapore. We stayed for several days, but saw nothing of Singapore as we anchored outside the harbor. We could only see land faintly in the distance.

The Italian liner Conte Verdi arrived at Singapore the same time we did and anchored about a mile from us. Italy had not yet joined the Allies. The Conte Verdi had come from Shanghai, bringing Americans from the interior parts of China and coast ports other than Shanghai. The Americans in Canton, Swatow, Amoy, Foochow and other interior cities such as Hankow, and cities to the north like Peking and Tienstin had been brought to Shanghai by the Japanese and put aboard the Conte Verdi. I think most of them had been interned in Shanghai about the middle of April. Very few Shanghai residents were aboard, as Shanghai residents were not interned. Only Shanghai residents who had actually been in jail, or connected with newspapers and the Red Cross were aboard the Conte Verdi. All in all, there were around 650 Americans aboard.

Of course, all of us on the Asama wanted to know who was aboard, as most of us had friends, and some relatives—husbands and wives—who had been in China. The Italian officers came aboard the Asama and had the passenger list, but the Japanese would not let any of us see it. There were no messages back and forth between the two ships at all as far as passengers were concerned. This was war, and the Japanese were not running any chances of any information being exchanged.

On the Asama we had some 60 South American diplomats aboard who were also being repatriated, although none of the South American countries were at war with Japan. Only the Chileans were permitted ashore. The rumors that went around the ship after they got back from their visit to town! I say rumors because I think that is exactly what they were. The most talked about story was that of British prisoners being stripped to the waist, coerced to work cleaning refuse, repairing streets and buildings, and doing all sorts of rough manual labor with the Japanese standing over them with fixed bayonets. Maybe it was true, but I have my doubts. The Japanese did not do this in Hong Kong, although I realize that this does not mean that they didn't do it in Singapore.

However, one of the main reasons for internment in Hong Kong was to break all communications that the enemy nationals had with the Chinese or other third-nation subjects in Hong Kong. The reason was to make the Chinese or third-nation subjects absolutely dependent upon the Japanese. Now, if they had put British soldiers to work in Singapore, they surely would've made some contact with the Chinese to get information in or out, possibly planning means for escape. There were plenty of Chinese and Malayans in Singapore who would work to support themselves. They could work much better than any Westerner could in that climate. My opinion is that the Japanese would much rather have them do the work than British soldiers, who could be watched strictly in a concentration camp, but not watched effectively if they were out in the streets working. Maybe some were made to work as a punishment, but I am extremely skeptical of the fact that the Japanese put all or large numbers of the British soldiers to work. At Stanley, they offered us work for extra food; maybe they had done the same in Singapore.

When the South Americans came back, all they brought with them was liquor, and they brought it by the case. They reported that all the stores were closed, and the city was dead. Well, they had found a few stores open to buy the whisky. I imagine that Singapore was just about like Hong Kong in that it had a large Chinese population. Although the Japanese were trying to get as many people to leave as possible to go back on the farms, it takes quite a little time to move a million and a half people. Hong Kong was by no means dead; the stores were open and doing business, although nothing as compared to what they had done before the war. When you have large concentrations of people, activity must go on. I don't believe Singapore was any exception. So much for the rumors; you can decide what most likely is true.

The Japanese name for Singapore was Shonan Port (the light of the east). One thing that did not happen in Singapore was that the Asama did not fuel. This was very significant to us. Here we were, right in the middle of the oil country, and no oil was taken aboard. The Asama was a diesel ship, and they had fueled in Yokohama for the round trip to Lourenco Marques and back! This could be done and was probably one of the reasons why we were short of water. Many water tanks had been filled with fuel. It was also a good indication that the fuel supplies had been pretty well destroyed by the Dutch. None of this Hong Kong business of leaving installations full of oil for the Japanese to get. There is no question but what the Japanese needed every bit of oil they could get. They would never take oil out of Japan if they could get it anywhere else; the oil used in Japan must all be imported. Right near rich oil country and no oil taken aboard was a good indication to me that a thorough and systematic job of destruction had been done before the Japanese actually arrived.

From Japan to Singapore, or rather Shonan Port, the Asama operated on Tokyo time. Singapore was at least 1,800 miles west of Tokyo, which meant the sun time was several hours different. We had breakfast at 7:30, and it was still dark. This meant that we had very long evenings, but that made no difference to us whatsoever. It is just an indication as to the length the Japanese will go to extend their sphere of influence. Every territory that they take over must have Tokyo time, regardless of where it is.

Ruth Briggs, Pasadena, California

It's now July, and Norman is somewhere on the high seas heading for Lourenco Marques, Portuguese East Africa. The Japanese businessmen in the United States were being held at the Greenbrier Hotel in West Virginia, a fancy place, I hear, while the Americans were in a prison! Now I'm on pins and needles, hoping the telephone will ring any moment to tell me when the ship comes in, and when he will board the Gripsholm. And, of course, when he will actually get home! I know I can't stay by it all the time and looking at it won't make it ring. The Company wrote to say that they could not pay our expenses to meet husbands in New York when the ship comes in. And, they said to watch the papers for ship arrivals, as schedules were kept secret. They also told us that we could write air mail letters directly to the Gripsholm at Lourenco Marques. So, I told everyone again where they could write. I hope the letters reach Norman and give him some comfort. I sure wish I could put myself in one so I could be there with him!

We had a wonderful birthday party on July 15 for Carol's second birthday and Pa Briggs. It was a nice surprise when she was born on his birthday. We had names all picked out, with Marcia being the name for a girl. But my brother Walter and his wife Edith had a baby girl two weeks earlier, naming her Marcia. So we had to go back to the drawing board for girl names. When she was born on Pa's birthday, it was easy—we named her for his sister, Irene Carroll, except we reversed the names to Carol Irene.

The party was fun, but several two-year-olds can be a handful. I set up tables on the porch for serving ice cream and cake. All had a good time—the grandparents, the children, and even the mothers. I thought Carol was a handful before, but now come the terrible twos. But she's generally a very happy little girl, and I'm lucky to have two wonderful children. I only wish Norman were here with me.

Chapter III
Exchange at Lourenco Marques

Leaving Singapore, we went southeast through the Sunda Straits which are between Sumatra and Java. The Sunda Straits are very narrow, and going through them was really beautiful. Sumatra was on the starboard, Java on the port side, and numerous small islands all around. We saw no local junks or sampans, but I am certain that these little islands were inhabited, because we could see little huts and other buildings on them. We saw one submerged boat, evidently the result of a battle, and could well understand why we went through the straits in the daytime and not at night. It was a perfect day and a beautiful sight. The only regret was the conditions that had forced us to view it.

We were through the straits by late afternoon, heading straight out across the Indian Ocean for Lourenco Marques. Everyone on the ship was greatly improved in spirits. We had seen the last of the Japanese occupied territory, so the chances of us going ahead were much better than for turning back. For the first time, we really believed this was repatriation and the deal was going to go through. In Saigon and Singapore there was too much ground that could be used for concentration camps. Now we had seen the last of land. The next port would be Lourenco Marques, so the chances were more than even that we would make it.

All the excitement and variation was over, so the ship settled into a routine. When I say routine, I mean routine, and what a rigid routine it was.

There were three things I never saw so much of in my life: card playing, Bible readings, and people talking to themselves. Of the 934 on board, everyone was doing one of those three things. I did not happen to see anyone doing all three at once, but I would not be a bit surprised, as most of us were either playing cards and talking to ourselves, or reading the Bible and muttering away. The Catholic Fathers were quite the card players. I would not be a bit surprised that now and then, between a bridge play, they would pick up their Bible, read a few lines and thus accomplish all three activities in one motion.

There were bridge games in every public room. It was very difficult to find space, in fact next to impossible unless you got up before everyone else to get squatters rights for a table. The smoking room was reserved exclusively for card games, mostly poker. Every night there would be four or five games of poker going on, but there were not sufficient poker tables to meet the demand. Our little session that we had in Stanley continued on, but we could only have a table every other night as we alternated with others. And so on life went—card playing, Bible reading, and muttering to yourself were the only forms of diversion.

On our second night out after going through the straits, the engines stopped. The Conte Verdi passed us, and we thought she was going to keep right on going, but when she got ahead of us she also stopped. Nobody knew what was going on. The two ships were signaling back and forth. What was it all about? Were negotiations broken down? Were we going back to Singapore? We drifted for about twenty minutes, when we then felt the propellers turning over. We were not turning around, but going straight ahead! Boy, did we all breathe a sigh of relief. The Conte Verdi gradually dropped behind us, taking up her regular position. In about an hour, we had regained our normal speed. We figured that everything was okay, just minor engine trouble that was corrected.

On account of the heat quite a few people were sleeping on deck. At 5:00 AM the deck crew would come along with fire hoses, washing down the decks. They did not give any advance notice, however. Whenever they saw anyone asleep, they would just turn the hose in that direction and watch the results. Of course, the person would scramble to get himself up, grabbing his bedding which would be soaked. The Japanese sailors would stand back and laugh.

It was a funny sight. Some people tried to make an atrocity story out of it. But on every ship I have ever been on, they always wash the decks down first thing in the morning. The Asama was no different in this respect. What do you think a bunch of American sailors would have done to a boat full of

Japanese? I myself thought this fire hose business was quite amusing. If people were dumb enough to go up there and sleep, well let them get wet. They knew what was going to happen. Of course, their plan was to wake up in time, but it did not always work out that way.

The attitude of the crew on the Asama was perfectly okay. There was no face slapping, kicking around, or any insolence whatsoever as far as I could see. Naturally, it was not a pleasure trip. No one asked anything of the crew; we let them alone, and they let us alone. They did what was absolutely essential. What more could you expect? At the table, if we wanted more bread, we asked for it, and they brought it.

The officers, of course, did not mingle with the passengers; I am certain they would not have been welcomed if they had. The deck stewards, however, seemed to get around a bit. I saw them playing shuffleboard and other deck games with some of the passengers. In fact, Ambassador Grew played shuffleboard every morning. On one or two occasions, the chief deck steward played with him. The Japanese liked to take pictures of these things, particularly so at night in the smoking room when the card games were going on. They would come in and take some pictures, all for propaganda purposes to show everyone how happy we were and how kind the Japanese were to let us enjoy ourselves. We were happy all right; we were getting out from under the clutches of the Japanese.

There was one group on board that had a good time, and that was the children. There was a special children's play room on the promenade deck which was a busy place. The parents formed a committee so there was always someone there to look after the children. The children were encouraged to stay in this part of the ship, which in the main they did. There were no servants, which most of the parents were used to from living in the Orient, so it was also good training for the parents to watch out for their children.

The days continued on one after the other, all just alike. Card playing, Bible reading, and muttering to oneself were still the main activities. Finally, on Wednesday morning, July 22, we sighted the coast of Mozambique. We were all up early, and was it ever cold! We knew it was winter in this part of the world, but this was the first cool weather we had felt in quite some time. The sun was out, but the wind was blowing a pretty stiff gale. It was too cold to stay out on the deck that was not protected. Those who had overcoats made good use of them.

There was a little cape or peninsula at the entrance of the harbor with a lighthouse on the point. A freighter was beached right in front of it. We presumed that it had been torpedoed and managed to beach itself rather than just trying to cut corners and running aground right square in front of the lighthouse. As soon as we rounded the cape and proceeded up the channel into the harbor, the weather changed from winter into summer. We were off the open ocean and the gale had subsided, making it much warmer. Lourenco Marques is 22 degrees south of the equator, so the climate is mild, but it did not feel like it outside in the channel.

As we continued down the coast, we spotted a big hotel on the cliffs. We then turned directly into the harbor, and there was the promised land—the port of Lourenco Marques, Portuguese East Africa. A few months ago, if anyone were to tell me that I would ever see this place, I would have told them they were crazy. But there was Lourenco Marques before us, and that was a beautiful sight!

It looked like an international safe haven, as there were about thirty ships in the harbor. The first ship that we saw in the distance was an American oil tanker. There was Old Glory flying from the stern. It was the first time we had seen that in many months. As we approached nearer, we could see that it was a pretty old ship. It needed painting and fixing up, but there she was, fully loaded and flying the American flag!

This tanker was right at the entrance to the harbor and was the first ship we passed. We passed very close and just as we came abreast of her, the captain lowered one of the windows on the bridge, leaned out, pulled on the whistle, and up the masthead ran a brand new American flag which he had saved for the occasion! Did we ever let loose! Absolutely everyone on the Asama shouted at the top of their lungs, waving hands, handkerchiefs, coats, shirts, and in fact everything that we could lay our hands on! It was one of the great thrills of my life. Here we had been through war and internment camp. Now we were about to be free, and there was the American flag. We showed the true American spirit—all spontaneous, nothing planned, and that was the true American part of it.

The whole crew of the tanker came out on deck, and we waved and shouted back and forth. As we continued on into the harbor, every ship picked up the spirit, blasting their whistles, giving the V for Victory signal as we went by. It was truly a royal welcome and made you proud to be an American. I shall never forget that event, and I think everyone else on board felt the same. Our thanks are due to the tanker captain. The Japanese stood by and watched all this. I wonder what they really thought. All of their public demonstrations are so highly organized with flag waving, bands, "banzai" and propaganda that they don't know how to react to a spontaneous uprising. I think they saw the true spirit behind it, and they didn't like it for it was something that they didn't have. They couldn't get it, and most important of all, they could not conquer it. It was a great thrill, one hundred percent American, and we were all proud of it.

We swung into the harbor proper, and there was the Gripsholm. We slowly moved in until we were right opposite her, then pulled ahead about a boat length and stopped. Tugs took us in charge and pushed the Asama into the pier where the Gripsholm was. We docked stern to stern, about twenty feet apart. Ropes were thrown over, we were made secure, and thus the first half of our journey had been completed.

No sooner had we tied up than the sterns of both ships were full. The Japanese on the Gripsholm were looking at us, and we were looking at them, both looking at our future home. We were looking forward with pleasant anticipation, but I doubt if they were. Some of our missionary friends hollered over to them in Japanese, asking about various people. There were not many of us interested in this, and soon we turned away.

But we did that too soon, for just then some of the crew of the Gripsholm came out and threw us oranges and apples. Boy, did we go for them! Everyone was on the back deck of the Asama. I am sure it must have lowered in the water a couple of feet, with the bow up proportionally. This did not last long, because they couldn't stand there and throw fruit to us all day. They assured us, however, that there was plenty on board, not to worry. The Japanese did not eat it all; there was plenty for us.

Shortly after lunch we heard that there was mail for us on the promenade deck. We all rushed up. I was fairly lucky to be one of the first in line. The mail had come out on the Gripsholm, and they sent it over to us on the Asama. The first news from home in more than seven months! I got my letters—29 in all— and were they ever appreciated! I think everyone who ever knew me had written me a line. All my family had written, there were pictures from home, and all were well. Everyone was busy that afternoon reading mail. We did not read our letters once, but several times. You would see people get their mail and then rush away hunting for some quiet spot where they could sit down and read it. Needless to say, everyone was extremely happy and joyful that afternoon and evening.

Later that afternoon our passports were taken up by the State Department, and we were given a landing card by the Portuguese Government. The purpose of taking our passports was so that we could not leave Lourenco

Marques. You could travel, but not when and where you wished. It was impressed upon us that we would not be entirely free until we landed in the USA.

Everyone wanted to go ashore, but we were not permitted off the ship at that time, and very few people were permitted on. These were Japanese restrictions, nothing to do with the international agreement or the Portuguese authorities. The three ships were tied up at the same pier in line—the Conte Verdi, the Gripsholm, and the Asama Maru. The Japanese had arrived two days ahead of us, and they were going and coming off the Gripsholm as they pleased. A few hours after the Conte Verdi tied up, they were permitted off and had the freedom of the city. Why couldn't we go ashore? We could get no answer, but we found out later that it was just pure Japanese cussedness and nothing else. They did it to be annoying. They were in authority, and they were going to retain their hold over us just as long as they could.

The next morning we were up early and told that the exchange would start at 9:00 AM. We were to line up with our baggage on deck and advised to take one bag with us as the rest would be put on the Gripsholm for us. As for myself, I only had two pieces of luggage and a blanket roll, so wherever I went, my belongings went with me.

The pier at Lourenco Marques was modern and up-to-date with traveling cranes and railroad tracks on the pier. The Portuguese ran in some empty freight cars, and the exchange started. We went off the stern of the Asama, passed along on the inside of the freight cars, and went aboard the stern of the Gripsholm. The Japanese got off the bow of the Gripsholm, passed along the outside of the freight cars, and went aboard the bow of the Asama. We thumbed noses at each other between the freight cars, and that was all there was to it. No checking, no ceremony, all very simple. The Gripsholm was cleared of the Japanese, and we were all aboard before noon on Thursday morning, July 23, 1942.

You should have seen the difference in the procession of these two groups of people. It was very easy to tell the treatment each group had received by just looking at them and seeing the personal belongings attached to each. Here we were with our clothes ragged and torn, our suitcases, cardboard boxes, straw baskets, and any container that we could get to hold our few personal belongings, tied up with rope, string, wire and anything that we could find. We were thin, drawn, and looked as though we had been through the mill, which we had. No doubt about that.

In contrast to us, the Japanese got off with snappy new American clothes, nice matched leather luggage. They looked well fed and happy. The women particularly looked very stylish with new hats and matched outfits. They surely presented a far different sight than we did. Well, they were welcome to it, as I think very few of them had any realization as to what they were going back to. I imagine that many of them had not been in Japan for many years. They were certainly going back to a different Japan than the one they had left. They were leaving all the good things behind them, and they had nothing but want, restrictions, and disappointment to look forward to. Yes, they were welcome to all that they had; they would need it. We were returning to a land of plenty, where we could get sufficient clothes and food. America, too, we would find different from the country we had left, but it would certainly be nothing like the conditions we were leaving behind—6 ounces of boiled rice and a little boiled lettuce each day. We were leaving these conditions behind, but the Japanese were going to it.

Ruth Briggs, Pasadena, California

Yes, I guess the terrible twos have begun, although I can't really say that Carol is really that terrible. She's just trying to assert herself and be a "helper" to me...at least that's how I interpret her.

Today was one of those days. I was doing the wash and, as usual, Carol was "helping." I am lucky to have one of the new wringer washing machines which really assists me in getting all the laundry done. Carol was on a chair handing me the wet clothes to put through the wringer, then into the basket to hang outside on the line.

The telephone rang, and I thought it might be news about Norman. I told Carol, who usually minds me, to not touch the clothes until I got back. It was a neighbor who called, asking if I could help her with an errand. Suddenly I heard Carol screaming, and I threw down the phone and went running. Carol's arm was in the wringer, up to her elbow! I unplugged the washing machine, and turned the lever that released the wringers, a process that seemed to take ages although I guess it was only a matter of moments. Carol's arm was flattened, with a bulging blood bubble formed at her elbow! I didn't know if I should put it under cold water or what, but I did know I needed to take her to the hospital.

The neighbor that had called me heard the commotion and came running over. She helped to calm me, wrapped Carol in a blanket, and called the hospital. It seemed forever to get to the hospital, Carol crying all the time. I didn't know if her arm was broken or permanently damaged or what.

My memory of the hospital is kind of hazy, but the doctors assured me that her arm wasn't broken. The wringer had pushed all the blood up, forming a big blood blister at her elbow. They drained it and told me that a scar would most likely form, but the ability and use of her arm should be normal. Thank goodness!

The next day, July 27, was much better. Carol was managing okay, not complaining too much. And then, I received two cables, one from New York, and ONE FROM NORMAN! Norman's came direct from Lourenco Marques: "Thanks letters meeting NY convenient ok otherwise coming immediately home. Well. Love all, Briggs." He had arrived, and was well! And, our letters reached him! Oh, what great news to hear directly from him. Next, I want to hear his voice. Then, of course, be with him forever!

The New York cable from the Company said they had received a cable from Lourenco Marques advising them all Standard Vacuum staff was aboard the Gripsholm and all were well. Personal mail was received and all send greetings to family and friends. So, now he's on the second leg of the trip to home!

Chapter IV
The Gripsholm

Once on the Gripsholm we had to stay in the public rooms or on the decks while they cleaned all the cabins. We were told that cabins would be assigned to us after dinner, and that a buffet lunch would be served immediately on deck.

Did we have lunch? It was the first real food we had seen since December 8th. Long tables were set up on A deck aft. When the stewards brought the food, the whole ship burst into acclaim. The excitement was almost, but not quite, as great as when we passed the tanker at the entrance to the harbor. There seemed to be no end to the platters of food that were brought forth. Bowls and bowls of salad, several cold turkeys, and all sorts of cold meats, fresh fruit, cheese, and all the bread and butter that one could desire. We just gorged ourselves. I am certain that everyone went back for seconds, and a few made a couple of trips after that.

There were, of course, several lines as 1,500 people could not all be fed at once. You could get hungry standing in line watching the food go by, but there were no complaints. There was more than plenty for all, and we knew that our turn would come.

When the whole 1,500 of us let go when we saw the food, the Japanese came running to the stern of the Asama to see what it was all about. They saw all right, and I think even their mouths watered. Not so much from the sight of food, because they had been fed amply, but rather from the fact that they were saying good-bye to it. Lean days were in store for them, and I think they felt it.

That was some lunch. On account of the conditions under which it was eaten, I have never had a better one, nor do I expect to. After being six months in a concentration camp, and then to be fed like that—all you wanted of the best food in the world—it was really an event of a lifetime. Try rice and boiled lettuce for six months, and then be given a chance at real food. What would your reaction be?

After lunch, we were told that we were free to go anywhere we wanted to in the city. Dinner wasn't until 6:00 PM for the first sitting and 7:00 PM for the second, so up to town we went. Real freedom!

The first thing I did was to get a haircut. Then I wandered up and down the main street, looking into the store windows and just generally inspecting the town. I returned to the Gripsholm around 5:00 PM. I certainly wasn't going to miss any meals, so I was ready for the first sitting.

After dinner I went up on deck to wait for the cabin assignments. The Gripsholm was a Swedish ship, run and operated by a Swedish crew, chartered by the American Government to take the Japanese from New York to Lourenco Marques and then bring us back to the United States. For some reason, the American Government sent eight pursers from the American Export Lines to assist the Swedes. In addition, the US flew out another person to take special charge of the billeting so that everything would go smoothly. I am certain that the Swedes wished they had never had their nine helpers, especially the one who was flown out to take charge, because what a mess they made. Big executive stuff, you know; fly an expert out to show how things are done.

The nine US helpers took over the combination library and reading room on A deck for their office. Billeting was to start at 8:00 PM. They had six tables set up, and they sat behind them with a mass of papers of the ship plans, passenger lists, and all manner of forms. At 8:00 PM they opened the door to let a single file enter. The billeting started by going to the first table, giving your name which was checked on the list, and some notations made. Then you were handed a piece of paper and went to the next table to check more references on the forms, and finally you were given a cabin number and berth.

The one line entering was divided into two once inside the room. At the absolute minimum it took one minute to deal with each person, but in reality the average was around three minutes. By doing some math, which the expert helpers obviously didn't do, even if the time were kept to the minimum one minute, only 120 people per hour could be billeted with that system. That meant, of course, that with 1,500 people to take care of, it would take 12 hours and 30 minutes. It was an impossible situation. We thought at least that they would have eight or ten lines and that everything would be in order. But, this was just the start of the real mess.

In the first place, they did not have the complete passenger list. People were in line whose names were not on the list at all. And assignments were messed up. A woman would go down to her assigned cabin and find three men there. Or a man would find women in the compartment. So back upstairs they would go to get a new assignment. Well, the helper at the table did not know how the mistake had been made. Instead of trying to find out, he just gave a new assignment. Nine times out of ten this would also be occupied by the opposite sex.

Outside on the decks everything was in a perfect uproar because everyone was trying to get preference in line so they could get their space and go to bed. The situation was just going from bad to worse, with things getting more bawled up all the time. Most assignments were generally wrong, so it was just confusion and more confusion. By 3:00 AM they just threw up their hands and told people to go and sleep wherever they could find space. Most of the people used their heads. When they found an empty bunk, they just went in and took it. There were no shortage of bunks, but even in spite of this, many people slept in the public rooms.

The next day, the big executive who had been flown out to especially take care of the billeting decided that the only thing to do was to discard everything and start in all over again from scratch. The people who had gotten assignments the previous night were told these were canceled and a new berth would be given. More help was called for, so they asked the men who were being repatriated who were with the American President Lines to give them help on billeting. The only difference this made was that the American President Lines people looked out for themselves and got a first-class cabin.

Well, they went through the whole thing again, only to find out that some of the people who had been assigned cabins on the first night refused to move. It also took them some time to get a complete passenger list, showing the name, age, and sex of the 1,500 Americans. The billeting started on Thursday night at 8:00 PM and was not finished until Saturday at midnight. In the meantime, people were sleeping wherever they could find space. A more complete mess you never saw in your life. The four Marx Brothers could not have gotten the thing anymore gummed up if they had tried. Probably any six-year-old child who could count up to ten could have done infinitely better.

When all the smoke was over and everyone had a berth, we discovered the same basic principle had been used as on the Asama. That is, the diplomats were given the best spaces, and then the first and second class was filled with women and children. There was much bad feeling over this from the men who took what was left in second and third class. We had taken the brunt of it on the Asama, and we thought we should be given some preference on the Gripsholm where conditions were much better. On the Gripsholm the largest number in any cabin was four people, and all the cabins had water in them. For those people who had first-class cabins for the first time on the Asama, why should they be in first class all the way? The weather was going to be much cooler from here, and the general conditions far better. Why not give someone else a chance in first class?

Furthermore, a number of the American firms had prepaid the passage in New York with the understanding that their employees should be given preference in space. I know Standard Oil always sent their employees first class. There was no attention paid to this whatsoever. When we received our baggage from the Asama, some had baggage labels with cabin assignments on them, but the cabin number had been erased. In any event, the whole thing was very poorly handled.

Of course the whole town heard about it. What a show we put on in front of the Japanese. So that is American organization, is it? The Swedes said they had never seen such a mess in all their lives. They had been running ships for generations and were used to having a full passenger list. When they picked up the Japanese in New York, their billeting was no problem. What a spectacle we put on! More ironic that we had sent a person especially to make this mess!

Although most of us endured the debacle, there was one amusing incident that happened during the mess of getting assignments. When the line from the library extended out into the lounge and it got to be about 2:00 AM, one of the women started to complain that she did not know what to do about Sonny. She carried on at great length about Sonny and how hard it was on him. A younger woman had gotten her assignment. As the older woman was complaining so much, the younger woman thought that Sonny must be a baby in arms, so she offered to give up her berth for the night so that Sonny would have a place to sleep. The older woman thanked her very much and assured all the people around that this was greatly appreciated. She would go and wake Sonny up so that he could go to bed and have a few hours of comfortable sleep. Imagine the surprise of all who had heard this offer made and accepted when they saw the mother walk over to the grand piano. Underneath was a long bundle of blankets. She shook the blankets, and then, section by section, like unfolding a carpenter's ruler, up comes Sonny who happened to be about 6 foot 2 inches and around 140 pounds. Sonny was fourteen years old. Imagine how the woman felt who had given up her berth for a supposed baby in arms! Well, it takes all kinds to make a world.

We were back in civilization again, because the paperwork had started; carbon copies by the million had to be signed. No one had any money, so we were given some, signing a promissory note for our passage. The trip on the Asama was free, provided by the Japanese Government. From Lourenco Marques to New York, the fare was $525, plus $50 for extra expense, such as baggage handling. We all signed a promissory note for $575. In addition, we signed a separate promissory note for the equivalent of $25 in local Portuguese currency to cover whatever expenses we might have while there.

But we were FREE to go into town, as we were told we would not be sailing for several days. The $25 was changed into 625 Portuguese escudos, and it certainly helped to transform our passengers. The little belongings people had were in a couple of suitcases and clothes had gotten pretty ragged. Everyone went into town and fixed themselves with new outfits. When I saw some of these people with their new clothes, I did not recognize them. Yes, we were quite the lads of the village, new squeaky shoes, loud ties, and mostly in the British national uniform—gray flannels and a blue coat with brass buttons. Some of the fit was not great, as everything was thrown together in a hurry, but it was a vast improvement, and everyone felt good to be in new, clean clothes.

The only things the Americans bought were clothes. Can you guess what the Japanese bought? They were in town two days ahead of us, and there was practically nothing left in the food stores. They bought sugar, big sacks of flour, and all the tinned goods they could lay their hands on. They also bought watches, fountain pens, and cameras by the dozen. Some even bought automobile tires. There was nothing movable or that could be carried that the Japanese did not buy. Taxis were going back and forth all day long between town and the Asama Maru. I guess the Japanese had some idea of the conditions they were going back to. I saw one Japanese walking back to the ship. Just as he was ready to go up the gang plank, he tripped and dropped 10 pounds of sugar. You should have seen the expression on his face! He looked at this watch, turned around and went back up town, presumably to buy more sugar.

We would pass each other on the streets and in the stores. No incidents took place as far as I know. The town was well policed, and we were not taking any chances of starting a gang fight, being arrested, and thrown into the cooler, only to watch the Gripsholm sail from a prison window. I think the Japanese thought the same. One day I was sitting in a restaurant when several Japanese came in and sat down at the next table. We looked across and through each other. Before I left, there were quite a few groups of both Americans and Japanese, but nothing happened. Perhaps the several Portuguese policemen scattered around the place had something to do with it. They were pretty efficient-looking policemen.

Did the Japanese have money? They had rolls and rolls of American currency. Compare that to the 100 Yen we were given when we left Hong Kong. Apparently, the US Government had let them take all that they had. I would not be a bit surprised if some had access to their company funds also. The night before they sailed, they hung around the gangplank of the Gripsholm wanting to buy any yen that we had. They were getting rid of all the US money, thinking that the Japanese Government might take it away from them when they arrived in Japan. The chances are they could get the goods they bought in, but American money was a different question. Japan could use this money in neutral ports to buy war supplies.

Within one week the little town of Lourenco Marques had 3,000 new customers, and good customers too! Americans bought because they had nothing, and the Japanese bought because they were stocking in preparation of going back to nothing. Did the stores ever make money! I don't know what the prices were before the circus came to town, but I'm sure they raised them. It was war time, but even so the prices seemed way out of proportion. Ordinary shirts which sell in the US for $1.00 or $1.50 were selling for $4.00 to $5.00 and were of inferior quality. The stores were making money from the Americans and Japanese. You can't blame them.

The town of Lourenco Marques was pretty and attractive. In fact, it reminded me very much of some of the smaller California towns. The climate is similar to southern California, maybe a little warmer. The town had a population of 50,000. Of this there were only around 1,200 Europeans, mostly Portuguese. The rest were native South Africans, very big and very black.

The streets were nice and wide, with the real downtown shopping section extending about four blocks each way from the main intersection. Most of the buildings were two stories high, but they did have several four-story buildings. They also had a big central market where you could buy all the local fruits and vegetables you wanted. The residential section of the town was quite nice, with modern bungalow houses.

Lourenco Marques was one the ports for Johannesburg, the other being the British port of Durban. Quite a lot of citrus fruit is grown nearby and shipped all over. Lourenco is also quite a popular winter and vacation resort. Looking out over the country beyond the city, it looked just exactly like southern California or Arizona. I shall always have very pleasant recollections of it.

Lourenco Marques was also thriving as it was a neutral port and a safe haven from the war. In port when we were there were ships from many nations. There were no war ships and no convoys were made up here, but Axis submarines would wait outside to get ships as they were entering or leaving the port. During our stay, we heard numerous stories of ships that had been torpedoed. The port was full of crews who had lost their ships. They counted themselves lucky, because many of their fellow crew members did not make it. We brought back on the Gripsholm thirty Swedes who had been members of a crew whose ship had been torpedoed. With the war, Lourenco Marques was a pretty busy place. Under normal conditions, I think it was somewhat of a dreamy, semi-tropical community.

There are many jokes about the Swiss Navy, but I actually saw a Swiss ship. During World War I the Swiss built up a fleet of ships to import their food supplies, especially grains. France and Italy were on our side then; the Swiss used ports there to transport the food products to Switzerland. What they were doing here, however, I was not sure. I doubt they are using any Axis ports because if they were, I don't think they would have gotten through the British blockade into Lourenco. Anyway, just believe me when I say there were Swiss ships.

When we were not in town, our favorite place to sit and hang out was at the head of the gangplank. It was our "community center." If you had made plans to go to town with someone, the place to meet was at the head of the gangplank.

I was sitting there one evening, and an incident happened that was the forerunner of more to come. A man came up the gangplank who was rather the worse for wear, having imbibed a little more than he could handle. He was weaving from side to side. The few of us gathered were betting as to whether he could make the grade or not. With the help of both handrails, and a Portuguese policeman (there was always one at the end of the gangplank) and a Swede steward, he finally made the deck.

Just as he made the deck, one of the missionary passengers, who was hunting for increased business and wanted to show a favorable report to his head office when he landed in New York, went up to him and asked our inebriated friend: "Have you found Jesus?" From the reply received, I don't think he had. Furthermore, the profounder of the question thought that it was the better part of discretion to retire and not follow up his original question with any more ground work.

We had many Catholic Fathers aboard. Generally they only wore their vestments on Sunday, wearing ordinary clothes the rest of the time. They liked to talk to the crew quite a bit, and some spoke some Swedish. One day in port, one of the Fathers in ordinary dress was standing on the aft deck, talking to some members of the crew. Another one of our passengers who was also looking for increased "sales figures" approached the crew. Just as luck would have it, he picked out the Father to start on. The promoter had several leaflets in his hand and asked the Father: "Could I not interest you in Christianity?"

The Japanese sailed on Saturday noon almost without ceremony. I say almost. About twenty-five Americans went over to the Asama Maru to wave good-bye. As the ship pulled away, they even bowed in Japanese fashion to show their respect. Now, I ask you, can you believe that one? If they felt that way, you'd think they would have the common decency to keep it to themselves. Many of us thought maybe they should have gone back on the Asama.

On Tuesday morning all shore leave was canceled, so we knew that we would be off fairly soon. At 10:00 AM the gangplank was taken in, and a couple of tugs took us in charge. Our departure was far different than our arrival—no whistles or commotion of any kind. We proceeded out of the harbor, down the channel. When we came abreast of the lighthouse, a little boat came out, we dropped the pilot, and then, with one long blast on the whistle, we bade final farewell to Lourenco Marques.

Ruth Briggs, Pasadena, California

Carol's arm is healing, although it has formed a big scab which I imagine will turn into a scar. But it doesn't seem to bother her anymore. She bounces around normally now as she did before. She has helped me with the wash again, but hasn't tried to put anything into the wringer. And I certainly don't leave her alone anymore for a minute!

Today was my brother Walter's birthday, so we all went to Santa Barbara to celebrate. Ed and his family were there too, so we all had fun, including the six girls.

It was fun watching the little cousins play together. And Kathie and Carol enjoyed playing with the other daddies too. Soon, hopefully, Norman will be home to play with them like a regular daddy.

I cherish times like this with my family, but it makes me miss Norman more. His parents have been really wonderful to me and such a help, with them living so close—only a few blocks away. I see them several times a week, and we always have Sunday dinner together.

Pa is good at entertaining the girls. He loves to draw them his little imaginary bug figures—the feegle-fogles. He and the girls make up different names for them, then the girls color pictures around them. Several days ago Carol came running in from the front porch, saying there was another feegle-fogle on it! We all went to look.. And there it was—a big praying mantis!

I got another letter from New York. They said they think that the Gripsholm will be docking in New York, although they still don't know exactly when, and last-minute changes of port are always possible. They said they would let us know the time and place as soon as they find out. I had written them earlier to ask if they were sending any of the men home from New York by air. They said they were considering it, but so far no specific arrangements have been made, and it was still a question as to whether any will be permitted to come by air.

So, I have to make some decision as to whether I will go to New York. And, if I do, that will hopefully be where the ship docks, although Standard Oil said they still weren't sure which US port the Gripsholm would go to..

Chapter V
Meetings, Music, and Rio

The ship first headed east, then turned directly south to the open ocean. Our next stop would be Rio de Janeiro. The first few days down the east coast of Africa were very warm and pleasant. Although I think everyone enjoyed Lourenco, I also think we were all glad to be on our way. With the billeting mix up, signing papers for money and tickets, buying a few necessary articles, the six days there had been very busy. No one had gotten a great deal of sleep.

We all felt a great letdown in the tension. We were out from under the Japanese. There was no question now but what repatriation was going to go through. For the first several days, everyone just lay around and collected themselves. There was ample deck space on the Gripsholm, especially on A deck aft. The steward got out the deck chairs, and there was a great scramble for them. A green and white awning was over the deck chairs, giving the ship a festive air. People enjoyed getting out to sit in the sun. We were entirely free, not a care in the world. War was all around us, but not here with us.

The first morning out a British plane came and circled us three times. He just gave us the once over, as he was evidently on patrol. The next morning we saw on the horizon the masts of several ships. These were certainly destroyers, according to our "experts" on board. Yes, sir, we had many experts on board; there was no question that we could not answer. These were the only war ships that we saw on the entire trip until we reached Rio. According to international agreement, we were granted safe conduct. Thus, no war ship of any nation should be within ten miles of us as they might draw fire from a belligerent ship and thus endanger the Gripsholm.

After the first couple of days, the weather got cooler. Going around the Cape of Good Hope it also got a little rough. The ship settled into a routine, all 1,500 or so of us—approximately 900 missionaries, 300 diplomats, and 300 business men.

As on the Asama Maru, we settled into three main activities: card playing, Bible reading, and muttering to oneself. However, we did have one additional activity and that was report writing. No one wanted to write anything on the Asama because we were afraid that we would be inspected and have it taken away from us. On the Gripsholm, typewriters were brought out and everyone started to write about his experiences. Some of the public rooms and decks sounded with the pecking of typewriters all day long. Those who did not have access to a typewriter wrote theirs out by hand. It's a wonder that the paper did not run out with the reams and reams of stuff that was written!

The US Government took over one of the small public rooms as an office. They were constantly asking for typewriters. They evidently did not have enough, but there were plenty up on deck. However, the holders of these would not let them go for Government business. I don't know as I blame them any. The time, effort, paper, and machinery consumed on deck and that in the Government office were about equal. Both were probably a waste. One was typing because he thought his experience was unique and the other just to make reports to file away which no one cared about or would read.

Another major activity consuming time was meetings. Did we have meetings! Of course, Sunday was the real field day, but the only difference between Sunday and any other day was that the meetings were a little more emphasized. Every public room was busy some part of the day with a meeting. Some of the rooms were tied up practically all day. Prayer meetings were also held on deck, both in the morning and late evening.

The Catholics would start off the first thing in the morning with Mass at 7:00. Of course, other denominations were not to be outdone. As soon as the Catholics finished, along would come the Presbyterians, Baptists, Methodists, Seventh Day Adventists, Lutherans, Christian Scientists, and then all sorts of others, such as the medical missionaries. If there was a denomination that was not represented on the Gripsholm, I would like to know what it was.

Some of the missionaries also tried to branch out to individuals. Going down to breakfast one morning, one zealous soul, holding out some printed pamphlets, asked, "Would you please read these few precious words this morning?" Well, I will not say any more, except all this extracurricular activity was entirely done by the Protestants.

We did have a few other activities of interest. Sometimes we had movies several times a week. They were shown in the main lounge, which would comfortably hold about 300 people. We usually had around 500 of us crammed in there. The curtains had to be drawn and the windows closed, and you all but suffocated. I went to one show, but passed the rest. How people stood it I am sure I don't know. The first show of the day was always for the children, but they didn't mind the heat.

We also had music, and good music it was. Of course, with 1,500 people there were quite a few piano players, even some professional ones. The wife of one of the South Americans was really an expert. She used to practice every morning about 11:00 AM. Her practicing was as good as any recital I have ever attended. It did not take long for the ship to get on to this excellent entertainment. She had quite an audience. The room was always crowded, and she did not mind it a bit, which was nice. It is not everyone who would practice before an audience day after day like she did. About twice a week she would give a little concert in the main public lounge. She would go on hour after hour, all from memory. It was really a marvelous feat.

There were one or two others that were pretty fair piano players. In addition, we had several dozen noise manufacturers and boiler makers. I was one who banged away at the piano from time to time. Others ranged from children 10 to 12 years old up to 3 score years and ten. I think there were about fifteen pianos in various parts of the ship. Sometimes they were all going at once. Children would be practicing, and others were just making a noise or trying to impress the rest of us that they could play. Then, of course, we had the jazz players who just didn't give a damn.

Several times in the evenings we had dancing, but this was just like the movies—too hot and crowded for me. However, the young lads and girls of the village seemed to enjoy themselves.

There was one group that made themselves particularly noticeable: the pacifists. There were around thirty of them, all either missionaries or teachers. From what I heard them say, they were pro-Japanese rather than pacifists. The leader of this group was a professor at one of the universities in Tokyo. He was cautioned several times about these meetings and the remarks he would make. He replied that this was a Swedish ship, operating under the Swedish flag. Therefore, the American Government had no control over him and he would speak and act as he saw fit. His rationale was that when the war was over, they wanted to go back to Japan. If they did anything against Japan now, they may not be permitted to go back. You might well ask why didn't they stay in Japan? The reason is that Japan did not want them either. As far as I was concerned, the whole crowd should have been thrown overboard some dark night. Or, why wait for a dark night? Needless to say, they kept pretty much to themselves.

Everyone felt freer on the Gripsholm than on the Asama, but even so, very few talked about their experiences. No one was interested in listening to what someone else had gone through. There was not a person on the ship who had been through a pleasant experience. The only difference was that some had worse experiences than others. On the Asama we did not dare talk, because we did not know who was listening. On the Gripsholm, we had no desire to rehash our experiences.

The passengers were divided into two groups: missionary and non-missionary. The cleavage was very sharp, distinct, and clear between these two groups, with feeling running very high. The reason for this was also very clear and distinct. Of the 1,500 people aboard around 900 were missionary and of that number approximately 500 were women and children. Of the business and diplomatic crowd, very few had their families. This was the root of the antagonism. By far the greater majority of the government and business people had complied with the expressed wish of the American Government. We sent our families home when the general evacuation order came out in the fall of 1940.

Sending our families home was a distinct hardship and sacrifice, and no one had wanted to do it. However, the conditions in the Far East were such that it seemed the wise thing to do to comply with the advice of the State Department. There is no question that every one of us were glad that we did. But would the missionaries send their families home? No, they made no sacrifices; they kept their families with them and remained at their posts. They could show no weakness to war or the threat of war. They were in Christian work. As an example to the community they served, they must stay on and show no concession. They had the same chance and advice as the business people, and were continually urged to send their families home. The situation in the Far East was very precarious, but they remained on with their families. So, these 500 women and children on board just meant that 500 men had to remain behind because there was not sufficient room. That was the entire issue. If it were only the missionary men, there would have been no complaints whatsoever. Unfortunately, around 500 men, who had wives and children waiting for them in America, had to stay behind in Shanghai because there was not sufficient room on the ship.

The businessmen were out there with the distinct knowledge and approval of the State Department. When war was declared, negotiations were immediately started to get the diplomats and businessmen repatriated.

Well, the missionaries ran for cover as fast as anyone else when the bombs began to fall and the scrap iron started to be thrown around. I wonder what the Christian Chinese and Japanese thought when the difficulties arrived and the missionaries did not stay to see them through. What reception will they get after the war is over? If the Orient ever needed Christianity, it certainly needed it now in the midst of all the trouble.

I am not condemning the missionaries as a class. There are many very fine people among them. There is no question that, as a group, they have done and will continue to do very valuable work for the progress of mankind as a whole. I do think, however, that the Christian organizations of America are open to severe censure and criticism for the stand they took on evacuation before the war was declared, and then to run for home at the first opportunity after it was declared. If the missionary organizations had said to the State Department okay, we refused to go when advised, so we will wait until the second ship that would have been a fair and equitable proposition. But to immediately run for the first ship and take up two-thirds of the space, leaving men behind who had complied with the orders of the US Government, seems to me neither human nor Christian.

Nevertheless, life continued on much the same, day in and day out, until August 11th when we arrived in Rio de Janeiro on a delightful day. As we came into the harbor, directly ahead of us was a perfectly huge ship. No one knew definitely, but it was either the Queen Mary or the Queen Elizabeth as there are only two boats of that size afloat. She was on troop transport duty bound for somewhere. Just as we were edging into the dock, the Queen pulled anchor and departed.

Each person had to get a landing card, so it was not until late afternoon that we were permitted ashore. We also signed another promissory note for the equivalent of $15 for our expenses ashore.

We had twenty-four hours in Rio, and it was all too short. We raced around seeing what there was to see—the colored sidewalks, the Copacabana, Sugar Loaf, and the sights of the town. Rio is a really beautiful city. Although the strains and stresses of war were evident, Brazil as a nation had not yet formerly entered the conflict.

I took the opportunity to cable my wife of my eminent arrival in New York, or at least I thought that was where we were headed. There could have been other ports for our destination, like New Orleans or Baltimore. We were never told any specific plans. I also cabled the office, asking them to inform my wife of our progress. I suspected they were being informed of the ship's route.

We were told to be back by 2:00 PM the next afternoon, and exactly at 4:00 PM we pulled away from the pier. However, there were two men who thought they would like to spend another night in Rio and did not think that the ship would sail as planned. They did decide, however, to come down and check up on it, arriving at 4:05 PM when we were about 75 feet away from the pier. Everyone was leaning over the rail, giving all sorts of useful hints and instructions, such as it could be made in two jumps, or come on dive in and we will throw you a rope.

They finally managed to get aboard one of the tugs that was pushing us out. When the tug got us into the middle of the harbor, the Gripsholm started under her own power and the tug could not get itself in a position that a safe transfer could be made. They tried to come alongside a couple of times, but the Gripsholm was moving too fast and the gangway entrance too high up.

Well, the two men transferred to the pilot boat. When we slowed down to drop the pilot, they climbed abroad. They had been following us in the pilot boat for about thirty minutes. The whole boat was shouting all sorts of little words of wisdom at them, like hoping that they would find Rio's jail better than Stanley.

Two days later we learned that Brazil had joind the war, demanding revenge on Germany for sinking her neutral ships.

Ruth Briggs, Pasadena, California

On August 5 the Company wrote that the Gripsholm was expected to arrive in Rio de Janeiro on August 9 or 10, and probably in New York City on or about August 25. I immediately wrote them asking about flying him home. They answered that, with the uncertainty of the arrival of the Gripsholm and the possible delay in debarkation of passengers, it was difficult to make air reservations. They said the FBI would be interviewing each passenger before he will be permitted to debark, which would take several days. They said the best thing to do would be to write him in care of the Postmaster in New York, addressed to the Gripsholm, to let him know where I was staying, or where relatives were staying so he could contact us when he could leave the ship. Oh dear, now I don't know what to do..

August 10—what a wonderful day!! I got a cable from Norman from Rio de Janeiro! He was there! He said he was all right, just minus a little weight. He thought the ship was headed for New York, but he really didn't know, as they kept destinations secret. So he urged me not to come to New York, because for all he knew the ship might head for New Orleans or Baltimore. He said whatever port they landed in, he would be on the first train to California. Oh, I was so hoping to meet him, but I guess he is right.

I wanted to get on the train right then. I called New York to see if they knew where or when the ship would be landing, but they said the same thing...the final destination was classified, and they didn't know either. But he's alive, that's the main thing. And coming home!

We celebrated Kathie's fifth birthday on August 23 and had a wonderful party, with not only her birthday to celebrate, but also that Norman was coming home. I had ten neighborhood children over for the party. Pa had made a little wooden pool for Kathie's birthday for the children to play in, so all the children brought their bathing suits. Carol, of course, had to be part of the action. When she saw everyone getting into the pool, she climbed in too. However, since I had always told her to take her clothes off if she wet them, she soon began to take her bathing suit off! I tried to explain that it was okay if her bathing suit was wet, but she insisted on taking it off. Nobody else seemed to mind, so the party went on. I did get her into clothes again for the ice cream and cake.

I gave Kathie a toy typewriter for her birthday, and the next day when I said I was writing a letter to Daddy, she said she wanted to write one too. So, she told me what she wanted to write, and I told her what letters to find. She wrote: "Dear Daddy I am 5 years old. When you come home I will give you a big hug and kiss. Love, Kathie." Later, Carol got hold of the typewriter and sort of messed up the paper, but I just cut the "letter" out to send with my letter.

The next day I received a letter from Norman, mailed from Rio! It was wonderful to hold the letter and see his handwriting! He said if the ship did dock in New York, he would probably stay one night with Margaret and Jack Slusser, then head straight home. He would also try to find out what the Company had in store for him regarding assignments, but he figured that they would give him at least a month's vacation to recuperate. He also said he would probably find himself in the Army. That I didn't even want to think about! He got all our letters in Lourenco Marques and read them many times. He said he couldn't believe the picture of the girls that I sent, that they were so big now! He said he wasn't mentioning what he had been through until he got home. Then he would tell the story, and never talk about it again.

Chapter VI
On to New York!

We were on our way on the last leg of the trip! New York, United States of America, here we come!

Several days out of Rio we sighted an empty floating raft and some wreckage one afternoon. This caused considerable speculation. About an hour later we sighted a thin column of smoke ahead on the horizon. Gradually, as we came nearer, it began to take form, but what was it—a barge, a boat, or what? We could see the glow of the flame now. Was it a torpedoed boat? By 6:00 PM we were abreast of it and slowed down to see if there were any survivors. Just as we were about to circle, one man hollered, remembering the billeting at Lourenco Marques, "Oh, I know what that is. That is some of those Washington officials coming out to help us disembark at New York." He was not far wrong at that.

Just what it was is impossible to say. It was a big U-shaped affair, looking like a ship that had broken in two. It was about 350 feet long and perfectly open at one end. It had been a raging inferno and the steel was all twisted and bent from the heat. It was right on the water line, and it would only be a question of time, a few hours at the most, when it would go completely under the water. There was no one on it, and no signs of life whatsoever. It was burning itself out. We didn't know if it was a tanker, a cargo vessel broken in two, or what. But it was something that had been attacked, and that is about all we knew.

We thought it might have been a submarine repair boat. The Germans have ships built like this, open at one end so that submarines can be taken right in, like a floating dry dock. The presumption was that this had been spotted by an Allied air patrol that dive bombed it. After we circled her once, we went back on our course, picked up speed, and got on our way.

It is fortunate we saw this in the daytime rather than at night. Although we would have seen the fire at night, it was a danger to navigation. I presume that even under war conditions, the Gripsholm reported its position. It was a reminder of war and the grim world that we are living in.

When we boarded the Gripsholm, we were not given any information on what route we were taking or our position from day to day. We knew that we were going from Lourenco Marques to the United States, but not by what route or when we would arrive. There were plenty of rumors, but no definite facts. We did not know we were going to Rio until the day before we arrived. We just presumed we would go to New York, but other ports were mentioned, like New Orleans, Baltimore, and Norfolk.

The Gripsholm was an Atlantic passenger ship, as all the space was given to passenger accommodations with very little freight. Pacific ships of about the same tonnage have just about half the passenger space. Including the crew, the Gripsholm had about 2,000 people aboard. All the cabins had four berths and everyone had a berth. We all had water in our rooms. The only difference was that in third class, where I was, we did not have piped-in water. We only had a container which was filled every day. We were comfortable, but this was not an ordinary trip in any sense of the word, nor was it conducted like one. The passengers could neither send nor receive radio messages.

The food was excellent, and there certainly were no complaints as we remembered what we had survived on at Stanley. It was not fancy, just plain good food. The food throughout the entire ship in the four dining rooms was exactly the same from the first to third class, unlike the Asama where the first class got a few extras.

We also had a store on the ship which sold candy, tobacco, and a few items of clothes and other novelties. Two days out of Lourenco all the candy was gone; the kids saw to that. There was also a barber shop for the men and a beauty shop for the women. They were busy all day long, and the women had to make an appointment about a week in advance.

The bar of the ship served both soft drinks and liquor. They ran out of Coca-Cola about ten days before New York, but there was sufficient liquor to float us in. We had no major trouble on account of liquor, no misbehavior due to people over-imbibing. I think there was quite an element on the ship that was somewhat disappointed at this, because they were looking for any excuse to make an official protest to have the bar closed. They never got their chance. However, it is really surprising that on a trip like this we had no trouble with liquor. Most of us were greatly surprised that there was a bar. If there had been any trouble, the captain would have immediately closed it of his own accord with no need of a protest from a self-appointed committee.

We also had fresh running water all the time in the public wash rooms, a great improvement over the Asama. We could not have fresh water baths, but we could have all the salt water baths that we wanted. Laundry was extremely difficult. For the whole trip, you could only send one small batch to the laundry. However, there was plenty of water to do your own washing, and this is what most of us did.

Dress on the ship was extremely comfortable. It was the only trip I have ever made that I did not have to get into a boiled shirt at least once. The Chinese looters did not want my boiled shirt, but I left it for them anyway, and they were welcome to it. I hope I never have to buy another one. Everyone wore sports clothes. It was not until we arrived in New York that we knew that there were so many good-looking people aboard. We all got dressed up in our best, that is, what we had been able to save from the looters or purchase in Lourenco or Rio.

For expenses on the ship everything was in US currency. We could get up to $50 by signing a promissory note. Tips were included in the ticket, but a few of us gave the table and room stewards a little extra. Since I have been home, I have read articles in which it was said that tips were refused. They took mine, as I expected them to, and I was glad to give it. The Swedes are fine people and we were all treated well.

The crew was excellent. They were under-staffed and worked long hours, but were always extremely courteous. I saw a few get a little out of patience now and then, but never once did they lose their sense of balance. With 1,500 people and a collection like we had, that is a major feat of endurance. I got talking to my cabin steward one day, and he asked me: "Why, why does the American Government spend all this money to bring THESE PEOPLE home?" A very good question.

We had boat drills four or five times on the trip. Each time we had to show up with our life belt on and report to our assigned evacuation spot. There was one argument from a passenger who wanted to stay in the cabin, as he thought it an excellent opportunity for somebody to go through the cabins on a private looting job. Thoughts of Hong Kong. If the boat had been torpedoed, his personal belongings would have been worth a lot! However, the steward took charge, and the next thing I saw was the person going upstairs to his life boat, a little bit subdued.

The last day at sea was the roughest day of the entire trip. All the port holes and windows on the promenade deck on the port side had to be closed. The waves were running pretty high, with the spray reaching the boat deck. It looked as though we were in for some really rough and tough going. Having been two months at sea, we should have been able to take it, but a few of the boys and girls couldn't. Fortunately, the weather let up by the middle of the afternoon, when it became quite calm and clear, although a little cool.

The last day at sea everyone generally reserves for packing, and this was no exception. However, most of us had very little. As far as I was concerned, ten minutes would have been sufficient.

We all had to have our temperature taken. I had never had to go through this process before entering the country, but then this was a special trip. We were all from the Far East where disease was prevalent under the best of conditions. Here we were 1,500 people who had been in concentration camps, jails, or held with other means of restraint. We all had been not only underfed, but also without any balance in the little diet we were given. It is truly remarkable that we came through as well as we did. However, if there is anything wrong with you, there is generally a temperature, so I guess it was a very wise thing to do. You should have seen some people running around here and there trying to get hold of a private thermometer to take their temperature before it was taken officially by the crew. Some people had visions of being confined in a US Quarantine Hospital. Although it would have been better than our treatment with the Japanese, we all had had enough of institutions. Some people had a temperature of half a degree above normal and asked all sorts of questions as to what to do to get it down. The ship had about 100 thermometers, so it did not take long to record our temperatures. We went through the line alphabetically, with a definite time set for each letter of the alphabet. As far as I know, we all passed with normal readings.

Monday night we tried to make more or less into a gala night. Even though we were arriving home, no one was in the mood for it. There was no captain's dinner or anything like that. The trip was far from an ordinary one, and the feeling on board was not particularly congenial amongst all. Everybody's main thought was in getting off the ship, and the sooner the better. We did have a dance out on the aft deck with an orchestra of the ship's passengers, but it was a little bit cool. Not a great deal of interest was shown in dancing, as everyone was looking by this time to see if shore lights could be seen.

The bar closed at 10:00 PM instead of midnight. The ship's officers were taking no chances with anyone being late for the various roll calls the next morning. By midnight we expected to be able to see the Ambrose Light shine, or at least see some signs of civilization, but we didn't. Whether this was due to war conditions, or whether we were just too far out, I don't know.

The next morning, Tuesday, August 25, we were called to report on the deck at 5:00 AM for quarantine inspection. Everyone was up on deck, there was no mistake about that. It was a cold, windy morning up on deck, but there was America. We could see the buildings of lower Manhattan! On one side we could look over to shore and see homes with nicely kept lawns and trees all green and fresh. On the other side was the city of New York.

I don't know which side looked the best; they were both good. It was America! No China, no Japan, no Hong Kong, and I hope I have seen the last of those places. The main question throughout the entire ship was WHERE IS THE STATUE OF LIBERTY?

This was the first time that I had ever entered the country through New York. The background looked familiar, but I knew that we were some ways out, and we yet had to pass the Statue of Liberty. There were quite a few people like myself who had never entered through New York harbor before, and there were some for whom this would be their first visit. Believe it or not, there were 25 or 30 people aboard who had never even seen America before. They were American citizens born in the Orient and were seeing their homeland for the first time. It was a thrill for all of us, but it meant more to some than to others.

We stayed at the quarantine station about an hour, then pulled anchor and headed out to sea for a mile or so. We had been pointed in the wrong direction and had to go out to get sufficient room to turn around. This we did, and then steamed right up the harbor. We saw the automobiles on Long Island, and than came the STATUE OF LIBERTY! Everyone looked toward Her and waved in salute. There was not a dry eye on the ship. The Statue of Liberty was a god, America was her shrine, and we would pass her in a spirit of reverence and thanksgiving for our safe return from the actual areas of warfare.

Breathes there the man with soul so dead
Who never to himself hath said,
This is my own, my native land?
Whose heart hath ne'er within him burn'd,
At home his footsteps he hath turn'd,
From wandering on a foreign strand?

Since leaving the quarantine station, we were escorted by four Coast Guard boats who continually kept circling around following the ship. We didn't know what they were doing. They immediately made a dash for everything that was thrown overboard and picked it up. It made no difference what it was, even the slightest piece of paper came under their inspection. Many on board were now not feeling so good. What was the meaning of this, and what process were we going to go though when we docked? I think some of the people who were busy with typewriters for the past month were not particularly proud of what they had written. Were they going to be taken to task for it now?

Shortly, notices were distributed around, saying it was necessary that everyone entering the country be checked very carefully. For this reason, it would take several days to clear the ship. More people were getting nervous. What kind of a country were we returning to, no longer free? The pro-Japanese on the ship were not feeling quite so cocky now. The American Government might have had nothing to say about the Gripsholm, but they were going to have a lot to say as to who got off it.

We came up the Hudson and stopped just opposite the Woolworth Building. A couple of tugs took us in charge and eased us into the American Export Line's pier on the Jersey side. Our traveling had ceased, but we were not yet free. No one knew when we would be.

We were told to keep one small overnight bag. They removed all the other baggage, putting it on the pier in letter order by your last name.

Then we were told that everyone on the ship had to be interviewed, even the diplomatic corps. They put them through faster, but every individual on the ship had five separate checks made on him by the FBI, and these were in addition to the checks on the immediate members of his family. The FBI and several other Government agencies, such as the Army and Navy Intelligence, came aboard, taking over all the public rooms on A deck as offices. They moved cases of files right in and enlisted the Coast Guard personnel to act as messengers, guards, and to do any running around that was required.

All day Tuesday they were busy with the diplomatic people. I think by midnight they were all clear of the ship. However, they were not the only people who received initial attention. All day long names of people were being called in groups of six or eight. These consisted of the pacifists, people whose passports were not in order, the people of Chinese and Japanese descent who were American citizens, and several other classifications. In fact, all the people who were considered "different" were called that day. At first we thought when we heard the names being called that it was somewhat of an honor, because we thought it meant that they would get off the ship before we did. They did, but not in the manner we thought.

They got all these "different" people together, and what do you suppose happened to them? A launch was brought alongside, and all of them were taken to Ellis Island. Right out of one concentration camp into another! Just exactly how many there were in this group, I do not know. Some people said 200, others 400, but I think 100 would be the more accurate number. All those that went to Ellis Island were not wanted for things they had actually done themselves, but to report and confirm the deeds of others. For instance, if you had been sitting at the table with one of the pacifists or pro-Japanese for the trip, you would probably be taken to Ellis Island and questioned concerning these people.

Wednesday morning we were informed that we would be taken alphabetically. Definite times were given for the first four letters. I certainly was glad my name started with a "B." Before being questioned by the FBI, we were to go ashore and get our baggage to go through customs. I located my things, and as I only had three pieces in total, I was passed through very quickly.

In checking my things, the officer asked if I had any letters, correspondence, or anything of a written nature. I was fully expecting this. I was one of the bright boys who had written up my Hong Kong experiences which ran into 80 handwritten pages. I handed this over to him, and he took it over to the Treasury officials who handled communications.

The Treasury person took this Hong Kong report, thumbed through it, looked up at me, and asked what I wrote all that for. While he said this, he tossed it over to one of his assistants, telling him to look through it. I replied that people would be asking me all sorts of questions. I had written it out so that I could say, if you are interested enough, here it is, read it. I did it to save myself talking my head off.

He was very haughty in his manner. When his assistant had given it back to him after looking though it about ten minutes, he asked if it contained many details of the fighting. When I replied affirmatively, he said that he would keep it and read it very carefully. He treated the whole thing with contempt. All the other questioning on the ship was very courteous and thoroughly in order. He was the only person who was a little bit officious. He took the report, my name and address, saying he would mail it to me later. It did come back, the last week in November, so I guess they read it carefully. But, they didn't make any comments.

After passing muster at that table, I was taken to another table. Here they wanted to know how much money I had. I turned over my wallet to them, which contained something like $112. If you had over $250, you had to give a detailed account of where you got it. They also asked me if I had any information about any counterfeit money that originated in the Far East. I said that I did not, and they let me go. The reason for the $250 limit was that in neutral ports, for instance Lourenco Marques, Axis agents were using American money to buy supplies and information. Anyone coming into the country with any large sum of American money had to explain how he got it. By this method, they hoped to get some check on how and where the American money abroad was being used.

With the baggage taken care of, I was permitted to go back on the Gripsholm for the session with the FBI. I went and took my place in line. When my turn came, they checked my name off a list and produced a file which contained details of my past actions. I was turned over to the Coast Guard orderly who took me out on the promenade deck which was lined up on both sides with card tables. I was shown to one, and my file handed over to the FBI man.

At the table were three men: FBI, Army Intelligence, and Navy Intelligence. They asked me some details of my experiences, where I had been stationed, the nature of my work, and wanted to know particularly if I had seen any atrocities. They said that any information that I could give the Government about the Orient or Japan in particular that would help toward winning the war would be appreciated. They also wanted to know if I had anything to report about anyone else on board. The interview lasted about 30 minutes. They were very courteous throughout the whole interview.

I was taken by the orderly to a couple of more tables, my name checked off the list, and more questions such as to when I last left America, on what ship, and to what address I was immediately proceeding. I was given my final clearance card, and told I was free to go. This was noon on Wednesday. I think the entire ship was cleared by Friday night, so I certainly was glad that my name began with a "B."

My cousin, Margaret Slusser and her husband Jack, were in New York to greet me. I stayed with them at their Long Island home that first night on American soil. Oh, how good that felt! The next day the company arranged a train ticket to get me home to California.

The trip that started in Hong Kong on Monday, June 29, was now completed on Wednesday, August 26, 1942. I was not yet home, but I got out of New York by train on Thursday and arrived in Pasadena Monday morning, August 31,1942, from which I had left for Hong Kong on August 14, 1941.

I had circumnavigated the globe for the first time, and I hope the last time. I still think the best remark that I ever heard about the Orient is: "You don't have to be crazy to live there, but it certainly helps a lot." You are welcome to it, for I have seen enough.

Ruth Briggs, Pasadena, California

The morning of August 31 couldn't come soon enough for me. I didn't sleep all the night before. I would be seeing Norman again…he was really coming home! The girls sensed the excitement too; although they slept. But they were up early when they heard me up getting dressed.

Ma and Pa went to meet the train with me, as well as Mrs. Enickieff, our friend from Japan. She and her husband had emigrated to Japan from Russia years ago. He worked for Standard Oil also, but since he was not a United States citizen, they could not bring him home. I felt sorry for Mrs. Enickieff, as he was still in Japan and she had no idea what his fate was. But she was a good friend, and was excited for me and very helpful with the children.

The train was pulling in! Soon the passengers were getting out, and we were looking all over for Norman. Then a thin man came toward us…Norman! Yes, it was Norman and I had my arms around him! Oh, did he look good and feel good to me. But he was very thin. Even though he had gained weight on the ship, he still had a way to go to get his over six foot frame normal again. He said he weighed in on the ship at 90 pounds! I will certainly enjoy cooking many meals for him again and hope we never have to be separated like this again.

Thank you, God, for bringing him home to me.

Epilogue

I guess I am crazy, because even though I vowed I never wanted to return to the Orient, I did. After reuniting with my family in Pasadena, I spent the next six months recuperating and gaining back my lost weight. My wife, Ruth, told me she had never lost faith that I was alive and would return home. Her prayers had worked.

My daughters, Kathie, now five years old, and Carol, now two, were beautiful to see. Kathie was almost four when I left, and Carol just one, so it was wonderful getting reacquainted with them, now real little persons. And the following July, 1943, little sister Norma joined the family.

Standard Oil let me rest for awhile to get my strength back, and then sent me to Madras, India, from late 1943 to late 1945. After the war was over, I stopped in Tokyo to check with the office there, where I would eventually be returning. Before going into the office, I made a stop at the Imperial Hotel. Walking into the bar, an old friend from my days in Japan before the war turned around, saw me, and said, "Briggs, where the hell have you been!"

I then returned to the United States to see my family again and report to the New York office. In 1946 I was sent to Shanghai for a year. After that and another home leave, I returned to Japan with my family in 1949.

Post Script

The family returned to Japan in 1949, living first in Kobe, then in Yokohama. The country was still very devastated by the war. Our house was the only one left standing in a mile radius, and had iron scrap junk piles on three sides of it. But the Japanese rebuilt fairly fast, and when we left in 1957, the country was on its way to industrialization.

My father showed no outward animosity toward the Japanese. He never talked about his internment, as it was a very painful time for him. When asked about it, he would say, "Yes, I was a guest of the Japanese government." He wrote his memoirs so he wouldn't have to relive the experience by talking about it.

He was happy to retire in 1957. The family spent a year in California with his parents, then went back to New Jersey to our house where we had lived briefly before going to Japan in 1949, returning every two and a half years for six months of home leave at the New York office.

Two years later my parents moved to Easton, Maryland, buying a house on the Chesapeake Bay. They lived there over thirty years. My father took great pleasure in the fact that he had been retired longer than he worked! He would sit out on his pier, which we named the Gin Deck, off the front lawn, raise his glass of Pink Gin, and proclaim, "My, my, this is the Land of Pleasant Living!"

He never traveled overseas after he retired, and never ate rice again. He was a man of great character, and nursed my mother through several long years of illness. He passed away suddenly in 1993 at the age of 88, in the woods, which he planted and loved, at the back of his home.

Carol Briggs Waite

Printed in the United States
59088LVS00004B/310-321

9 781424 113019